design activism

design activism

beautiful strangeness for a sustainable world

Alastair Fuad-Luke

publishing for a sustainable future
London • Sterling, VA

First published by Earthscan in the UK and USA in 2009

ISBN: 978-1-84407-644-4 hardback
        978-1-84407-645-1 paperback

Typeset by Domex e-Data, India
Cover design and page design by Rob Watts

For a full list of publications please contact:

Earthscan
Dunstan House
14a St Cross St
London, EC1N 8XA, UK
Tel: +44 (0)20 7841 1930
Fax: +44 (0)20 7242 1474
Email: earthinfo@earthscan.co.uk
Web: **www.earthscan.co.uk**

22883 Quicksilver Drive, Sterling, VA 20166-2012, USA

Earthscan publishes in association with the International Institute for Environment
and Development

A catalogue record for this book is available from the British Library

Library of Congress Cataloging-in-Publication Data

Fuad-Luke, Alastair.
  Design activism : beautiful strangeness for a sustainable world / Alastair Fuad-Luke.
     p. cm.
  Includes bibliographical references and index.
  ISBN 978-1-84407-644-4 (hardback) -- ISBN 978-1-84407-645-1 (pbk.) 1. Design--
Social aspects. 2. Sustainable design. I. Title.
  NK1390.F83 2009
  745.4--dc22
                                    2008046521

At Earthscan we strive to minimize our environmental impacts and carbon footprint
through reducing waste, recycling and offsetting our CO_2 emissions, including those
created through publication of this book. For more details of our environmental policy,
see www.earthscan.co.uk.

This book was printed in Malta by Gutenberg Press
using soya-based inks. The paper is FSC certified.

Mixed Sources
Product group from well-managed
forests, and other controlled sources
www.fsc.org Cert no. TT-CoC-002424
© 1996 Forest Stewardship Council
FSC

To my parents, Eric and Pam

Contents

Figures and Tables

Figures

Tables

Acronyms and Abbreviations

AfH	Architecture for Humanity
AHRC	Arts and Humanities Research Council
CNC	computer numeric controlled
DfE	design for the environment
DfS	design for sustainability
EF	ecological footprint
EMUDE	Emerging User Demands for Sustainable Solutions
FAO	Food and Agriculture Organization
GDP	gross domestic product
HDI	human development index
HDPE	high density polyethylene
HIPC	heavily indebted poor countries
HPI	Happy Planet Index
html	hypertext mark-up language
HVAC	heating/ventilation/air-conditioning
ICSID	International Council of Societies of Industrial Design
ICT	information communication and technology
IP	intellectual property
IPCC	Intergovernmental Panel on Climate Change
IT	information technology
ITDG	Intermediate Technology Development Group
LCA	life cycle analysis
LCT	life cycle thinking
LDCs	least developed countries
LETS	Local Exchange Trading System
LGBT	lesbian, gay, bisexual and transgender
MDF	medium-density fibreboard
MDP	measure of domestic progress
MDRI	Multilateral Debt Relief Initiative
MEA	Millennium Ecosystem Assessment
MIPS	materials intensity per unit service
NEF	New Economics Foundation
NPD	new product development
OAN	Open Architecture Network
ODA	Official development assistance
OLPC	One Laptop per Child
OS	open source
PC	personal computer

PD	participatory design
ppm	parts per million
PPP	purchasing power parity
PSS	product service systems
QoL	quality of life
SCP	sustainable consumption and production
SD	sustainable development
SMEs	small and medium-sized enterprises
T&L	teaching and learning
TBL	triple bottom line
TCP/IP	Transmission Control Protocol/Internet Protocol
TOES	Towards Other Economic Systems
UCD	user-centred design
UNDP	United Nations Development Programme
WCED	World Commission on Environment and Development
WWF	World Wide Fund for Nature

Acknowledgements

I thank all the individuals and organizations with whom I've conversed and dialogued about design and sustainability over the last decade, as without them this book could not have emerged. In particular, I am very grateful to the designers and other professionals who generously gave permission to use images, illustrations and other materials, all of which help bring the topic of design activism to life. Thanks are also due to Guy Julier, Ann Thorpe, John Wood, Carolyn Strauss and my colleagues on the DEEDS project. Tamsine O'Riordan, formerly an editor at Earthscan, received my book concept with enthusiasm that was then supported by the sterling work of Hamish Ironside with Michael Fell and Claire Lamont. The Earthscan team co-designed the book cover and layouts with graphic designer Rob Watts (Rogue Four Design), to create an accessible work. I am grateful for the diligent proofreading by Christine James. I thank my wife, Dina, who encouraged and sustained me during the months required to bring this book to fruition.

Preface

'The real JOY of design is to deliver fresh perspectives, improved well-being and an intuitive sense of balance with the wider world. The real SPIRIT of design elicits some higher meaning. The real POWER of design is that professionals and laypeople can co-design in amazingly creative ways. The real BEAUTY of design is its potential for secular, pluralistic expression. The real STRENGTH of design is this healthy variance of expression. The real RELEVANCE of design is its ability to be proactive. The real PASSION of design is in its philosophical, ethical and practical debate.'

Alastair Fuad-Luke[1]

Design is a key agency in materializing, and designing, our lives. For, as many observers have noted, what is already designed exerts a huge influence over the design of our lives, and what comes next. Design converts nature's capital and man's (human and financial) capital into 'man-made' capital by giving it form, by embedding meaning (by vesting the form with symbolic capital), by defining societal values and, ultimately, by designing our perception of reality. Design contributes to the evolution of individual human capital and defines our collectively held social capital. Design is the medium through which these capitals are transformed into materialized and symbolic languages. For the past 250 years design has endorsed the notion of economic progress by making the newly materialized forms 'culturally acceptable', in symbolic, aesthetic and functional terms.[2]

Today, the vast majority of the world's nations endorse the universal mantra of capitalism. It has become the default model for economic and material progress. This model is founded on the doctrine of free trade espoused by Adam Smith in his famous treatise *An Inquiry into the Nature and Causes of the Wealth of Nations* published in 1776.[3] His basic thesis was that trade should not be restricted, that the betterment of the self is achieved by hard work, that this work accrues financial and man-made capital, and that this self-achievement automatically betters everyone in society. His writings were influential and struck a favourable note with a British society undergoing a radical transformation at the birth of the Industrial Revolution, a shift accompanied by massive migration from the countryside to the emerging industrializing cities. Smith's philosophy and premises still underpin economic theory and practice today. Yet, Smith's world was very different with a world population of 0.79–0.98 billion, compared with today's current total of 6.721 billion.[4] Nature looked fecund and boundless in the late 18th century, ripe for exploitation, available for capitalizing man's purpose. Nature could easily support the population growth needed to keep growing the industrial economy. The game plan has not changed. Yet today, the plan looks a little shaky. Nature's ability to sustain this exploitative onslaught, and sustain humankind's vision of economic progress, is in serious doubt. Nature is dying. Parts of the global society of humankind are also dying. Ethnic groups and languages are disappearing, and the poor become invisible. Economic disparity between rich and poor has steadily risen since the 1950s and the emergence of the consumer economy,[5] and more than a third of the world's population (over 2 billion people) still live in abject poverty, earning less than US$2 per day.[6] This world of inequality is facing unprecedented economic, ecological *and* sociological crises.

According to the Millennium Ecosystem Assessment Overview conducted by the United Nations, the capacity of the world's great ecosystems (agricultural, coastal, forest, freshwater and grasslands) to provide certain essential services (ranging from food and fibre production to water quality and quantity, biodiversity and carbon storage) that support life, is declining.[7] Coupled with an increase in world population and a rise in global temperature, this is creating the most serious threat to global ecological stability ever known to humankind. Urgent attention is needed to restore the capacity of these ecosystems to keep delivering the services humans demand to sustain the quality of their lives. There is a growing realization that the call for 'sustainable development' (SD), which stills sees economic growth as part of developing human progress, has done little to avert recent negative environmental or social trends. SD is now being challenged by a new vision of 'positive development', a more holistic approach to restore ecosystem services.[8] This demands a transition of societies that is equally as profound as the one experienced in the late 18th century at the emergence of the Industrial Economy, itself a result of earlier transformations in the Renaissance and the Enlightenment. It demands that we reflect on our current notions of economically endorsed forms of beauty (and their implicit symbolic and exchange values) because these forms actually *threaten our lifeworld*. This threat is raised by dissenting voices who gently or vigorously contest the dominant (unsustainable) paradigm, reminding those who care to listen that all is not well; that an urgent conversation is needed about our global environments, about unequal distribution of money, food and hope; that the powerful's vision of capitalist economic progress is flawed; that multiple realities tell 'divergent', and sometimes negative stories about 'progress'; that the consumer end-game is near; that post-peak oil is a reality now; that life as we know it is about to change significantly or, perhaps, irrevocably. These are the voices of the activists – and they are growing globally.

Are there many designers among the activists? There are indeed some that articulate their thoughts and convert them into positive societal and environmental change. But they are few, just at a time when many are needed. Designers are, after all, licensed to imagine, to realize what John Wood calls 'attainable micro-utopias', to make the unthinkable possible.[9] Design is a motive force in suggesting and realizing new materializations for our world. Design can reconnect the disconnected and make new connections. Design can challenge the underlying, implicit ethics of the explicit forms we create. Design can create new memes (units of cultural transmission that elicit new behaviour). Design can find the best fit between economic viability, ethical and cultural acceptability and ecological truth. Design can seek genuine mutual benefits to humankind *and* nature. Design can breathe new life into the everyday by reconnecting the conceptual with the natural and the natural with the artificial. Design can ask 'what now?' and 'what next?'. Design can disturb current narratives. Design can rupture the present with counter-narratives. Design can contribute to reformist approaches. It has the ability to catalyse societal transformations. Design is critical imagining. Design generates considered possibilities for a new, 'beautiful strangeness' (with new values embedded or implicit). Design can readjust our notion of beauty to embrace a multitude of truths – economic, political, social, ecological, ethical, technical, symbolic, institutional, philosophical and cultural. To rise to this challenge, design must set its own agenda for positive change.

This book charts the territory of the design activist – a person who uses the power of design for the greater good for humankind *and* nature. A person who is a free agent; a non-aligned social broker and catalyst; a facilitator; an author; a creator; a co-author; a co-creator; and a happener (someone who makes things happen). Most of all, this book is for everyone who believes that design (especially when we design together) is an essential human expression that will help us *all* to move towards more sustainable futures. This text is also contesting the future of design, because design's current vision is not telling the ecological or sociological truth, nor is it a truly representative democratic tool for society. So, the design activist also contests who contributes, who designs and who decides 'what now' and 'what next'.

Notes

1   Alastair Fuad-Luke (2006) from the opening review of Positive Alarm, Platform 21, a project of Premsela, the Dutch design foundation, www.platform21.com
2   Findeli, A. (2001) 'Rethinking design education for the 21st century: Theoretical, methodological and ethical discussion', *Design Issues*, vol 17, no 1, Winter, pp5–17.
3   Smith, A. (1776, 2001) *An Inquiry into the Nature and Causes of the Wealth of Nations*, Adam Smith Institute, London, www.adamsmith.org/smith/won-intro.htm, accessed 15 September 2008.
4   Wikipedia (2008) 'World population', http://en.wikipedia.org/wiki/World_population, accessed 15 September 2008.
5   On 12 November 2003 the Worldwatch Institute issued a Vital Signs Facts report on the widening of the rich–poor gap, stating that, while the global economy expanded sevenfold since 1950, between 1960 and 1995 the disparity between

rich and poor in the 20 richest and 20 poorest nations more than doubled ('Rich-Poor Gap Widening', www.worldwatch.org/node/82, accessed 15 September 2008). UK income distribution between 1977 and 2006 shows a long-term trend of the income inequality between the highest and lowest income earners ('Income Inequality', www.statistics.gov.uk/cci/nugget.asp?id=332, accessed 15 January 2009).

6   World Development Bank data on absolute poverty.
7   UN (2003, 2005) Millennium Assessment Reports.
8   See, for example, Birkeland, J. (2008) *Positive Development: From Vicious Circles to Virtuous Cycles through Built Environment Design*, Earthscan, London.
9   Wood, J. (2007) *Design for Micro-Utopias: Making the Unthinkable Possible (Design for Social Responsibility)*, Ashgate, Farnham.

Scoping the Territory: Design, Activism and Sustainability

'Sentiment without action is the ruin of the soul.'

Edward Abbey, environmental author

'Design, never a harmless play with forms and colors, changes outer life as well as our inner balances.'

Richard Neutra[1]

'Design activism' has a delicious tension. We carry an understanding of 'design' and of 'activism' but joining the words together imbues a certain ambiguity. To say 'design activism' is to imply that it already exists and has an established philosophy, pedagogy and ontology, i.e. it circumscribes a system of principles, elicits a wisdom and knowledge, has a way of teaching and has its own way of being. This may be an ambitious claim. Defining design activism and its effects has the potential to result in a pluralist, messy and contestable result. However, this book hopefully gives some credence to the existence of an emergent design activism and its healthy potential to help us deal with important contemporaneous societal issues.

Defining 'Design' Today

'Design' and 'activism' are words carrying a similar burden. They are conjured in the mind and transport our thinking in diverse ways; they are malleable, easily borrowed and corruptible. A recent discourse about design terminology[2] provides an insight into the complex world of design today by citing a wide variety of adjectives or nouns as a prefix or suffix to 'design' (Table 1.1). This terminology refers variously to the type of design author, the design context or discipline, the design approach, historical design precedents, and an arena for practising design. Moreover, the editors find it 'impossible to offer a single and authoritative definition of ... design'.[3] Flexible verbal accounts of 'design' reveal that design is tied to cultural perceptions that are contemporary and yet very personal.[4] It seems that design is difficult to pin down and is everywhere. Indeed, a glance at the long list of design disciplines reveals that design has penetrated every facet of our materialized and virtual worlds (Figure 1.1). Design also embodies diverse historical and contemporary styles, invokes a wide range of disciplines, has legal protection (registered designs and intellectual property, IP) and is practised by professionals

Table 1.1
Prefixes and suffixes associated with the word 'design'

Prefixes – anonymous, architectural, audiovisual, auteur, automobile, Bel, broadcast, character (films, comics, games), collaborative, conceptual, corporate, critical, cross-cultural, digital, eco, engineering, environmental, event, exhibition, fashion, food, furniture, futuristic (futurism, streamline design), game, gender, good, graphic, green, industrial, information, interaction, interface, interior, jewellery, landscape, lighting, mechatronic, media, non-intentional, olfactory (scent), packaging, participatory, photographic, poster, product, protest, public, radical, re-, registered, retail, retro, safety, screen, service, set, shop, signature, slow, sound, stage, strategic, streamline, textile, time-based (animation, performance), title (film credits), transportation, TV, universal, urban, web
Suffixes – criticism, education, history, management, planning, research, theory

Source: Erlhoff and Marshall (2008)[5]

(of varying public status from unknown to known, but not yet famous), iconic or avant-garde designers (famous, auteur or signature designers) or by anonymous or non-intentional designers.

Design crosses a diverse range of subject fields and disciplinary borders (Figure 1.2) giving design a unique reach among the creative disciplines, while simultaneously adding more complexity and blurring the discursive space. Figure 1.2 combines the work of Prasad Boradkar, who suggests that design operates on things and systems,[6] and D. Fallman, who sees design in dynamic tension between design practice, design studies and design explorations.[7] A further layer of complexity is added to the designing of 'things and systems' by considering the four sustainability dimensions – economic, ecological, social and institutional – proposed by Joachim Spangenberg.[8] Design also embraces myths and meaning, philosophy, science, teaching/education, anthropology, sociology, material culture studies, media and cultural studies, economics, political sciences, economics and ecology. It is design's ability to operate through 'things' and 'systems' that makes it particularly suitable for dealing with contemporary societal, economic and environmental issues.

Design, therefore, is manifest in all facets of contemporary life. Design is executed by designers that are trained, professional and offer expertise. Yet it is also engaged by designers that are unknown (anonymous, non-intentional) and who gain their expertise from outside the design professionals' world. This dualism would seem to be equally apt for 'activism'. There are well-known activists who have a public profile and earn their living as professional activists[9] and there are also many unknown activists beavering away out of the public gaze. The nature of contemporary 'activism' is elaborated on below, but a definition of design that

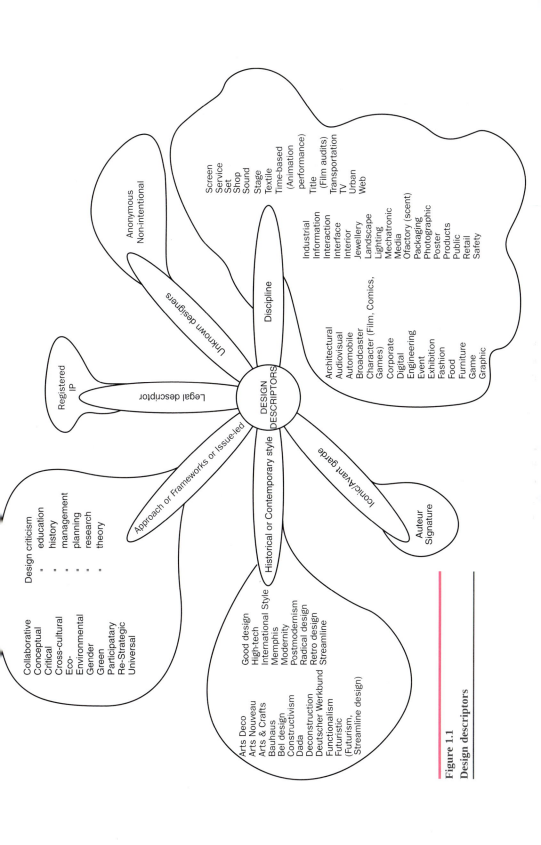

Figure 1.1
Design descriptors

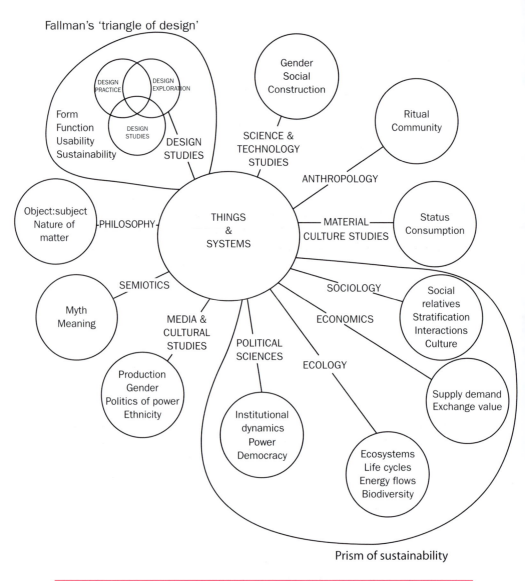

Fallman's 'triangle of design'

Prism of sustainability

Figure 1.2
Design in relation to other disciplinary studies focusing on 'things and systems'

embraces this professional/non-professional dualism can be found in two seminal works published in the late 1960s/early 1970s. In 1969, Herbert Simon[10] noted:

> *'Everyone designs who devises courses of action aimed at changing existing situations, into preferred ones.'*

And in his polemical book, *Design for the Real World*, Victor Papanek[11] opened with the words:

'All men are designers. All that we do, almost all the time, is design, for design is basic to all human activity.'

Papanek's views still receive considerable debate, both positive and negative,[12] as some designers draw very clear boundary lines between the work they do as professionals and the kind of design executed by other professionals or laypeople. Those who practice design activism tend to blur these boundaries considerably.

Both Simon and Papanek are frequently cited by those keen to stress the important contribution that design does and can make to contemporary issues affecting societal development and environmental stability.[13] Simon's all-encompassing definition of design seems most fitting to the territory of design activism because activists can originate from a spectrum of status, from activist professionals to unknown activists. A working definition of design is therefore proposed:

Design is the act of deliberately moving from an existing situation to a preferred one by professional designers or others applying design knowingly or unknowingly.

Defining 'Activism' Today

'Activism' is a broad church. As our industrial economies and concurrent societies have metamorphosed into 'post-industrial', 'consumer' and 'knowledge' economies, expressions of activism have taken on more pluralistic forms, aided and abetted by information communication and technology (ICT) platforms, especially the internet.[14] Activists, that is those carrying out the activism, can belong to social, environmental or political movements that are localized or distributed, and that are based upon collective and/or individual actions. They are often allied to, or are, the founders of social movements, defined by Tarrow[15] as:

'Collective challenges [to elites, authorities, other groups or cultural codes] by people with common purposes and solidarity in sustained interactions with elites, opponents and authorities.'

Other activists orientate around special interest groups gathered around specific issues with an anthropocentric focus (e.g. AIDS, pro-life anti-abortionists, anti-war, fathers' rights, feminism, anti-poverty) whereas others take a more biocentric focus (e.g. animal rights, environmentalists, anti-nuclear power).[16] The professional activism industry is dominated by not-for-profit, charitable and non-governmental organizations working across the political, social, environmental, institutional and economic agendas. Lobbyists working on behalf of corporations and political parties also have an activist role in influencing these agendas.

All activists are involved in inculcating change that favours their 'world-view', i.e. how they see the current paradigm(s) and the associated issues. Change implies moving from 'state A' of a system to 'state B'. This may involve a transformation of the system and its target audiences or social groups, but often also involves the transformation of the individual activists too. Both these notions of transformation can be embedded in a working definition of activism:

> *Activism is about … taking actions to catalyse, encourage or bring about change, in order to elicit social, cultural and/or political transformations. It can also involve transformation of the individual activists.*

As such, activism operates on social, cultural and political capital to elicit a change to the stock by catalysing new flows of stock. This construct of 'capital', 'stock' and 'flow' offers a potentially useful way of viewing the potential and real effectiveness of activism.

Activism and the Five Capitals Framework

Activism operates on a variety of forms of capital that contribute in different ways, and by different means, to the globally shared notion of 'capitalism' which has come to dominate economic and political thinking. The Forum for the Future's Five Capitals Framework[17] is posited here as a means of examining where activism aims to exert an effect on different capitals. The five capitals are natural, human, social, manufactured and financial (Table 1.2). Natural capital is the capital that underwrites every other form of capital since it is the capital from which all life springs. Human capital is held in each individual human and is therefore another primary capital. Social, manufactured and financial capitals are derived from the two primary forms of capital – natural and human. There are three other forms of capital – man-made (material) goods, cultural and symbolic capitals – which are also important to consider beyond the Five Capitals Framework as design plays a particularly important role in regulating their flow (see Figure 1.3). Design mediates, to some extent, the flow of all these capitals. So it is important to understand the diversity and complexity of contemporary activism, so the designer can locate areas for activist work in a larger landscape.

Activism affects the perception and quality of stock of these capitals, especially those capitals that are socially orientated – social, cultural, human, institutional – around which societal and 'political' change pivots. Political in this sense is not a narrow view of political parties and their respective philosophies and beliefs, but is a wider view of the citizen contributing to a broad political dialogue within society, where the question being asked is 'in what sort of society do we want to live?'.[18] Design is implicitly embedded in this question and so all design can be considered political.

Table 1.2
The Five Capitals model and other capitals

Capital	Description
The Five Capitals	
Natural (environmental, ecological)	'Any stock or flow of energy and matter [from the natural world] that yields valuable goods and services.' Resources – renewable, e.g. timber, grain, fish, and non-renewable, e.g. fossil fuel; sinks – absorb, neutralize or recycle waste; services, e.g. climate regulation by air, cloud, wind.[19] Resources are the main measured stock and it is our difficulty or unwillingness to measure and/or value other natural capital stocks that makes the capital in the larger 'environment' at risk from over-exploitation.
Human	Adam Smith defined human capital in his 1776 economic treatise, *An Inquiry into the Nature and Causes of the Wealth of Nations*, as 'the acquired and useful abilities of all the inhabitants or members of the society'.[20] He indicated that each person acquired this human capital during his/her education, study or apprenticeship; that acquisition had a real cost; and that human capital resides within the person. Physical, intellectual and psychological skills and dexterity, and judgement, are all forms of human capital. Forum for the Future expands this list to embrace spiritual and emotional capacities.[21] While Smith was largely thinking about how human capital contributed to improvements in financial, manufactured and natural capital held in land, more modern definitions see human capital as something each one of us brings to any work, play, nurturing or loving situation, i.e. today we have a much more holistic view.
Social	Social capital holds a wide variety of meanings (Wikipedia, social capital)[22] but most agree that it concerns connections between and within social networks that encourage civic engagement, engender trust, create mutual support, establish norms, contribute to communal health, cement shared interests, facilitate individual or collective action, and generate reciprocity between individuals and between individuals and a community. Bridging social capital is inclusive[23] as it is outward looking and tries to join people from different social units or groups, e.g. the civil rights movement. In contrast, bonding social capital is exclusive as it looks within the social unit or group to reinforce an identity, e.g. a church group, social club or urban gang. Not all social capital is therefore positive as some forms of social capital divide societies while other forms strengthen societies. Social capital is represented by two important subsets – institutional capital and cultural capital – that have considerable influence on whether social capital is used to deliver positive growth or negative impacts on the whole or parts of societies.
Financial	Financial, or economic, capital is represented by money and other financial instruments which in themselves are merely a representation of other forms of wealth (capital) equating to one or all of the following: a medium of exchange; a standard of deferred payment; a unit of account; or a 'symbolic' store of value.[24] Porritt argues that financial capital is governed by markets and institutions that are, in effect, social networks with stocks of specialist information and expertise, and that transactions take place based on norms and trust.[25]

Capital	Description
Manufactured	Manufactured capital is man-made material artefacts that 'contribute to the production process, but do not become embodied in the output of that process'.[26] This includes buildings, infrastructure and technologies. Buildings include the built environment of villages, towns and cities; infrastructure is the physical fabric that society depends upon including systems for transportation, education, health, energy, water and waste disposal; technologies include tools, machines, information technology (IT), biotechnology and engineering that enable the production of goods and services. Infrastructure is sometimes referred to as infrastructural capital, and is held in public, public/private or private ownership for the purpose of the common good.
'Other' capitals	
Man-made (material) goods	Man-made goods originate because natural capital is converted by manufactured capital using social, financial and human capital. This form of capital is at the heart of the 'consumer economy' that emerged in the 1930s in the US and found momentum worldwide in the 1950s, and finally evolved into the 'global economy' in the 1990s. This type of capital is introduced here because it is the primary capital with which design works and is implicit in the debate around sustainable consumption and production (SCP), a concept that tries to balance stock and flow of natural capital with other capitals and with an increasing world population that continues to put yet more demand on depleting stocks. SCP is really asking how many man-made goods natural capital can support, now and in the long term.
Cultural	Cultural capital first emerged as a sociological concept in the early 1970s[27] and was later developed by Bourdieu[28] to indicate three manifestations: *An embodied state* where cultural capital is held in the individual as a culturally inherited and acquired set of properties that confers a certain social relation within a system of (social) exchange – this is part of human capital but requires social capital for its verification. *An objectified state* where individuals that possess more cultural capital have acquired material and symbolic goods that are deemed rare or worthy by society – these goods have both financial and symbolic capital and are derived from man-made goods capital. *An institutionalized state* recognizing the cultural capital conferred by institutions on individuals, such as an academic qualification, that enables the individual to achieve certain financial value in the marketplace – so this form of cultural capital is bound up in particular forms of social capital. As individuals move around society and are exposed to different forms of social capital, the currency of their cultural capital shifts. Certain states of cultural capital will have high value in certain social units or networks, whereas other forms of cultural capital will be perceived as having little or no value. Such value decisions are qualitative.
Symbolic	Capital is symbolically represented in all forms of anthropocentric capital – financial, manufactured, man-made goods, social, cultural and human capitals – because it forms the basis by which we recognize the sociological or anthropological status of individuals in society or within social units or groups. Symbols confer meaning and value, and therefore status. Those meanings and values are both collectively and personally held and negotiated, so will shift within and between different societies and cultures, and over time.

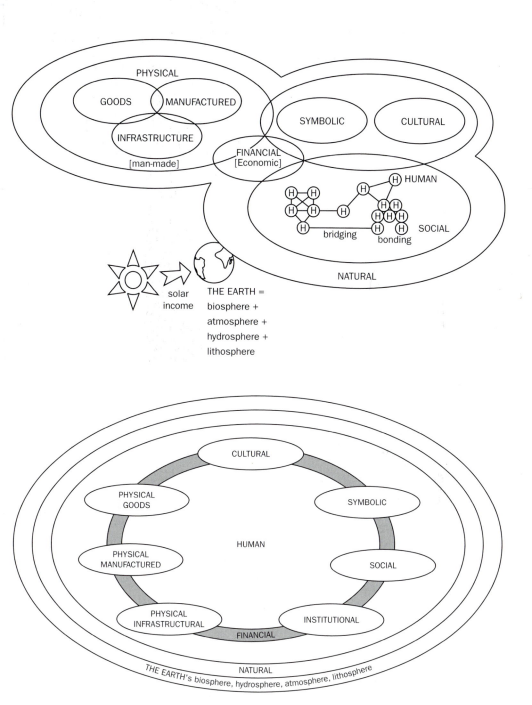

Figure 1.3
Anthropocentric views of ten key 'capitals'

All the above capitals can be affected in either a positive or negative way, depending on the aim or objective of the activism. So capital can be grown or diminished and/or redistributed differently. Figure 1.3 shows how the various capitals relate to each other, in particular how financial (economic) capital works across all the other forms of capital because money and other financial instruments are merely a representation of other forms of wealth (capital) equating to a medium of exchange, standard of deferred payment, unit of account or a 'symbolic' store of value.[29] Physical capital embraces manufactured, infrastructure and material goods. In the Five Capitals model, 'manufactured capital' is man-made material artefacts that 'contribute to the production process, but do not become embodied in the output of that process'.[30] This includes buildings, infrastructure and technologies. Social capital embraces both human capital and the capital of humans gathered in institutions, and interfaces with ideas of cultural capital and symbolic capital.

Recent interpretations of human capital have included physical, intellectual, emotional and spiritual capacities.[31] Danah Zohar indicates that the notion of 'spiritual capital' goes beyond any religious or institutionalized vision of 'spirituality', rather it addresses fundamental searches for 'shared meanings, value and ultimate purpose' and that this is critical if we are to achieve 'sustainable capitalism and a sustainable society'.[32] Forms of activism are also an attempt to disrupt existing paradigms of shared meaning, values and purpose to replace them with new ones, and so activism perhaps embodies a sense of developing the spiritual capacity of individual human capital, that is collectivized in social capital.

The activism landscape

It is possible to construct a map of contemporary activism focal points and issues by referring to the Five Capitals Framework (Figures 1.4 to 1.8) and by also considering the capital of man-made (material) goods (Figure 1.9). These 'mind-maps' are conceived as a starting point for the reader to extend or modify this activist landscape, rather than a definitive mapping. Certain focal points or issues are common to the maps for several capitals. For example, alternative economic approaches such as co-operatives, social enterprises and non-monetary models feature in financial capital and man-made (material) goods capital. The concept of 'low-carbon economy' features in financial capital and in natural capital.

There are five key areas of activism centred around financial (economic) capital (Figure 1.4):

- international development
- alternative economies
- corporate lobbyists
- intellectual property ownership
- alternative banking.

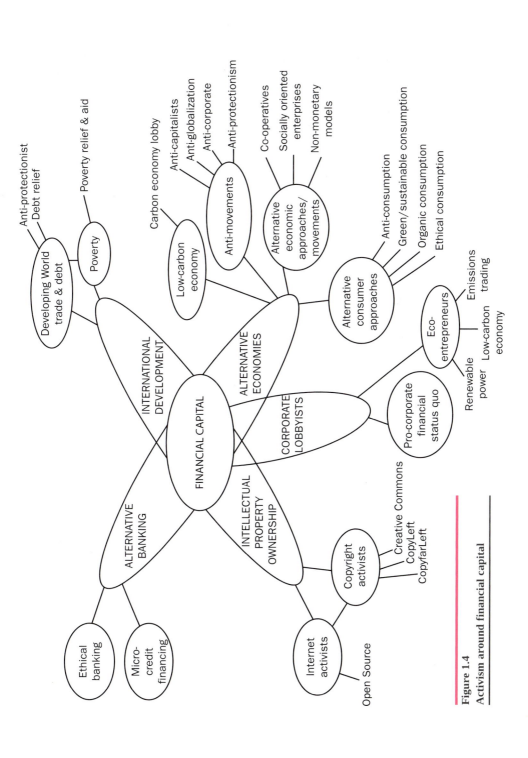

Figure 1.4
Activism around financial capital

Figure 1.5
Activism around natural capital

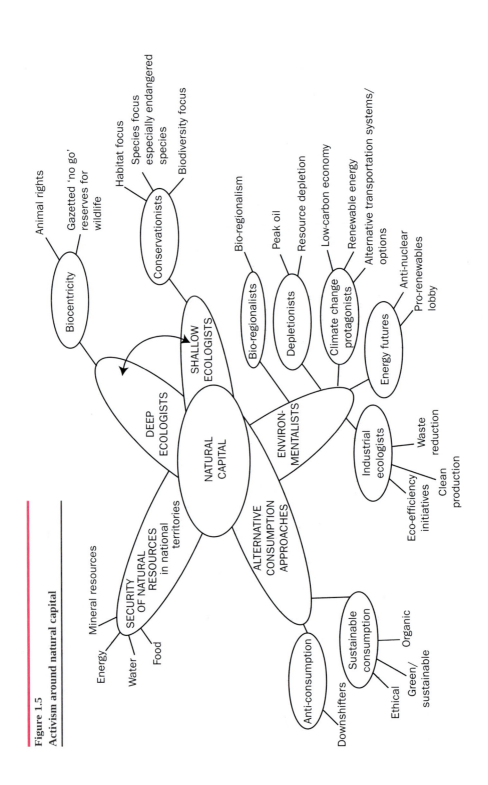

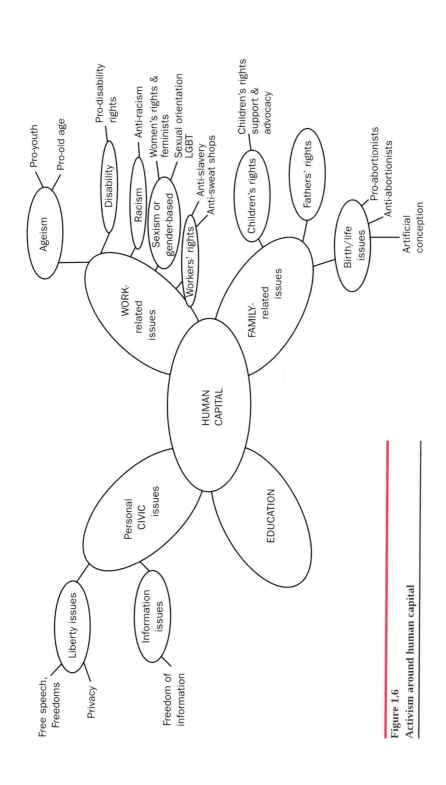

Figure 1.6

Activism around human capital

Figure 1.7
Activism around manufactured capital

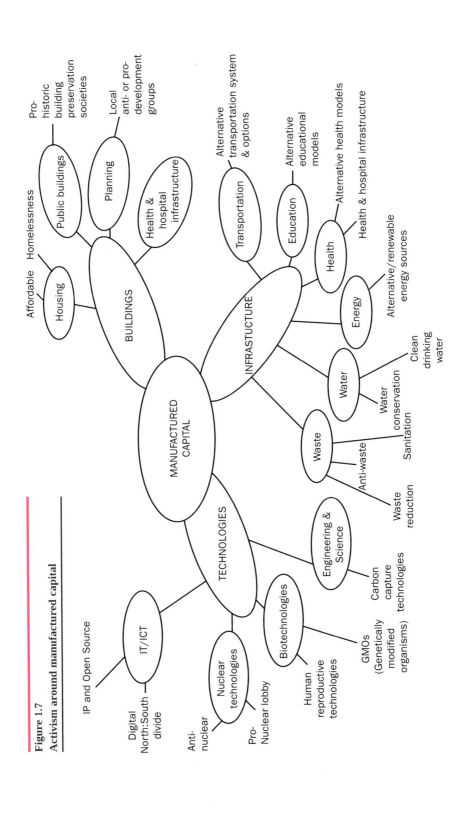

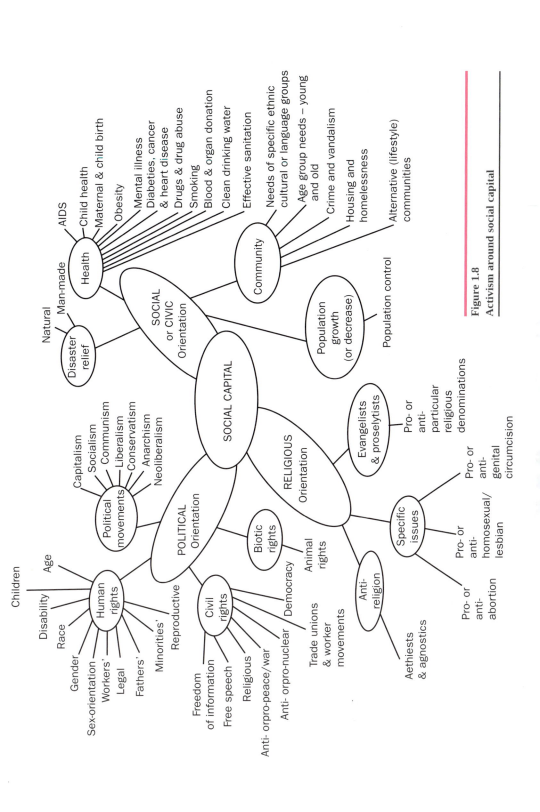

Figure 1.8
Activism around social capital

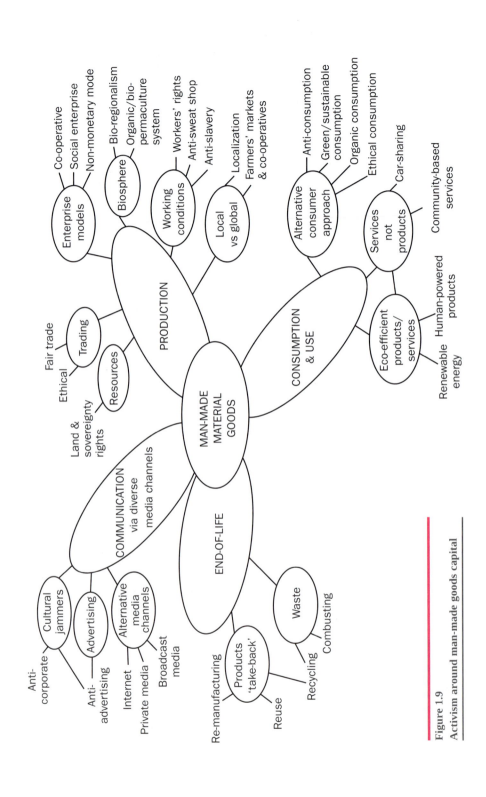

Figure 1.9
Activism around man-made goods capital

Natural capital distinguishes between the approaches of the 'deep' and 'shallow' ecologists, environmentalists, alternative consumption movements and those concerned with the security of natural resources in national territories (Figure 1.5). The foci of activism around human capital are based around rights and issues concerned with work, family, education and personal civic rights and issues (Figure 1.6). Manufactured capital is centred around buildings, infrastructure and technologies (Figure 1.7). The focal points and issues around social capital are the most numerous and complex but orientate around three main areas – social/civic, political and religious domains (Figure 1.8). Lastly, the activism associated with man-made (material) goods capital is orientated around the life cycle of production, consumption and end-of-life, and how these material goods are communicated through diverse media channels (Figure 1.9).

Reference to this schematic model reveals an activism landscape that is varied and far ranging. While many of the focal areas of activists are clearly anthropocentric, and gather around changing social, cultural and/or political thinking, structures and activities, other activists address biocentric causes including representation to support 'endangered species' and biodiversity, animals and their rights, and the conservation or restoration of specific habitats. The scope for the design activist to contribute to this activism landscape is huge. The areas where design activists are already contributing is discussed in later chapters.

Activism in architecture, design and art

In a broader design context there is a strong emergent interest in how design is engaging with issues both locally and globally.[33] This is explored further in Chapter 4. However, there is a paucity of literature addressing the notion of activism in many of the design disciplines (which this book sets out to address), with the exception of architecture and graphic design which have received more attention regarding the nature of their activism. The literature ranges from examining the thoughts and outputs of individual architects or graphic designers to looking at broad trends and approaches. For example, Whyte examines in minute detail the work of the German architect Bruno Taut and the 'Activists', emerging out of Expressionism into Functionalism in the late 19th and early 20th centuries.[34] In reality the Activists, informed by 'social idealism', had little effect on inculcating real social change as its proponents remained aloof architectural visionaries rather than grassroots political revolutionaries. Dovey explored the nature of power structures mediating the built environment and the architecture activism deployed in this mediation process.[35] Farmer examined the green/ecological timeline through architectural design history.[36] More recently, several works have examined architectural practice in the improvement of lives for the poor and displaced in the US, the developed North and the developing South.[37,38] There is a rich seam of texts that look at all facets of the ecological, bioclimatic and environmental dimensions of architecture[39] – all relevant topics for the architect activist wishing to tread more lightly on the planet's resources.

Graphic design, firmly rooted in the arena of design communication, has long been associated with social and political discourse and propaganda. Recent studies indicate a rude health for graphic design activism from the early struggles of the suffragette movement in the 1860s to the present day.[40] The voices of graphic designers regularly bubble up during times of social and political change, both in the service of clients' needs and with concerns raised by the designers themselves, the latter being good examples of design-led activism.[41] Showing a continued thirst for responsible graphic design, the *First Things First* manifesto launched by Ken Garland in 1964 was recently republished by self-proclaimed 'culture jammers' Adbusters in 1999,[42] who have their own particular brand of graphic design activism particularly targeting transnational corporations.[43] This is an indication that graphic design still has a very central role to play in activism's wider purpose.

While the subject of this book is design, a brief consideration of art's relationship with activism is helpful at this juncture. Although art would seem to occupy a prime position to influence social and political discourse, Felshin queries the uneasy relationship that 'art activism' has with 'art'.[44] The notion that art activism is challenging the culture of art *and* a wider socio-cultural platform is realized in the conceptual art of the late 1960s and early 1970s[45] with its temporal, often performance-based interventions or activities, and its interventions in mainstream media. The approach of many of the artists in this era involved collaborative participation between other artists and a wider public, making the outputs only achievable with a dialogic exchange. In doing so they contested the notion of the art object and its 'commodity-driven delivery system' and led to new meaning for the art work being located in its contextual framework not in an autonomous object.[46] This meant that new physical, institutional, social or other contexts could become the focus of an art work and, arguably, led to the emergence of the early environmental and land art from the likes of Robert Smithson and George Trakas. Lessons from this earlier art activism offer some insights into where commodity-driven design may care to set its ambitions (see Chapters 5, 6 and 7) including new arenas for participation.

Motivation and Intention

What motivates the activist? Personal motivation may embrace needs, desires, goals, a certain philosophical approach, or other intrinsic factors. Activists can also be driven by a strong sense of altruism or morality, aimed at delivering benefits for the greater societal good (although there may not be a consensus on what this 'good' constitutes). Aside from these intrinsic factors, external circumstances can provide strong motivational forces. A trigger or stimulus from the existing system

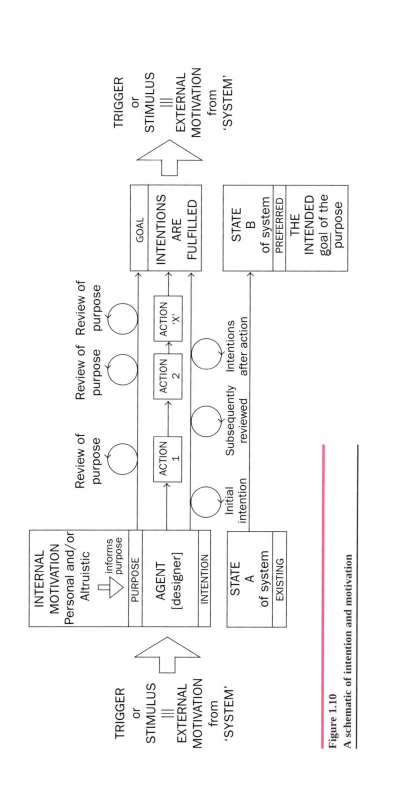

Figure 1.10
A schematic of intention and motivation

can motivate. Activists tend to gather around social movements, interest groups around specific causes, a set of beliefs or perceptions that something is unjust, dangerous or of concern to future generations. Of great importance is how the activists frame their beliefs/perceptions as this contributes to defining their purpose or goal-orientation and hence their intention achieved through specific actions to reach the goal (Figure 1.10). Intention informs a series of iterative actions that continually allow interrogation of the purpose in order to reach the goal. The achievement of the goal is attainment of the original purpose. However, the effectiveness of the intention and purpose needs to be measured against the change in system from 'state A', the original state, to 'state B', the altered state.

While activists take on the role of 'change agents', trying to influence and change the behaviour of others, they may also experience what is known as 'transformational activism', a concept where the activists and the subject(s) of their activism undergo a personal internal transformation as well as expressing it outwardly. This suggests that being an activist is part of a personal developmental and life journey to realize a state of being, as well as a desire to contribute to a greater societal good.

As will be seen in later chapters, those who apply design in an activist cause need to have a clear idea of their purpose or intention and its potential effectiveness. This is particularly important when considering the targets of the activism and the intended beneficiaries.

Issue-Led Design and the Sustainability Challenge

The list of adjectives used as descriptors for design (Table 1.1) have been rearranged to reveal certain orientations (Figure 1.1): two major orientations emerge. It is clear that 'design' can be orientated towards a specific *discipline* and that certain *approaches/frameworks* can be applied. Particular considerations will be associated with specific design disciplines. So, for example, automobile design frequently deals with safety, ergonomics, aesthetics and fuel efficiency; fashion design has to consider drapability and durability of fabrics, colour trends, etc. Certain considerations apply across all disciplines, such as cost, availability of materials, clients' needs and so on. What is interesting is that the design approaches/frameworks can, in general, be applied to any discipline. Furthermore, each design approach/framework embeds its own characteristics related to particular contemporary issues (Table 1.3). In other words, many design approaches/frameworks are already 'issue-led'. In that sense design is already 'activated' in trying to address contemporary issues. Is there a meta-challenge, an overarching challenge, tying this seemingly disparate lexicon of design approaches/frameworks together? 'Sustainability' may be conceived as that meta-challenge – a concept that had its first tentative expressions more than 60 years ago, although it was then referred to in terms of man and his total environment.[47]

Table 1.3

Characteristics and contemporary issues associated with particular design approaches/frameworks

Design approach/ framework	Typical characteristics	Key contemporary issues
Collaborative	Participatory processes and methodologies	Cultural, social, political – participation and democracy
Conceptual	Speculative future scenarios, futurology	Cultural and social transformation
Critical	Speculative design proposals, provocation, intervention	Cultural and social critique
Cross-cultural	Issues of hegemony, cultural power, values	Cultural, social and political aspects of globalization/ localization
Eco-	Issues related to the environmental and sustainability impacts of design	Environment, sustainability
Design criticism	Informing and shaping views of design/public worlds by reflective writing	Any contemporary issues
Design education	Design and delivery of specialist courses in 'design'	Any contemporary issues
Design history	The study of the history of design	Any contemporary issues
Design management Design planning	Processes to implement or plan design within a business or organizational context	Any contemporary issues
Design research	Allocation and management of design-related resources	Any contemporary issues
Design theory	The study of design theory by reflection on its actions, processes and outcomes	Any contemporary issues
Environmental	A framework that encourages a reciprocal relationship between the design object (on a micro- or macro-scale) with natural systems	Environment, sustainability
Gender	The analysis of objects with regard to their genderization	Cultural, social, political
Green	Considers issues of the environmental impacts of design	Environment, sustainability
Participatory	A collaborative approach to the design of products, services, spaces or systems that involves actors/stakeholders in the design process	Cultural, social, political – participation and democracy
Protest	A loose movement of mainly younger designers commenting and reflecting on current social/political issues	Cultural, social, political, environmental issues

Design approach/ framework	Typical characteristics	Key contemporary issues
Re-	'Refining, improving, or reinterpreting an already existing functional design'	Economic, environmental, cultural (consumerism)
Slow	'An approach that encourages a slower, more considered and reflective process, with the goal of positive well-being for individuals, societies, environments and economies'	Any contemporary issues
Strategic	An approach aimed at levering maximum competitive advantage to businesses or organizations by using design at a strategic level of operation or management	Economic +/- corporate social responsibility (social and/or environmental)
Universal	An approach that encourages designs that should be equally accessible and can be experienced by the largest possible number of people. Synonymous with design for accessibility, design for all, transgenerational design and inclusive design	Cultural, social, political – participation and democracy
Metadesign	Design that designs itself, within the whole, in order to redefine and synergize social and technical infrastructures, collaboratively and co-adaptively.	Cultural, social – participation and democracy
Co-design	Design that brings users, actors and stakeholders into the design process on the basis that everyone likely to use a design has a voice in its conception	Cultural, social – participation and democracy
Sustainable design	Design to deliver sustainable development and deliver the 'triple bottom line' – by balancing profit, people, planet	Balancing economic, ecological and social considerations
User-centred	Design that focuses on the needs of the users and involves them in the design process	Cultural, social – participation by users
Empathic design	Combining qualitative methods of engaging with users with quantitative user data	Economic, cultural, social – participation by users
Experience design	Designing human experiences foremost and products, processes and services that deliver that experience	Economic, cultural, social

Sustainability is grounded in ecological praxis and systems thinking. It challenges the capitalist system of production and consumption that assumes unlimited growth.

The concept of sustainability gathered renewed interest in 1980 when the term 'sustainable development' was first articulated by the International Union for Conservation of Nature and Natural Resources[48] with the most cited definition being quoted from Gro Harlem Brundtland's 1987 report, *Our Common Future*:[49]

> *Sustainable development is 'development that meets the needs of the present without compromising the ability of future generations to meet their needs'.*

Since then, substantive efforts have been made to agree on what sustainable development actually means, but it remains a 'contestable concept like liberty or justice'.[50] Sustainability has many flexible definitions, depending on the context and the field of study. Deeply rooted in the concept of sustainability is the question of equity, between and within generations[51] and, the deep ecologists would argue, for an equity between humans and other life forms. Environmental economists, who by definition are engaged with improving ecological efficiency (improved economic viability with reduced negative environmental impact) tend to address sustainability by the maintenance or non-depletion of the Earth's 'natural capital', i.e. all that nature's biotic (living) and abiotic systems provide to man-made systems of capital. Yet this ignores the social and institutional dimensions of sustainability that strive to deliver equal shares of these capitals. Simon Dresner notes that 'sustainability is an idea with a certain amount in common with socialism'.[52] This socialist orientation ensures that many activists, of diverse persuasions well beyond the environmentalists, are attracted to the concept of sustainability.

There are dozens of definitions of sustainability, the most apt from a design point of view being the one adopted by Domenski et al in 1992 to reference the idea of the 'sustainable city', which is a complex design outcome:

> *'Sustainability may be defined as a dynamic balance among three mutually interdependent elements: (1) protection and enhancement of natural ecosystems and resources; (2) economic productivity; and (3) provision of social infrastructure such as jobs, housing, education, medical care and cultural opportunities.'*[53]

Designers of all persuasions may recognize the daily balancing act that they already carry out which acknowledges the mutual interdependence of the three elements. This definition recognizes the services that nature provides and the duty of care man has to nature, invokes productivity rather than economic growth, and links sustainability to our overall social condition and health. In fact these three elements, the ecological, the economic and the social are often used in Venn diagrams to represent eco-design and sustainable design with their eco-efficiency and triple bottom line (TBL) agendas – people, planet and profit (Figure 1.11). In 1992 in Rio de Janeiro, the United Nations Conference on Environment and Development organized the Earth Summit bringing together nearly 200 nations to discuss the (perilous) state of the world's environment.[54] The Agenda 21 framework of action, emerging from the Earth Summit, added important considerations to the sustainability debate – the idea about participation, open government and institutional roles. The institutional element adds a level of complexity and gave rise to the sustainability prism (Figure 1.11) which links the ecological, economic, social and institutional dimensions.[55] Moving from the bilateral agenda of eco-efficiency to the tripartite agenda of TBL shifts the number of possible relationships from one to three. Inclusion of the fourth institutional dimension suddenly generates six possible relationships, and so a level of complexity. Nonetheless, the sustainability prism becomes a more holistic framework for balancing considerations of the different dimensions and revealing opportunities and threats.

Sustainability is seen as the pre-eminent challenge of the 21st century, although it remains a quixotic and contentious concept. As a result, Janis Birkeland now prefers to talk about 'positive' rather than 'sustainable' development in the context of urban planning and design:[56]

> *'Positive development refers to physical development that achieves net positive impacts during its life cycle over pre-development conditions by increasing economic, social and ecological capital.'*

This definition specifies the direction of the development and how it should affect economic, social and ecological capital. Design can have a positive impact on these capitals and has already evolved over the past three decades to rise to the sustainability challenge. The question is how much of this design response can be considered as 'design activism'?

Defining the Design Activism Space

An understanding of the wider activism landscape, as illustrated in Figures 1.4–1.9, reveals a broad territory for designers to consider where, when and how they can contribute to socio-cultural and political change, and in doing so help build positive capital in each of the capitals identified. There are many actors, agents and stakeholders in this activist landscape that intentionally or unintentionally use design, design thinking and other design processes to deliver their activism. Intentional use of design may involve the commissioning of professional designers by organizations or individuals with an activism orientation. It may also involve the use of design thinking and processes by those that are not professional designers in

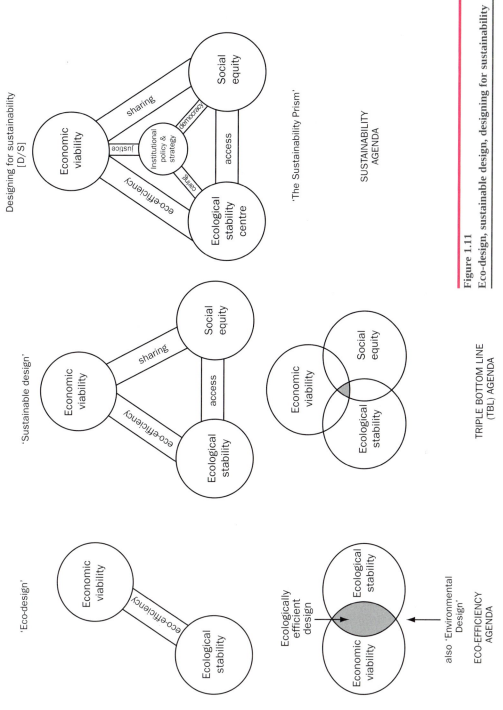

Figure 1.11
Eco-design, sustainable design, designing for sustainability

these same organizations. Both these applications of design may be considered as 'design-orientated activism' emanating from 'traditional' activist organizations. When designers themselves intentionally use design to address an activist issue or cause, whether working alone or within a not-for-profit design agency specifically set up with altruistic objectives, it can be considered as 'design-led activism'. This distinction is confirmed by the preliminary results of a survey of the design press initiated by Ann Thorpe, a researcher at the Open Unversity in the UK.[57] This book predominantly focuses on expressions of activism by designers, i.e. design-led activism, and the spaces that this occupies, in order to investigate the current state of the art.

Drawing lines between 'avant-garde' and 'activism'

Isn't all 'avant-garde' design a form of activism, as it represents the vanguard, the leading edge? The answer partly depends upon the purpose, intention and motivation of the designers and the scope of ambition to address the culture of design and/or the wider societal culture. Definitions of the avant-garde have remained remarkably consistent over the past 50 years, ranging from the 'pioneers or innovators in any art in a particular period'[58] to 'any group of people who invent or promote new techniques or concepts, especially in the arts',[59] although others would widen the scope of avant-garde activities to experimental work in art, music, culture or politics.[60] The avant-garde offers an alternative world-view, a counter-narrative to the dominant narrative. Poggioli observed that the avant-garde is solitary, loves its ivory tower, while courting an aristocratic body of the initiated, and that the 'tragic position' of the avant-garde art is that it must fight on two fronts simultaneously against the bourgeois culture of which it is an offspring and against popular culture.[61] If this general characterization of the avant-garde is true, then the focus appears to be on changing an elite culture first before that group can then in turn extend influence over a wider socio-cultural or political group. Of great importance is whether the avant-garde is intent on serving him/herself and/or is indeed looking to benefit others. Knowing the intention of the avant-garde is again of primary importance in determining the extent of their activist ambitions.

Social movements embody activism by group action – a collective aspiration to maintain or change the existing situation. Those that seek change may be at the leading edge of societal or political change and so would seem to share some similarities with the more maverick character of the avant-garde. Yet, in the blurring of boundaries between one social class and another that occurred throughout the 20th century, and with the further democratization of channels of influence through the social networking phenomenon of the internet, the primacy of an elitist avant-garde to exert influence has perhaps been eroded. Does the avant-garde still exist in a design activist sense? And if it does, what causes and forms of activism does it favour?

A preliminary definition of 'design activism'

Having scoped the broad territory of 'design' and 'activism', acknowledging that activism is focused around contemporary social, environmental and political issues, and seeing how current design theory and practice sit within the sustainability debate, it is possible to offer a tentative preliminary definition of design activism.

> *Design activism is 'design thinking, imagination and practice applied knowingly or unknowingly to create a counter-narrative aimed at generating and balancing positive social, institutional, environmental and/or economic change'.*

The emphasis on 'counter-narrative' is important as it suggests that it is somehow different from the main narrative, either that which is explicitly and collectively agreed upon by society as being 'mainstream' or being implicit in accepted behaviour (the underlying paradigm). The implication is that design activism voices other possibilities than those that already exist with a view to eliciting societal change and transformation. While those who unknowingly apply design thinking, imagination or practice in the cause of design activism are important – the unknown, non-intentional designers – it is those who knowingly use design, i.e. the design-led activists, who are the subject of investigation below.

Notes

1   Neutra, R. (1954) *Survival through Design*, OUP, Oxford, p314.
2   Erlhoff, M. and Marshall, T. (eds) (2008) *Design Dictionary: Perspectives on Design Terminology*, Birkhäuser-Verlag, Basel/Boston/Berlin.
3   Ibid. p104.
4   For example, see Julier, G. (2000, 2008) *The Culture of Design*, Sage Publications, Los Angeles, London, New Delhi, Singapore, 1st and 2nd edns, for historical and emerging perceptions of design and design culture; and a blog, Designfeast, www.designfeast.com/ for how the design conversation is changing.
5   Erlhoff and Marshall (2008), op. cit. Note 2.
6   Boradkar, P. (2007) 'Theorizing things: Status, problems and benefits of the critical interpretation of objects', *The Design Journal*, vol 9, no 2, pp3–15.
7   Fallman, D. (2008) 'The interaction design research triangle of design practice, design studies, and design explorations', *Design Issues*, vol 24, no 3, MIT Press Journals, Cambridge, MA, pp4–18.
8   Spangenberg, J. H. (2002) 'Environmental space and the prism of sustainability: frameworks for indicators measuring sustainable development', *Ecological Indicators*, vol 57, pp1–14.
9   For example, Al Gore, author, climate change lobbyist and ex-presidential candidate, US; Tony Juniper of Friends of the Earth, UK; Jonathon Porritt, author, chair of the Sustainable Development Commission, UK; Alex Steffen, Worldchanging, US.
10 Simon, H. (1996) *The Sciences of the Artificial*, MIT Press, Cambridge, MA; a republication of the original 1969 version.

11 Papanek, V. (1974) *Design for the Real World: Human Ecology and Social Change*, Paladin, St Albans, UK, p17.

12 See for example, Lewis, H. and Gertsakis, J. with Grant, T., Morelli, N. and Sweatman, A. (2001) *Design + Environment: A Global Guide to Designing Greener Goods*, Greenleaf Publishing, Sheffield, p19; and Morelli, N. (2007) 'Social innovation and new industrial context: Can designers "industrialize socially responsible solutions?"', *Design Issues*, vol 23, no 4, Massachusetts Institute of Technology, Cambridge, MA, pp3–21.

13 Thackara, J. (2005) *In the Bubble: Designing in a Complex World*, MIT Press, Cambridge, MA, p2; Whiteley, N. (1993) *Design for Society*, Reaktion Books, London; Morelli, N. (2007), ibid.

14 Tarrow, S. (2005) *The New Transnational Activism*, Cambridge Studies in Contentious Politics, Cambridge University Press, Cambridge.

15 Tarrow, S. (1994) *Power in Movement: Collective Action, Social Movements and Politics*, Cambridge University Press, Cambridge.

16 Wikipedia (2008) 'Activism', http://en.wikipedia.org/wiki/Activists; Google Directory (2008) 'Society>Activism', www.google.co.uk/Top/Society/Activism/

17 Porritt, J. (2007) *Capitalism as if the World Matters*, revised paperback edition, Earthscan, London.

18 Bonsiepe, G. (1997) 'Design – the blind spot of theory, or, Theory – the blind spot of design', conference text for a semi-public event of the Jan van Eyk Academy, Maastrict, April 1997.

19 Porritt (2007), op. cit. Note 17.

20 Smith, A. (1776) 'Of the Nature, Accumulation, and Employment of Stock', book 2, chapter 1, paragraph 18, available at www.adamsmith.org/smith/won-b2-c1.htm, accessed September 2008.

21 Porritt (2007), op. cit. Note 17.

22 Wikipedia (2008) 'Social capital', http://en.wikipedia.org/wiki/Social_capital, accessed September 2008.

23 According to Putnam, R. (2000) *Bowling Alone: The Collapse and Revival of American Community*, Simon and Schuster, New York, cited in Porritt (2007), op. cit. Note 17.

24 Wikipedia (2008) 'Financial capital', http://en.wikipedia.org/wiki/Financial_capital

25 Porritt (2007), op. cit. Note 17, p197.

26 Ibid. p183.

27 Bourdieu, P. and Passeron, J-C. (1977) *Reproduction in Education, Society and Culture*, Sage Publications, London; translated by Richard Nice from the French (1970) *La Reproduction*, Paris, Éditions de Minuit.

28 Bourdieu, P. (1986) 'The Forms of Capital', from J. E. Richardson (ed) *Handbook of Theory of Research for the Sociology of Education*, Greenwood Press, available at http://econ.tau.ac.il/papers/publicf/Zeltzer1.pdf, accessed September 2008.

29 Wikipedia (2008), op. cit. Note 24.

30 Porritt (2007), op. cit. Note 17, p183.

31 Ibid. p8.

32 Ibid. p169.

33 See, for example, Steffen, A. (ed) (2006) *Worldchanging: A User's Guide for the 21st Century*, Abrams, New York; Mau, B. with Leonard, J. and the Institute without Boundaries (2004) *Massive Change*, Phaidon, London; Thackara, J. (2005) *In the Bubble: Designing in a Complex World*, MIT Press, Cambridge, MA.

34 Whyte, I. B. (1982) *Bruno Taut and the Architecture of Activism*, Cambridge University Press, Cambridge.

35 Dovey, K. (1999) *Framing Places: Mediating Power in Built Form*, Routledge, London and New York.

36 Farmer, J. (1996) *Green Shift: Towards a Sensibility in Architecture*, edited by K. Richardson, Architectural Press, Oxford.

37 Bell, B. (ed) (2004) *Good Deeds, Good Design: Community Service through Architecture*, Princeton Architectural Press, New York.

38 Sinclair, C. and Stor, K. with Architecture for Humanity (2006) *Design Like You Give a Damn: Architectural Responses to Humanitarian Crises*, Thames & Hudson, London.

39 Some popular sources include: Wines, J. (2000) *Green Architecture*, edited by P. Jodidio, Taschen, Köln; Behling, S. and Behling, S. (2000) *Solar Power: The Evolution of Sustainable Architecture*, Prestel, Munich/London/New York; Lloyd Jones, D. (1998) *Architecture and the Environment: Bioclimatic Building Design*, Lawrence King Publishing, London; Vale, B. and Vale, R. (1991) *Green Architecture: Design for a Sustainable Future*, Thames & Hudson, London; Slessor, C. (1997) *Eco-Tech: Sustainable Architecture and High Technology*, Thames & Hudson, London; McHarg, I. (1992) *Design with Nature*, John Wiley & Sons, New York, first published by the Natural History Press in 1969; van der Ryn, S. and Cowan, S. (1996) *Ecological Design*, Island Press, Washington, DC.

40 Cranmer, J. and Zappaterra, Y. (2004) *Conscientious Objectives: Designing for an Ethical Message*, RotoVision, Mies, Switzerland, pp10–29.

41 Heller, S. and Vienne, V. (eds) (2003) *Citizen Designer: Perspectives on Design Responsibility*, Allworth Press, New York; Heller, S. and Kushner, T. (2005) *The Design of Dissent: Socially and Politically Driven Graphics*, Rockport Publishers Inc, MA, with cover design by Milton Glaser and M. Ilic.

42 See the orginal Ken Garland's original manifesto, http://en.wikipedia.org/wiki/First_Things_First_1964_manifesto; Adbusters, www.adbusters.org; Wikipedia, 2008, 'First_Things_First_2000_manifesto', http://en.wikipedia.org/wiki/First_things_first_2000_Manifesto

43 Lasn, K. (2006) *Design Anarchy*, Adbusters Media Foundation, Vancouver, British Columbia.

44 Felshin, N. (1995) *But is it Art?: The Spirit of Art Activism*, Bay Press, Seattle, WA.

45 Ibid. p10.

46 Ibid. p19.

47 Vogt, W. (1949) *Road to Survival*, Victor Gollancz, London, quoted in Bell, S. and Morse, S. (1999) *Sustainability Indicators: Measuring the Immeasurable*, Earthscan, London, p7.

48 Dresner, S. (2008) *The Principles of Sustainability*, 2nd edn, Earthscan, London, p1.

49 World Commission on Environment and Development (1987) *Our Common Future*, Oxford University Press, Oxford.

50 Dresner, S. (2008), op. cit. Note 48, p2.

51 Ibid. p2.

52 Ibid. p4.

53 Dominski, A., Clark, J. and Fox, J. (1992) *Building the Sustainable City*, Community Environment Council, Santa Barbara, US, quoted in Bell, S. and Morse, S. (1999) *Sustainability Indicators: Measuring the Immeasurable*, Earthscan, London.

54 Rio de Janeiro 'Earth Summit' was organized by the United Nations in 1992 and was reported in a wide range of publications including Bell and Morse (1999), op. cit. Note 53 and Dresner (2008), op. cit. Note 48.

55 Spangenberg, J. H. and Bonniot, O. (1998) *Sustainability Indicators – A Compass on the Road towards Sustainability*, Wuppertal Paper 81, Wuppertal Institute, Wuppertal (was reprinted by the Organisation for Economic Co-operation and Development (OECD) and thus spread rather widely); Spangenberg, J. H. (2002) 'Environmental space and the prism of sustainability: frameworks for indicators measuring sustainable development', *Ecological Indicators*, vol 57, pp1–14.

56   Birkeland, J. (2008) *Positive Development: From Vicious Circles to Virtuous Cycles Through Built Environment Design*, Earthscan, London, pXV.

57   Thorpe, A. (2008) 'Design as activism: A conceptual tool', in *Changing the Change: Design Visions, Proposals and Tools*, Changing the Change conference, Turin, Italy, June 2008, Umberto Allemandi & Co, pp13, www.allemandi.com/cp/ctc/book.php?id=115&p=1, p11.

58   Fowler, H. W. and Fowler, F. G. (eds) (1964) *The Concise Oxford Dictionary of Current English*, 5th edn, Oxford University Press, London.

59   Wiktionary (2008) 'Avant garde', http://en.wiktionary.org/wiki/avant_garde

60   Wikipedia (2008) 'Avant garde', http://en.wikipedia.org/wiki/avant_garde

61   Poggioli, R. (1968) *The Theory of the Avant Garde*, translated by G. Fitzgerald, Belknap Press, Cambridge, MA, p37, p216, cited in Whyte (1982), op. cit. Note 34.

Past Lessons: A Short History of Design in Activist Mode, 1750–2000

'Designing is not a profession but an attitude.'　　　　　　　Laszlo Moholy-Nagy

Design as 'Giving Form to Culture'

The history of design activism is woven into a wider history of design. What can we learn from that history and how has it informed what design activism is today? What were the motives and intentions, and who were the target audiences and beneficiaries of the designers? How do the findings fit with the central idea of activism as an act to create positive social and political change?

It is important to enquire whether designers were specifically interested in changing the culture of design, i.e. the culture specifically belonging to the world of design, or a wider expression of culture as it belongs to the wider society, or indeed whether they were targeting both. Guy Julier differentiates between design culture as an object of study – as a process, as context-informed practice, as organizational or attitudinal, as agency, and as pervasive but differentiated value – and as an academic discipline (Table 2.1).[1] Today's omnipotent design culture, at least in the 'developed' North,[2] plays a comprehensive role in suggesting and/or setting new values and, hence, inculcating societal change. Whosoever controls the designers – in modern capitalism that role generally falls to business and government – controls to a large degree the expressions and evolution of the design culture. The idea of design culture as an agency of reform (or even revolution) directing design towards greater and more direct social and environmental benefit, indicates the necessity to include wider societal representation and control of design activities. Does design history reveal these past 'agents of reform'?

How far back we care to take the 'past' in referencing design is a moot point. 'Design' appears to have entered language and been given etymological birth in the Italian Renaissance as *disegno*, communicating the idea of drafting or drawing,[3] but arguably did not find its way into general use until the first rumblings of the pre-industrial revolution in the mid-18th century.[4] However, Sparke notes: 'The designed artefact is on its simplest level … a form of communication and what it

Table 2.1
Interpretations of 'design culture'

an 'object of study'	
A design culture located in communication; something that is all around; an attitude; a value; a desire to improve things; existing at the local level; embedded in the working systems, knowledge and relationships of designers and design users; as a form of agency, 'encultured' design; directed towards future global change and a generator of (new) value; as a means to herald changes in a wider world; a ubiquitous presence; study of the material and immaterial aspects of everyday life; articulated through images, words, forms and spaces *and* it engages discourse, actions, beliefs, structures and relationships; motivated by concepts of value, creation and practice	
As 'process'	A design culture described by the contextual influences and contextually informed actions within the development of a design; systems of negotiation that define and frame design artefacts; process produced within and by a network of everyday knowledge and practices that surround the designer
As 'context-informed practice'	A design culture concerned with collectively held norms of practice influenced by geographical context of the local and/or the globalized, dominant, mainstream forms of practice; as a forum and platform; embraces notions of 'creative industries' as agents in business organization and 'brand stewardship'
As 'agency'	A design culture as an attitudinal marker for an organization and/or design engaged towards direct social and environmental benefits; a 'way of doing things'; context as circumstance not a given; a change agent
As 'pervasive but differentiated value'	A design culture going beyond traditionally held notions of 'excellence', 'innovation' or 'best-practice' able to create specific and designerly ambience
As an 'academic discipline'	
Not 'design culture' but 'Design Culture', to sit alongside Visual Culture, Cultural Studies, Media Studies and even Design History; moving from an emphasis of the 'reading' of an image to a culture that is three-dimensional, equally tactile as visual and textual, all engulfing, lived in and directly encountered rather than as a (sole visual) representation; 3D visual artefacts that are not only 'read' but experienced within structured systems of encounter within the visual and material world; the study of design primacy for establishing symbolic value, a productive model of styling, coding and effective communication; designing an 'aestheticized state', commodifying the visual to meet modern capitalism's imperative; where in the new conditions of design culture, cognition becomes as much spatial and temporal as visual, embracing reality and virtual reality	

Source: Julier (2008)[5]

conveys depends on the framework within which it functions.'[6] This acknowledges that any artefact communicates and embeds design, and that designed artefacts pre-date the era of the Renaissance, the Enlightenment and the Industrial Revolution on which so much design history is focused.

How has the role of design shifted through these eras? Figure 2.1 brings together the work of the Postmodern critic Charles Jencks with some concepts developed by brand consultant Will Murray.[7] Jencks, in his landmark book *What is Post-Modernism?*,[8] indicated that human concepts of time and space have gone through several phases. The first phase concluded around 1450 with the emergence of the Renaissance and the concept of 'linear' time–space, the notion of progress. This era signalled the end of 'cyclic' time–space that had kept man in empathy with nature's rhythms. The birth of the Industrial Revolution literally accelerated the idea of progress and rapidly evolved design praxis (theory and practice). A further gear change in the time–space model happened in 1960 when the earlier ideas of 20th century modernity (with its roots in the late Medieval period and then the Enlightenment) were rejected in favour of a populist, pluralist Postmodernity with a concurrent ideological shift from mass consumption to individualized consumption. Murray looks back even further and suggests that societies are actually 'economies'. As one society merges into another society we are really seeing shifts in economic models as a fundamental driver. Over the past 10,000 years there has been a consistent trend – the lifespan of these economic models is getting shorter (Figure 2.1).

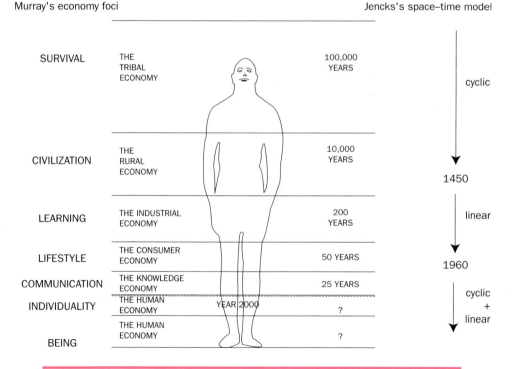

Figure 2.1
How has the role of design changed over time with successive economies and space–time models?

As design helps materialize a 'culturally acceptable' form to represent the economic model,[9] then design has evolved with these economic models and with our psychosocial perceptions of this rapidly changing world and its new time–space perceptions.

Design has occupied this central role as mediator of cultural acceptability and therefore provides a regulatory service in production and consumption. This role has shifted in three major phases between 1750 and 1990.[10] The first phase, 1750–1850, heralded spectacular developments in agricultural equipment, the steam engine and early models of industrial manufacturing in the great ceramics companies of the Staffordshire Potteries, such as Wedgwood. The second phase, 1851–1918, commenced with the world's first trade fair, the Great Exhibition at Crystal Palace, London, representing an industry servicing the production and consumption boom of the European powers as they exploited their colonies for raw materials and labour. World War I, 1914–1918, shifted the global order and heralded the third phase in the history of industrial design, 1918–1990, where various design movements and groups juggled for supremacy throughout the 20th century. In each of these phases, the products (objects of production) become texts in 'circuits of culture'.[11] These artefacts are texts, representations that live within cultures, inform identities and social relations, and generate feedback to the next generation of production. John Wood sees design as a 'wise regulation of dynamic elements' where 'form giving' controls not only flows of materials in goods and products, but also controls the awareness and regulation of perceived value and hence the next cycle of 'form giving'.[12] Tony Fry neatly encapsulates all these circuits and flows with the beautifully simple phrase, 'design designs'[13] recently interpreted as 'design as preconfiguration and directionality' with the capability to influence what we choose to design and what happens next.[14] Perhaps this preconfiguration could be interpreted as 'memes' – units of information and units of cultural transmission that explicitly and implicitly guide behaviour. Wahl and Baxter suggest that real forms are in themselves memes, but also carry a second meme, a vMEME or value meme.[15] In giving form to the dominant socio-political and socio-economic norms, design simultaneously confers meaning and values, and affirms the dominant paradigm. Contention of the dominant paradigm implies the existence of a counter-narrative(s). Do these examples exist in design history and, if affirmative, how do they reveal themselves under the lens of sustainability as acts of design activism? How have these instances attempted to preconfigure and direct design, and the wider, culture?

A summary of the main design movements, groups and initiatives is given in Appendix 1 together with a brief analysis of the motivations, intentions, target audience and beneficiaries of their activities. Their achievements are also viewed through the lens of sustainability, so the outcomes are viewed in relation to positive economic, ecological, social and institutional contributions.

1750–1960: Mass Production and (Sporadic) Modernity

The steam engine came of age in 1740 in Great Britain heralding a new energy source to drive new visions of mass production involving the local, regional and international transportation of materials, often over great distances, to a centralized factory. Here labour, formerly deployed on the land but driven from it by the introduction of mechanized equipment, worked with new steam-driven machinery to produce the goods for populations at home and overseas, the latter busily expanding and exploiting the first truly global business of Empire. In 1759, Josiah Wedgwood established his innovative ceramics business in the Potteries in Staffordshire, England.[16] He was the first entrepreneur to achieve mass production of beautiful, affordable tableware, and set a model for mass production that still exists today.

In just 100 years, the physical, psychological, emotional and spiritual landscape of Britain had changed dramatically.[17] This was lauded and celebrated in the Great Exhibition of 1851 in London's Crystal Palace – a building that was remarkable in itself for being a modular flat-pack construction of steel and glass predominantly made in Birmingham, central England and transported to the capital by canal barge and horse-drawn transport. Surely this represented a positive design contribution to society, a vision of man taming nature and forging progress? Not everyone agreed. Early dissenters included Augustus Pugin and John Ruskin who critiqued the poor quality of the industrial goods on display at the Great Exhibition and the crass ornamentation, which they perceived as a cacophony of visual discord. These were the first design activists prepared to stand up to the Industrial Revolution juggernaut. Pugin and his colleagues set the tone for later dissenters who found their voice through William Morris, who established his own company in 1861 – Morris, Marshall & Faulker & Co – intent on promoting a revitalized vernacular simplicity combined with excellent craftsmanship. Morris and his colleagues extolled the virtues of these new ideas of craft as a means to promote social cohesion. Here were the founders of the late 19th-century British Arts and Crafts movement, the first design reformers intent on contributing to positive social change through improved design of artefacts, textiles, wallpapers and buildings. Sadly, their ambition outstripped their effectiveness. Morris and his followers encouraged artists to get out of their academies and immerse themselves in more prosaic production activities. He also galvanized the Arts and Crafts Guilds to organize themselves, and set standards of quality for both design and production. However, the outputs of their efforts could only be afforded by the bourgeois. More progressive thinkers in the movement, such as Charles R. Ashbee and Gordon Russell, established rural furniture manufacturing operations in an attempt to create more affordable products. Yet, the rampant industrialization and commercialization of Victorian life was largely untouched by these initiatives. There was, however, an unseen legacy. This early design movement is credited with stimulating and provoking thoughts among artists and designers throughout Europe, laying the foundations for various expressions of Art Nouveau and, in the first decade of the 20th century, the Vienna Workshop, Austria, and Deutscher Werkbund, Germany. The Deutscher Werkbund, 1907–1935 and 1947–present, emerged out of the expressive Jugendstil (representing Art Nouveau) to become the first significant organization to exploit and communicate the power of design as a vehicle for improving people's lives. The early reforms of the Werkbund were celebrated by Heinrich Waentig noting that 'a simple form, imposed on everyone, could produce 'the most complete and noble overcoming of class conflicts', clearly enunciating the socialist ambitions of this design movement.[18] Functionalism demonstrated a new German idealism, but also drove darker ambitions of imposing artistic imperialism that emerged over the course of the next two decades.

Existenzminimum and other socially orientated housing projects by the Deutscher Werkbund

With the rise of national German folk culture and a concurrent socialist ideology, the Werkbund's remit was focused on achieving good design with utilitarian production methods that maximized quality but retained affordability. A leading exponent of this affordable but functionalist design, with its socially conscious imperative, was Richard Riemerschmid accompanied by Bruno Paul, Peter Behrens and Josef Maria Olbrich working alongside established and respected manufacturers. Members included artists, designers and architects, including Walter Gropius, later to become the founding director of the Bauhaus. After a landmark exhibition in 1914 in Cologne – the Deutsche Werkbund-Ausstellung, showing Gropius's steel and glass factory (and its improved conditions for production and the workforce) – the Werkbund's popularity was assured and by 1915 it had attracted nearly 2000 members. In 1924, under the helm of Riemerschmid, the Werkbund published *Form ohne Ornamen* (*Form without Ornament*) heralding the foundation of early Functionalism. In 1927, the architect Mies van der Rohe coordinated, on behalf of the Werkbund, architects from all over Europe to work on the *Weissenhofsiedlung*, a housing estate in Stuttgart. Interiors were fitted with the steel tubular furniture of van der Rohe, Mart Stam, Marcel Breur and Le Corbusier – some of the avant-garde of Modernism. A similar ideology was rolled out for the *Existenzminimum* apartments for low-wage earners in Frankfurt, Stuttgart, Dessau, Breslau and Berlin. While the idea of social housing was not new (in England visionary social housing was the ambition of the US philanthropist George Peabody, who formed the Peabody Trust in 1862, and W. H. Lever who developed a model village at Port Sunlight by Lever Brothers in 1888), the belief that design of space, light and the component furnishings could elevate the quality of life of the inhabitants was radical.

Bauhaus myths and realities

The illustrious history of the Bauhaus, its directors and students, has rightly garnered much attention from the design historians in its pivotal role in establishing the rationality and efficiency of the Modern movement's modes of design and production. In effect, this was the third era of modernity culminating in the 'designability of everything and everyone' – the first and second eras of modernity stretching from the Middle Ages to the Enlightenment.[19] Yet the Bauhaus was a quixotic institution subject to at least five phases of growth and change, often instigated by each director responding to internal and external political pressures. It was during the directorship of Hannes Meyer, from March 1928 to July 1930, that the Bauhaus enjoyed its most socially proactive phase. Meyer was a steadfast proponent of affordable design and architecture for the working classes with his slogan 'popular requirements instead of luxury requirements'.[20] Meyer was perceived in retrospect as one of the most important Functionalists in the architecture of the 1920s.[21] In 1929, he oversaw the design of the Trades Union School, Bernau, Berlin and the fixtures and fittings for the People's Apartment. The furniture was so diligently conceived that it could have easily been mass produced. A touring exhibition for the cities of Basle and Mannheim, organized by Meyer, included Gustav Hassenflug's folding table and Marianne Brandt and Hin Bredendieck's redesigned bedside light for the Kandem company (Figure 2.2). The aesthetic of these products reveals a seductive simplicity akin to the contemporary designs of a present-day IKEA showroom. This reflected Meyer's beliefs that design could elevate the welfare of the people and it could harmonize the requirements of the individual with the community. Meyer's commitment to socialist ideals even led him to take a group of students to the Soviet Union in 1930 under the banner of the red Bauhaus brigade – an act that may have eventually led to his dismissal later that year as the political climate changed in Germany.

It seems Meyer was, under the preliminary terms of design activism defined so far, the Bauhaus's lead design activist. Despite his intentions, the measurable benefits of his endeavours were probably limited. While the quality of the Bauhaus's output is uncontested, and the contribution made to the pedagogy of art and design is not in dispute, many of the activities only influenced a relatively small number of manufacturers and built developments. In short, the Bauhaus did not seem to *directly* touch many in society, although its ripples were surely felt. Perhaps the disbandment of the Bauhaus in 1933 meant that the full social potential of the experiment could not be felt. The dispersal of many Bauhaus luminaries to the US and other countries following the swing towards Fascism and World War II undoubtedly provided many international benefits, but the momentum of design as a positive social force was lost and along with it the central ideal of Modernism to improve the human condition. The radical underlying social agenda of the Bauhaus was rapidly commodified in the International Style, which was soon recognized as

Figure 2.2
Furniture for the 'People's Apartment', Bauhaus touring exhibition 1929

a vehicle for transnational companies to flag their modern ideals, but not necessarily their social mores.

From the 1930s to the 1960s, in the growing world of consumer products, Modernism took a few twists and turns through Streamlining, Organic Design, Utility Design, Good Form and Bel Design, and Good Design. Two of Organic Design's great exponents deserve a mention for their consistent attempts to humanize the overtly functional codes of Modernism and their introduction of organic forms. Frank Lloyd Wright in the US cut his teeth with his Prairie Houses in and around the suburbs of Chicago, revealing his empathy for natural materials and light, born out of a sympathy for the Arts and Crafts. He brought a holistic approach combining the best of Modernism with nature's own genius in each location, and later championed outstanding examples of Organic Design, such as the Guggenheim Museum (1943–1946 and 1955–1959). The other luminary was the Finnish designer, Alvar Aalto. Aalto's genius was to see the use of natural materials and light as a humanizing element in design that offered psychological benefits over man-made synthetic materials. The Paimio Sanatorium, 1928–1929, for tuberculosis patients, is one of his most well-known early works. His eclectic forms for grand

and modest public buildings, and a number of experimental private houses, indicated his human-centred version of the Modern movement, and ambition to improve people's well-being through the very fabric of the architecture. While both these architects strove for buildings that made genuine attempts to improve well-being, and undoubtedly influenced the culture of architecture, their contribution to wider social benefits seems less easy to confirm.

In the pre- and post-World War II years, there was little dissent from the Modernist mantra, just the occasional voice or head raised above the parapet. Early environmentalists had spotted some of the problems inherent in industrialization and consumerism, and the insatiable demands on nature's resources and ecosystems. Aldo Leopold's *Sand County Almanac* introduced the concept of a 'land ethic', calling for man to adjust his presumption as nature's conqueror to one of citizen sharing the Earth with a wider biotic community whose stability was in the citizen's interest.[22] An early advocate of treading more lightly on the planet's resources was Richard Buckminster Fuller, a maverick whose work ranged from mathematics to architecture and industrial product design. Buckminster Fuller was environmentally and socially aware, proposing numerous concepts and realizing diverse projects that addressed eco-efficiency and affordability – many emerging from his Dymaxion Corporation, a name derived from 'dynamic' and 'maximum'. Projects included prototype housing (Dymaxion House, 1927; Witchita House, 1945) and cars (Dymaxion Car, 1934). He popularized the concept of the light-weight, efficient geodesic dome and was not alone in his concerns for the welfare of the planet. In the mid-1950s, architect Richard Neutra unveiled his concerns in *Survival through Design* and Vance Packard wrote a withering trilogy of books exposing the deceit and lies of the consumer economy (*The Hidden Persuaders, The Status Seeker,* and *The Waste Makers*).[23] But it took an angry post-World War II generation, and the emergence of new voices in 'youth' and 'teenagers', to foment social change and, finally, an interrogation of the dicta of the Modernists. They rejected the notions of an elite circumscribing and moralizing about what constituted 'good design' and embarked upon a design fiesta that marked the birth of the consumer economy, still with us today.

1960–2000: From Pop and Postmodernism to Postmodern Ecology and Beyond

The 1960s heralded a social, technological and environmental watershed. Here was a discursive climate from which an explosion of fresh ideologies resulted. The father of British Pop Art, Richard Hamilton, posited the idea that values are explicitly and openly debated in a genuinely democratic society: 'An ideal culture, in my terms, is one in which awareness of its condition is universal.'[24] The elitist Modernist principles adapted by so many of the industrialized countries had failed to respond to the paradigm-shifting consequences of the emergent post-war consumer economy and its resultant outputs of mass culture and mass taste.[25] A new design language, 'pop design' emerged with its central tenets of diverse expression, symbolism, ephemerality and fun.[26] Parallel to the mass-market exploitation of pop design to sell yet more, there was an emerging coalition of Italian designers and architects whose ambition it was to leave Modernism behind and to forge a new experimental era. The various individuals, groups and activities of the Italian Radical Design and Anti-Design movements operated from 1967 until the late 1970s/early 1980s.[27] Well-known Radical Design groups such as Archizoom, Superstudio and Gruppo Strum critiqued the rationalist approach and contested design's role in consumerism. A counter-architecture and design group Global Tools, 1974–1975, explored non-industrial techniques, inspired by the Arte Povera movement in Italy. In the mid-1970s, expressions of Anti-Design, from the likes of Studio Alchimia, led by Alessandro Mendini, revitalized design with an overt political, fun and deconstructionist message. There is no doubt that these Italian movements, and especially the theorist practitioners Andrea Branzi, Riccardo Dalisi and Lapo Binazzi, prepared the ground for a healthy pluralism and the seedbed for the emergence of Postmodern thought. This celebration of cultural pluralism recognized the ecology of the human condition, something Rationalism and Functionalism had ignored at its peril. In doing so, design genuinely sought to improve relationships between objects, spaces, the built environment and human fulfilment. Sadly, the genuine efforts of these proto-Postmodernists were easily subverted by commercial exploitation. The Italian manufacturer Alessi SpA was a knowing contributor to the debate, hiring early Postmodern luminaries such as the US architect and designer Michael Graves to create cutting-edge design for the cognoscenti, but their objectives were primarily driven by a commercial expediency. Questions of greater import around the deleterious effects of mass consumption on society and the environment were left to an emergent group of Postmodern ecologists and 'alternative' designers.

Out of the early Postmodern debate did emerge a genuine desire to involve people in the realization of design projects. An exemplar of this more participatory approach is the Byker Wall Estate in Newcastle-upon-Tyne by the architect Ralph Erskine with the local community (1973–1978). Yet it was the ecological imperative, rather than the social one, that garnered more attention during the 1970s.

The Postmodern ecologists

As the photographs from the Apollo space missions in the 1960s first revealed the beauty and fragility of planet Earth and Buckminster Fuller coined the expression 'Spaceship Earth', the environmental movement found new momentum. Buckminster Fuller was an early advocate of resource conservation throughout the 1960s. In 1963 he proposed an inventory of world resources,[28] but it was 20 years later just before his death in 1983 that the likes of the World Resources Institute and other organizations took up the call in earnest. However, the social turbulence of the 1960s and new energy in the environmental movement stirred the global design community.

The manifestos and ambitions of the Postmodern ecologists are clearly expounded by Jencks and Kropf[29] with Ian McHarg setting the foundation stone for this school of thought in his 1969 treatise, *Design with Nature*,[30] firmly stating that the values of the economic system must embrace biophysical realities and human aspirations. The economy sits within a greater ecology, biotic and human, and to ignore that is perilous. It had taken two decades to synthesize the underlying concerns of Vogt, Leopold, Neutra, Packard and early environmentalist/scientists such as Rachel Carson (and her shocking revelations about environmental damage in *Silent Spring*[31]) into formative propositions for the design community. And it took a further two decades to progress the cause of Postmodern ecology, the main tenets of which are explored in Figure 2.3a and Figure 2.3b. Advocacy varies from biocentric to humanist perspectives and some manage to combine both perspectives to encourage more symbiotic relationships between man and nature. Their voice is still growing and perhaps with more urgency today as issues such as climate change and 'peak oil' impact on architecture and the design of transportation and food production systems.

The alternative designers

Parallel to the development of a strong line of Postmodern ecological architectural praxis, other design disciplines contributed to a critique of mainstream design and culture in the 1960s and 1970s. They were inspired in part by the Situationists International, a self-appointed group of cultural critics, led by Guy Debord, famous for their distribution of graphics and posters in the May 1968 Paris riots. Their critique of the commercial appropriation of all aspects of everyday life, and the acquiescence of creative professionals in this appropriation, not only tapped into the Zeitgeist but confronted all those involved in design with some searching questions.

First Things First – manifesto for graphic designers
A challenge to graphic designers, and those responsible for advertising and early brand management activities, was originated by Ken Garland in 1964, when he published the *First Things First* manifesto.[32] This manifesto stimulated much debate in the graphic design industry varying from a positive shift towards the search for creating new meaning and a wholesale rejection of the manifesto for being naïve and idealistic. This shift from profit-/self-/form-centred design to human-centred design was a big challenge to the graphic design community. The urgency of this call got lost in the euphoria of popular culture and pop design coupled with the economic turbulence of the 1970s. However, the legacy lives on in organizations like Adbusters who, with Garland's approval, updated and published a revised version of the *First Things First* manifesto in 2000.[33]

Victor Papanek and Design for Need

In 1969, the same year that McHarg published *Design with Nature* aiming at architects and landscape architects, the International Council of Societies of Industrial Design (ICSID) initiated some soul searching among industrial designers. ICSID held a conference in London entitled 'Design, Society and the Future' encouraging designers to consider the economic, social and moral consequences of their work. In 1971, Victor Papanek launched his polemical book, *Design for the Real World*, striking deep into the design profession.[34] Papanek's pitch was straightforward – designers needed to take responsible decisions, spend less time designing ephemeral goods for the consumer economy, and spend more creative time on generating solutions to the real needs of the disadvantaged 80 per cent population of the planet. He was lauded and rejected in equal measure across the design world. Just a few years later, the Middle East oil price rise crisis in 1973–1974 gave another jolt to collective design thought. It even heralded the introduction of life cycle thinking (LCT) and life cycle analysis (LCA) by US design engineers challenged by the political administration to quickly find ways of becoming more energy efficient. In 1976, the Royal College of Art set up an exhibition and symposium called 'Design for Need' with Papanek as keynote speaker. This debate prompted the emergence of fresh design approaches – universal design, inclusive design and user-centred design, setting a lasting impact

Figure 2.3a
Design themes from Postmodern ecology

on design culture. However, this call to arms left the general modus operandi for industry unaffected.

Alternative, appropriate and DIY technology

A mish-mash of 'alternative design' groups aspired to a simpler life, downshifting from the consumerist society and its multiplicity of negative impacts. Communities sprung up all over the world, reaching out for Stewart Brand's *Whole Earth Catalog*, a toolbox of ideas and equipment, to create an autonomous way of life.[35] Some of these initiatives still flourish today, although they have all had to find some common ground to maintain relevance to mainstream culture. Examples include the Centre for Alternative Technology in Wales; Paolo Solari's Arcosanti, an evolving town in the Arizona desert, US; and various eco-villages including Findhorn, Scotland. Second-generation experiments for alternative holistic design include sophisticated ecological community planning such as the Center for Maximum Potential Building Systems' Advanced Green Building Demonstration in Austin, Texas, US, 1994–1997 and the Laredo Demonstration Blueprint Farm in Laredo, Texas, US, 1997 onwards.[36]

Other trends were visible in product design. In Germany in 1974, Jochen Gros formed the group Des-in which experimented by designing using recycled materials

---

1991 Team Zoo/Atelier Zō
Principles of Design
Expression of region
Diversity
Emotional sensory response
Experience of time
Balancing & enjoying nature
Aimas moko – undefined,
vague or ambiguous
Area of transition
Jiku – axis, orientation

1992 Willaim McDonough
The Hannover Principles
Co-existence of humanity & nature
Interdependence & distant effects
Relationships between spirits & matter
Responsibility – human well-being
Responsibility – viability of natural systems
Safe objects of long-term value
Eliminate concepts of waste
Evaluate full life cycle
Rely on natural energy flows
Understand the limitations of design
Improve by sharing knowledge

1994 Ken Yeang
Bioclimatic Skyscrapers
Design with climate
Life-cycle energy costs
Users' sense of well-being
Energy-conserving agenda
Abiotic/biotic relationships
Variable deep air zones
Transitional spaces
Building skin
Homeostatic systems

1991 Brenda & Robert Vale
Green Architecture
Earth, water, fire, air
Actions and consequences
Conserving energy
Working with climate
Minimizing new resources
Respect for users
Respect for site
Holism – Holistic approach
Common ground – user/architech

1993 Peter Calthorpe
The Next American Metropolis
Timeless qualities of culture & community
Walking distance neighbourhoods
Pedestrian Pockets – circulation local
Transit–Oriented Developments – circulation beyond local
Affordable, mixed use
Pedestrians make communities meaningful
Energy and habitat protection & enhancements

1992 Sim Van der Ryn
and Stuart Cowan
Ecological design
Mirror nature's deep connections
Solution grows from place
Ecological accounting informs design
Design with nature
Everyone is a participant-designer
Make nature visible

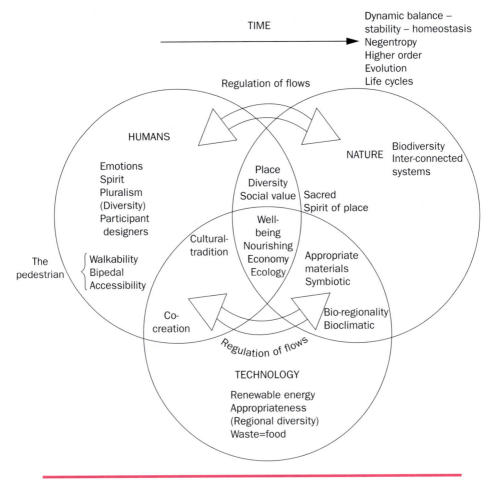

Figure 2.3b
A model of nourishment and well-being in the new Postmodern eco-economic landscape

and alternative production methods. These experiments had little effect on German industrial product design, locked into the functionalist and production aesthetic of the Ulm School of Design, but did raise the consciousness within the design community to wider responsibilities.

Yet another branch of this alternative design thinking were the 'alternative' or 'appropriate' technology groups who focused on issues of shelter, sanitation and potable water for poor communities in the North and South. The Centre for Alternative Technology in Wales[37] was set up in 1973 by Gerard Morgan-Grenville and continues to to provide support, advice and training for those interested in everything from off-the-grid living to permaculture studies. The Intermediate Technology Development Group (ITDG) was founded in the UK in 1966 by

E. F. Schumacher, author of *Small is Beautiful*, a seminal book on the value of locally focused economies.[38] The ITDG still encourages design engineers to find practical, affordable solutions – a direct and lasting response to the call made by Schumacher and Papanek – and a vocation recently celebrated by the Cooper-Hewitt Museum in New York in its exhibition 'Design for the Other 90%'.[39]

Out of this diverse range of alternative movements came the advocates of a particular form of ecological design – permaculture design – a holistic, minimal, interventionalist and ecological design approach. The founders of permaculture design were Bill Mollison and David Holmgren in the mid-1970s.[40] They have continued to refine and develop the design principles over the past 30 years[41] with emphasis on three underlying ethical principles – care of the Earth, its people and a fair share for everyone. Since 2002, permaculture thinking and practice has stimulated new forms of grassroots localization, like the Transition Towns movement aiming to 'power down' in response to the double whammy of climate change and peak oil.[42]

The eco-efficiency activists

From the early to mid-1980s, designers from a wide range of disciplines examined how they could aspire to create more eco-efficient buildings, products and services. This repositioning of their design philosophy sets them in a positive activist mould whose aim is to reduce the environmental footprint and impact of their creations. Quite simply, they adopted a new client – the environment.

Architectural responses tended to follow certain strategies: an update of vernacular traditions and techniques with sensitive culturally relevant design; reuse and recycling of materials; embedding of the latest eco-technologies to reduce a building's environmental load. Occasionally the strategies were hybridized. This work is well documented in architectural publications and will not be further considered in detail (see examples cited pp17–18 and Note 39 on p29). There are rarer examples where ideas of socio-cultural sustainability are blended seamlessly with eco-efficiency and a powerful design aesthetic. The Jean-Marie Tjibaou Cultural Center, 1992–1998, in Nouméa, New Caledonia by the architect Renzo Piano, is an exemplar.

In the late 1980s there was a shift in Western European countries towards a concept of the 'green consumer'.[43] John Elkington penned a ten-point code for green designers for the Design Council in the UK in 1986. This galvanized certain sections of the industrial product design community, especially design engineers, who were helping companies to bring 'green design' products to the market.[44] Through the early 1990s this approach to product design acquired the catch-all description of 'design for the environment' (DfE) and a well-developed toolbox emerged.[45] DfE, also referred to as 'eco-design', was seen as a promising approach to encourage companies, especially small and medium-sized enterprises (SMEs) in the Netherlands to improve their environmental standards, and to stimulate the debate among designers.[46] Van Hinte and Bakker[47] flagged the potential of design to communicate potential eco-design futures by proactive interventions, provocations, experimental prototypes (one-offs) and propositional or protest artefacts (see pp83, 85 for definitions). Their curatorial observations signalled a fresh avenue for exploration that was already being exploited by an exciting group of Dutch designers, Droog Design[48] concerned with ecological, social, psychological and behavioural aspects of sustainability.

What are the Lessons Learnt?

This short perambulation of 19th- and 20th-century design history (see Chapter 4 for post-2000 design activism) sheds some illumination on the various expressions of design and whether they held any activist intentions. This canon of design history often reveals an inwardly focused design culture examining the self, egoism, the design community and its culture, rather than being orientated towards more altruistic ambition for specifically defined social, ethnographic or global causes. In general, designers seem to have been driven by personal and/or avant-garde ambitions although some of the mavericks and activists described above did counter design's tendency for navel gazing. They were, however, few in number until the emergence of the consumer economies that rose out of the ashes of World War II. This seemed to release design from the pre-war constraints of Modernism, Functionalism and Rationalism. The euphoria of the economic miracles of the 1950s, and purposeful positioning of 'Good Design' (UK), 'Bel Design' (Italy) and 'Good Form' (Germany) by governments and their design bodies, was rudely supplanted by radical alternative design movements and popular consumer design in the 1960s. Concurrently, the reality of the downsides of the consumer economy began to bite as the extent of global environmental problems, coupled with the mid-1970s oil crisis and the general waning of European manufacturing, were felt. During the 1970s, some designers realigned themselves towards more altruistic purposes, but a paradigm shift in design philosophy was not to be realized (and we are still waiting). Some 30 years later, at the turn of the millennium, the majority of product, lighting and furniture designers were still largely untouched by more altruistic concerns connected with environmental and/or social issues.[49]

The target audiences for many of the design movements, groups and individuals cited above were predominantly aimed at designers, with a view to changing the way they think, approach their work and deliver their form-giving, rather than at specific targets external to the world of design. This implies a clear focus on changing design culture in research, education and practice. While difficult to quantify, the reality of effecting change in wider cultural settings often appears to have had a negligible, notional or rather diffuse impact at the social level. The main beneficiaries were often the designers themselves, the evolution of design culture and the growth of industrial and commercial enterprises. There are some notable exceptions, from the Deutscher Werkbund, and Hannes Meyer's Bauhaus in Dessau, to the Design for Need movement of the 1960s and the work of individual luminaries in the 1970s, including architect Ralph Erskine, and some of the more socially conscious alternative design movements from the 1970s to the present day.

Design evolved and was generally synergistic with the growth of the Industrial Revolution, the ambitions of the Machine Age, Functionalism and the Modern movement. Design indulged in its own Postmodern fiesta, fetishizing over form (arguably this continues apace) and has bounced around consuming a plethora of short-lived ideologies for the past 40 years. Alain Findeli[50] neatly summarizes a century and a half of these design cycles as a preoccupation with the rhetorical tools of aesthetics (late 19th/early 20th century), ergonomics (mid-20th century) and semiotics, which he notes is really 'aesthetics again' (in the late 20th century). While the heroes and heroines charting counter-narratives to the accepted design paradigm are few, they reveal a valuable lesson to aspiring design activists today – be very clear about your intentions, specify the target of your ambitions, and measure the results to ensure that the beneficiaries really do benefit.

By focusing on environmental positives, rather than socio-cultural ones, the story of design history looks somewhat different. While the British Arts and Crafts movement raised the spectre of massive environmental damage wrought by the Industrial Revolution, its impact in addressing it was minimal, although as a design phenomenon it was seminal in the evolution and reform of design culture in the late 19th and early 20th centuries. After almost 70 years of very little environmental focus by designers there was a flurry of 'alternative design' champions in the 1970s, but the positive impacts were marginal and soon faded. A steady, but minority, uptake of Postmodern ecology practice since the late 1970s/early 1980s and the application of DfE since the mid-1980s has made progress and elicited a quiet design activism of its own, but remains a 'minority sport'. An additional challenge is that eco-efficiency in buildings, services and products will not, in itself, guarantee future sustainability because of the well-documented 'rebound effect' where people spend the money released by eco-efficient goods or services on other things, and so negating any gains, or where the sales of eco-efficient products actually increase to deliver more overall environmental impacts. The eco-efficiency and eco-tech agenda will not alone rescind the likely repercussions of 150 years of economic growth. Significant shifts in individual and collective behaviour are required in combination with eco-effective design.

There is a growing need for new design heroes and heroines to provide some guidance to meet the enormity of the scale of the environmental, social and economic crises in the global, and regional/local, economies (see Chapter 3). While there have been, and are, some lucid voices from the design community,[51] and the aforementioned maverick designers and architects, the silence from wider design education and practice communities is notable. Ironically, while design is acknowledged as a powerful communicative force, it has failed to communicate its own social and environmental ambitions to society, and so remains perceived as merely a servant to powerful economic imperatives. At the end of the millennium, Rachel Cooper's rhetorical question, 'Is design in a philosophical crisis?', seems apt and timely.[52] Perhaps sustainability offers *the* opportunity for design to find its real voice. It appears that design activists may have to multi-task by focusing on saving society, the environment *and* the future of design.

Notes

1   Julier, G. (2008) *The Culture of Design*, 2nd edn, Sage Publications, London, pp3–6.
2   The reference 'North' refers to the developed, Westernized countries largely found in the Northern hemisphere; the 'South' refers to the developing or emerging countries largely found in the Southern hemisphere. The design theorist and critic Guy Bonsiepe prefers use of the word 'peripheral' countries to describe the 'South' because it identifies 'the core cause of under-development, which is the lack of autonomy to act'. The 'central' countries represents the North, which exercises tremendous power and control over the periphery. Bonsiepe, G. (1999) *Interface, An Approach to Design*, Jan van Eyck Academie, Maastricht, p100.
3   Hauffe, T. (1998) *Design: A Concise History*, Lawrence King, London, p10.
4   Sparke, P. (1987) *Design in Context*, Guild Publishing, London.
5   Julier (2008), op. cit. Note 1, pp3–11.
6   Sparke (1987), op. cit. Note 4, p8.
7   Jencks, C. and Kropf, K. (eds) (1997) *Theories and Manifestoes of Contemporary Architecture*, Wiley-Academy, Chichester; Murray, W. (2000) *Brand Storm: A Tale of Passion, Betrayal, and Revenge*, Financial Times/Prentice Hall, London.
8   Jencks, C. (1986) *What is Post-Modernism?*, Academy Editions, London.
9   Findeli, A. (2001) 'Rethinking design education for the 21st century: Theoretical, methodological, and ethical discussion', *Design Issues*, vol 17, no 1, MIT, Cambridge, MA, pp5–17.
10   See the trilogy of books that charts the design history from 1750 to 1990, from the Industrial Revolution to Postmodernity: Ponte, A. (ed) (1990) *1750–1850 The Age of the Industrial Revolution*; Ausenda, R. and Ponte, A. (eds) (1990) *The Great Emporium of the World*; and Ausenda, R. (1991) *The Dominion of Design*, all published by Electra, Milan.
11   Richard Johnson's 'circuit of production and consumption' and Paul du Gay's 'circuit of culture' quoted in Julier (2008), op. cit. Note 1, pp66–69.
12   Wood, J. (2003) 'The wisdom of nature = the nature of wisdom. Could design bring human society closer to an attainable form of utopia?', paper presented at the 5th European Design Academy conference, 'Design Wisdom', Barcelona, April, available at www.ub.edu/5ead/PDF/8/Wood.pdf, accessed September 2008.
13   Fry, T. and Hart, A. (1999) *A New Design Philosophy: An Introduction to Defuturing*, New South Wales University Press, Sydney.

14   Fry, T. (2008) *Design Futuring: Sustainability, Ethics and New Practice*, Berg Publishers, Oxford; Willis, A.-M. (2008) 'Design, redirective practice and sustainment', keynote talk at *360 Degrees*, a conference organized by the School of Architecture and Design, University of Brighton, UK, 19–20 September, on behalf of the DEEDS project, www.deedsproject.org.

15   Wahl, D. C. and Baxter, S. (2008) 'The designer's role in facilitating sustainable solutions', *Design Issues*, vol 24, no 2, pp72–83.

16   Ponte (1990), op. cit. Note 10.

17   Ausenda and Ponte (1990), op. cit. Note 10.

18   Ibid.

19   Erlhoff, M. (2008) 'Modernity', in Erlhoff, M. and Marshall, T. (eds) *Design Dictionary*, Birkhäuser Verlag, Basel/Boston/Berlin, pp262–266.

20   Eisele, P. (2008) 'Bauhaus', in Erlhoff, M. and Marshall, T. (eds) *Design Dictionary*, Birkhäuser Verlag, Basel/Boston/Berlin, p41.

21   Bauhaus Archiv and M. Droste (1998) *Bauhaus 1919–1933*, Taschen, Köln.

22   Leopold, A. (1968) *A Sand County Almanac*, Oxford University Press, Oxford (first published 1949).

23   Neutra, R. (1954) *Survival through Design*, Oxford University Press, Oxford; and Vance Packard's trilogy – *The Hidden Persuaders* (1957) and *The Status Seekers* (1959) both published by Penguin Books, Harmondsworth; and *The Waste Makers* (1960) David McKay Co, London.

24   Richard Hamilton cited by Whiteley, N. (1993) *Design for Society*, Reaktion Books, London, p167.

25   Sparke (1987), op. cit. Note 4, p214.

26   Sparke (1987), op. cit. Note 4, p217.

27   Fiell, C. and Fiell, P. (1999) *Design of the 20th Century*, Taschen, Köln, pp39–41, pp589–590.

28   Who is Buckminster Fuller?, www.bfi.org/our_programs/who_is_buckminster_fuller/design_science/design_science_decade

29   Jencks and Kropf (1997), op. cit. Note 7, pp133–168.

30   McHarg, I. (1992) *Design with Nature*, John Wiley & Sons, New York (first published by the Natural History Press, 1969).

31   Carson, R. (1962) *Silent Spring*, Hamish Hamilton, London.

32   Reproduction of the original *First Things First* manifesto by Ken Garland in 1964, www.xs4all.nl/~maxb/ftf1964.htm

33   Revised *First Things First* manifesto published by Adbusters in 2000, www.xs4all.nl/~maxb/ftf2000.htm

34   Papanek, V. (1974) *Design for the Real World*, Paladin, St Albans, originally published in 1972 in the UK by Thames & Hudson, London, written in 1971.

35   The story of Stewart Brand's counterculture education and tools, that were made available via publications and educational tours, is outlined in Wikipedia's article 'Whole Earth Catalog', http://en.wikipedia.org/wiki/Whole_Earth_ Catalog, accessed September 2008.

36   Wines, J. (2000) *Green Architecture*, Taschen, Köln, pp152–155.

37   Centre for Alternative Technology, www.cat.org.uk/information/aboutcatx.tmpl? init=4

38   Intermediate Technology Development Group, http://practicalaction.org/? id=about_us; and, Schumacher, E. F. (1973) *Small is Beautiful: Economics as if People Mattered*, Harper & Row, London.

39 Cooper-Hewitt National Museum, http://other90.cooperhewitt.org/; and Smith, C. (2008) *Design for the Other 90%*, Cooper-Hewitt Museum, New York.

40 Mollison, B. and Holmgren, D. (1979) *Permaculture One*, Tagari Publications, Australia; Mollison, B. (1979) *Permaculture Two*, Institute of Permaculture, Australia.

41 Mollison, B. and Slay, R. M. (1997) *Permaculture: A Designers' Manual*, Tagari Publications, Australia; Holmgren, D. (2002) *Permaculture: Principles and Pathways beyond Sustainabilty*, Holmgren Design Press, Australia.

42 Hopkins, R. (2008) *The Transition Handbook: From Oil Dependency to Local Resilience*, Green Books, Dartington, Totnes; see also Transition Towns, www.transitiontowns.org

43 Elkington, J. and Hailes, J. (1988) *The Green Consumer Guide*, Victor Gollanscz, London.

44 Mackenzie, D. (1991) *Green Design*, Lawrence King, London.

45 See for example, Lewis, H. and Gertsakis, J. (2001) *Design + Environment*, Greenleaf Publishing, Sheffield; Tischner, U. (2001) 'Tools for ecodesign and sustainable product design', in M. Charter and U. Tischner (eds) *Sustainable Solutions*, Greenleaf Publishing, Sheffield, pp263–281.

46 Van Hemel, C. G. and Brezet, J. C. (1997) *Ecodesign: A Promising Approach to Sustainable Production and Consumption*, United Nations Environment Programme, UNEP, Paris.

47 Van Hinte, E. and C. Bakker (1999) *Trespassers: Inspirations for Eco-efficient Design*, Netherlands Design Institute and 010 Publishers, Rotterdam.

48 Bakker, G. and Raemekers, R. (1998) *Droog Design: Spirit of the Nineties*, 010 Publishers, Rotterdam.

49 See for example the personal statements of 100 'iconic' designers in Fiell, C. and Fiell, P. (2003) *Design for the 21st Century*, Taschen, Köln, where only 5 per cent of designers referenced both social and environmental concerns, and only a minority clearly felt that environmental concerns were a focal point their daily work.

50 Findeli (2001), op. cit. Note 9, p15.

51 For example, the writings and voices of Ezio Manzini, Stuart Walker, Guy Bonsiepe, Klaus Krippendorf, Victor Margolin, Richard Buchanan, Tony Fry and John Thackara.

52 Cooper, R. (2002) 'Design: Not just a pretty face', *The Design Journal*, vol 5, no 2, p1.

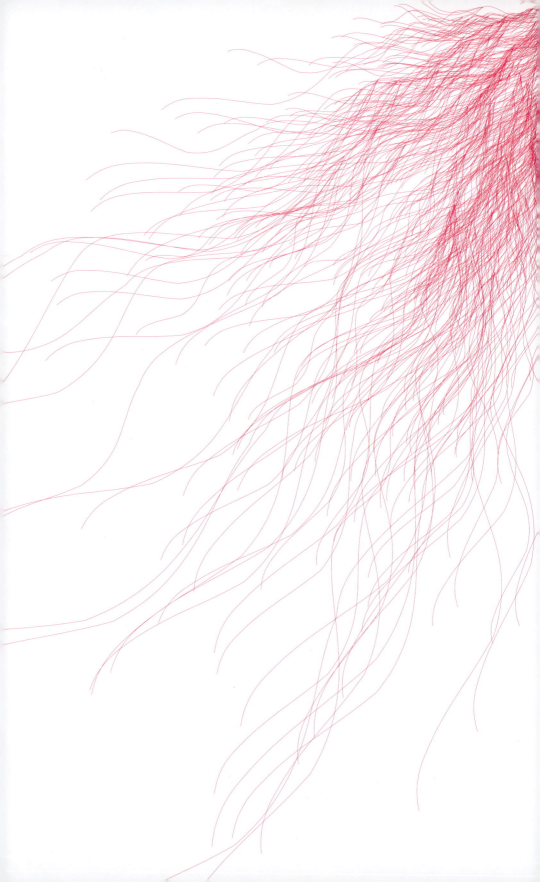

Global–Local Tensions: Key Issues for Design in an Unsustainable World

This chapter charts how our world is changing in order to highlight the key issues that all designers need to engage with now and tomorrow. The extent and speed of these changes to our global environment, to the human condition and to the man-made and natural world are astounding. All trends point to a reduction in biodiversity and a deterioration of the life-giving support provided by global ecosystems. One species – humans – are causing the demise of tens of thousands of the estimated 5–10 million species that inhabit planet Earth. If all humans were benefiting from this exploitation of natural capital then the global human consciousness could sleep easier. But in reality there are billions of people in abject poverty living in conditions where improving quality of life (QoL), and thereby the potential for human development, remains a considerable challenge. There is a daunting task ahead, during the early to mid-21st century, to try to balance the Earth's ability to provide biological sustenance with a growing human population, and to simultaneously nurture a 'better life' for humans. This task is made immeasurably more difficult against a background of climate change.

Significant changes are taking place within the global 'commons' – such as climate change,[1] changing sea levels,[2] water availability from the hydrosphere[3] – *and* within more local socio-economic, political and bio-regional circumstances (see for example the challenge in China).[4] Change is global and local, and inseparable, because even local economies are caught up in the global economy and the phenomenon of globalization. Aside from this global–local dualism, there is another major dualism that needs to be highlighted. 80 per cent of the world's population, 5.4 billion out of a total of today's 6.7 billion people, still struggle to maintain a QoL due to low income, and are subject to the vagaries of variable potable water supply, poor sanitation and disease, often coupled with socio-economic and political instability.[5] Based on data from 2005, almost 2.6 billion people are caught in 'absolute poverty' – defined as an income of less than US$2 a day – and 5.12 billion earn less than US$10 per day.[6]

It is proposed that this majority of the world should therefore be called the *under-consumers* – they actually need to consume more to elevate their very basic standard of living. The remaining 20 per cent of the world, the rich, are the profligate *over-consumers.* This 20 per cent of the population uses approximately 83 per cent of the world's resources,[7] a situation that most societies would recognize as grossly unfair. The basic human 'physiological and safety needs' as envisaged by Abraham Maslow or 'subsistence needs' as framed by Manfred Max-Neef, in their respective needs typologies,[8] are met for this global minority. However, meeting these needs requires phenomenal quantities of raw materials, finished products and energy, all originating from finite natural capital (often the natural capital of other poorer nation states, in the form of imports). The excessive consumption patterns of this minority are causing a severe strain on global life-supporting ecosystems, generating new social problems and pre-empting options for future generations worldwide.[9]

Is there any good news? A 2006 report by the World Wide Fund for Nature (WWF) noted that, of the countries with total populations exceeding 1 million, Cuba was the only country in the world that was living within its ecological capacity *and* encouraging improvement of the human development index (HDI) of its citizens to what the United Nations Development Programme (UNDP) considers 'high human development', an HDI of 0.8 where 0.2 is the lowest and 1.0 the highest.[10] This is not to say that Cuba is a model for a sustainable nation state, but there are valuable lessons in Cuba's development over the past two to three decades that have taken place *despite* international economic and trade embargoes and limited oil imports. In a sense, Cuba has already made the transition to a post-peak oil economy *because* it was denied oil imports, and the embedded economic model that the oil economy supports, that other countries took for granted. What has happened in Cuba has required a re-learning about the ecology of the country's land mass and a social journey to understand how to live better on that land.

A Precarious Balance in a Changing Climate

The world came together to discuss the global environmental crisis in 1972 at the United Nations Conference on the Human Environment,[11] but it took another 20 years for widespread recognition of the criticality of the situation. In 1992, representatives from more than 190 nations gathered in Rio de Janeiro for the United Nations' Earth Summit.[12] The urgency of the debate had, in part, been accelerated by a landmark report, *Our Common Future*, prepared by the World Commission on Environment and Development (WCED) some five years earlier. The WCED definition of sustainable development – 'development that meets the needs of the present without compromising the ability of future generations to meet their own needs' – is one of the most frequently cited definitions.[13] It encourages anyone thinking about development to address key issues now and to take a long-term view.

The Earth Summit generated a raft of agreements and principles, including Agenda 21, which called for a radical shift in socio-economic and political governance to more open and participatory forms in order to effectively combat the most severe global environmental problems. Other important documents included the *Framework Convention on Climate Change, Convention on Biological Diversity, Statement on Forest Principles* and the *Rio Declaration*.[14] Principle 15 of the *Rio Declaration* was the 'precautionary principle', which states that even if there were an absence of scientific consensus that an action or policy may cause severe or irreversible harm to humans or the environment, the onus falls on those who would advocate taking the action to prove it is not harmful. It was intended to encourage self-editing action among the world's nations to develop in a way that would not irrevocably harm the Earth's ecosystems or social systems on which we all depend. In Rio, the United Nations also laid the foundations for further international research, negotiation and agreements on combating climate change. The continued work of the UN's Intergovernmental Panel on Climate Change (IPCC) helped guide the path towards development of the Kyoto Protocol in 1997. The Protocol achieved an international agreement between the industrialized nations to reduce greenhouse gas emissions by 5.2 per cent, compared with 1990 data, in the period 2008–2012.[15]

What has happened since the Rio Earth Summit? Negotiations on climate change have been protracted and largely ineffectual in changing trends due to the abstention of some developed nations, notably the US and Australia, and some emerging nations, notably India and China, from making positive contributions to the process. Talks in Bali in late 2007 – about what happens after the Kyoto Protocol's first period ends in 2012 – did win some consensus, brought Australia into line, got China and India involved, and ended with the Americans being isolated (again).[16] The real crunch is in Copenhagen in 2009 when the post-2012 deal will be brokered. Pre-industrial concentrations of carbon dioxide were 280ppm (parts per million); today it is about 385ppm rising at 2ppm per annum. By 2009 there may be more evidence as to the criticality of imposing a threshold of 450ppm of carbon dioxide, which the IPCC predicts will result in a 2°C rise in global temperature – a global temperature rise not experienced on the planet for over 3 million years. Lynas actually sees carbon dioxide concentrations of 450ppm as beyond a key threshold because at this juncture significant positive carbon feedback cycles kick in, with an acceleration of melting of ice at the poles and in frozen soils in northern latitudes of Russia and Canada, releasing vast quantities of methane, a powerful greenhouse gas.[17] Lynas notes that global emissions must peak at 2015 under a 400ppm target to keep the temperature rise below the 1.1–2°C increase. On current international agreements this simply does not look feasible.

The Fourth Assessment Report of the IPCC, released in 2007, specified a number of scenarios for climate change.[18] The most optimistic – the low-emission scenario – forecasts a sharp reduction in greenhouse gas emissions to keep global warming to 1.1°C, the most pessimistic predicts a rise of 6.4°C by 2100. The impact of each scenario reveals an increasingly polarized world where freshwater distribution changes radically, ecosystems become degraded, food production systems disrupted, coastlines severely damaged and human health takes a downturn (Figure 3.1). Lynas gives a graphic account of what this may mean for humans and other forms of life.[19] Whether you are a dissenter[20] or an advocate[21] there are two events in recent memory which demonstrate that significant climate change is already dramatically affecting people's lives. Hurricane Katrina arrived in New Orleans in August 2005 making millions homeless in the city and the environs of the Gulf of Mexico. Nearly half a million refugees continue to live in Texas today.[22] Another rather less spectacular incident, that remains more of a footnote in the international media, is the case of the Carteret Islands in the Pacific Ocean. In November 2003, the Papua New Guinean government backed a progressive evacuation of the Carteret Islands

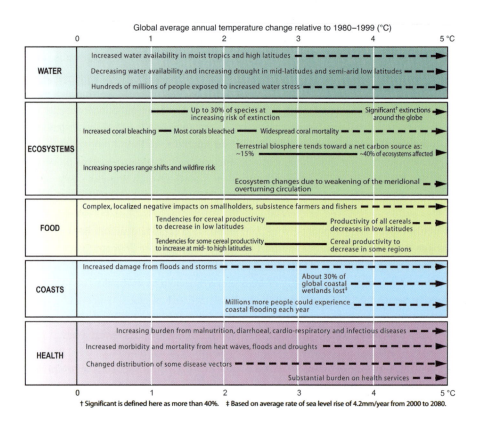

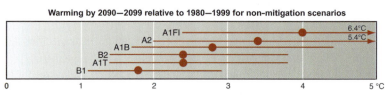

Figure 3.1

IPCC impacts associated with global average temperature rise

over a decade as the islanders became the world's first 'climate refugees'.[23] Over the next few years, rising sea water levels will further contaminate drinking water and agricultural activities. Evacuation is now under way and it is expected that by 2015 the islands will be uninhabitable. These rather insidious changes may be a foretaste of things to come.

Invoking the precautionary principle seems an eminently sensible position regarding climate change, for ourselves, future generations and for a wider living world. As Al Gore noted, climate change is *the* inconvenient truth because most models of economic development do not factor in the true costs of climate change, and most governments are not asking basic questions about how the economic model(s) need to change.[24] The publication of Sir Nicholas Stern's report for the UK government on the costs of climate change certainly focused the economists with its prediction that it would take 1–2 per cent of world GDP to avert the worst consequences of climate change if we act now, and 15–20 per cent of world GDP if we do nothing.[25] Whereas governments had hardly heard the voices of diverse climate change activists over the previous decade, Gore and Stern made them sit up.

The definition of who and what are the major contributors to carbon dioxide and other greenhouse gas emissions is a science fraught with different approaches. The top five nations vary according to the metric used (Table 3.1). Key to the debate to reduce carbon emissions is the political position of the US, the European Union, Russia, China and the Middle Eastern states. If they do not reach agreement then the expectation of increasing levels of carbon dioxide and irrevocable climate change in the 21st century will forge a new global reality. The main sectors contributing to carbon dioxide emissions are industry (40 per cent), buildings – homes, offices and so on (31 per cent), transportation (22 per cent) and agriculture (4 per cent). Design can be a powerful intermediary for new and retrofitted solutions in all these areas.[26] Solutions are most likely to involve eco-efficient technologies *and* behavioural change, for example, Lynas[27] suggests:

- halve the distances people drive each year and double the vehicle fuel economy (this is a 'Factor 4' gain)
- dramatically increase the energy efficiency of buildings
- dramatically increase the efficiency of fossil-fuelled power stations
- construct 2 million 1MW wind turbines to generate electricity
- cover 2 million hectares of land with solar panels
- stop the destruction of tropical rainforests and dramatically increase tree planting elsewhere
- choose between carbon dioxide injection and capture in underground reservoirs and investing in 1400 new gas power plants to produce electricity
- move towards a slower lifestyle strategy by not driving or flying, shopping locally, growing one's own food and focusing on local communities.

Table 3.1

Three metrics to measure the nations contributing most to carbon dioxide emissions (data year 2000)

Percentage of global emissions (CO_2 + other greenhouse gases from fossil fuel burning, and CO_2 from cement production)	Emissions per capita (tonnes of carbon equivalent per person)	Carbon intensity (tonnes of carbon emitted in CO_2 per millions of dollars in GDP/PPP)
US 20.8	Qatar 18.5	Ukraine 483
China 14.8	UAE 10.1	Russia 427
EU (collectively) 14.0	Kuwait 9.5	Saudi Arabia 260
Russia 5.7	Bahrain 7.0	Poland 230
India 5.5	Australia and US 6.8	Iran 223

Source: Henson (2006)[28]

There is a broad coalition of activist organizations that are lobbying governments to take more action to avert the worst forecasts of global warming, from well-known environmental organizations, such as Friends of the Earth,[29] to single-issue organizations, such as Plane Stupid,[30] fighting to prevent new airports being built in the UK. Governments are also taking action at a national and regional level, for example, the UK government initiated The Carbon Trust as a means to accelerate the move towards a low-carbon economy.[31] It therefore seems important for designers to take on a larger role in addressing climate change issues. Those who have looked at improving the energy efficiency of technologies using non-renewable energy sources (oil, gas, coal), or who create new designs using renewable energy sources (wind, solar, water, geothermal), or who reduce the energy requirements of their products, or who use light-weighting to reduce materials, or who encourage recycling at 'end-of-life', are all 'default' design activists since their intention is to reduce dependence on non-renewable energy sources and/or help transition towards genuinely sustainable energy-based economies. However, eco-efficiency improvement in products, services and buildings can only go so far. Designers will need to encourage positive eco-efficient behavioural changes to significantly reduce per capita carbon footprints.

Resource Depletion

One of the most dramatic psychological shifts we need to make about the future is our perception about the amount and condition of natural capital in the world. A screaming headline in a UK national newspaper, 'Two-thirds of world's resources "used up"' was written by a respected newspaper science editor, Tim Radford, on the publication of the Millennium Ecosystem Assessment (MEA).[32] The statistics are thought provoking: 24 per cent of the land surface is now appropriated for agriculture; 40–50 per cent of all available fresh water running off the land is used by humans; groundwater sources are being used up faster than they are replenished; the Yellow River in China, the Nile in north Africa and the Colorado in the US now dry up completely for parts of the year; 12 per cent of bird species, 25 per cent of mammals and 30 per cent of amphibians are threatened with extinction during the next century. And then we are running out of an energy source that, literally, fuelled the last 100 years of the industrial and consumer revolutions – oil from fossil fuels. All designers, as specifiers, are implicit in resource use and so have a key role to play in averting resource depletion. Current rates of consumption of resources actually mean we require the equivalent of two planets for energy, construction materials and metals to maintain growth and development.[33] Sometime in the 1980s, the rate of consumption of global resources exceeded the capacity of natural capital to regenerate itself by 25 per cent and consumption rates are still increasing. Over the past decade, rates of consumption have increased due to an increasing world population (from 6 billion in 2000 to 6.7 billion in 2008) and phenomenal economic growth in India, China and Asia in general. Short-term adjustments are needed to improve eco-efficient use of these resources by 50 per cent, or a factor of two times (Factor 2) and much higher factors will be required for longer-term social, political, economic and environmental stability.

Oil and peak oil

The spectre of running out of fossil fuel reserves, and having to find alternative energy sources was first raised by a geologist, Marion King Hubbert in 1956, working then for Shell and from 1964 onwards for the US Geological Survey. He predicted that US oil would reach peak production in 1970 and decline thereafter.[34] It peaked in 1971. He further predicted a similar phenomenon for the world oil supply by the turn of the millennium, a view supported by the Association for the Study of Peak Oil and Gas (Figure 3.2). His thinking has come to fruition some 50 years later, with a growing acceptance of the concept that we have just passed/reached 'peak oil', i.e. we have used more than 50 per cent of the world's oil reserves. This realization has garnered many commentators and activists to talk about life after peak oil[35] and 'energy descent' to transition to a post-peak oil economy.[36] Peak oil also means peak synthetic plastics, as oil is the main raw ingredient for these materials. It is presently difficult to conceive a world without oil and plastics, but perceptions will undergo some adjustment in the next generation or two. Receiving less debate, but possibly more important than the depletion of one energy source (the world's oil reserves), is the depletion of essential minerals, land for food production and potable water.

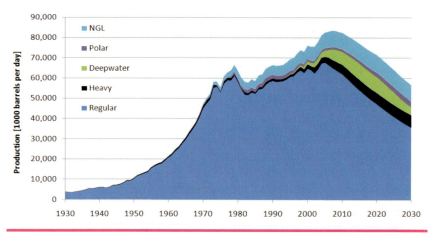

Figure 3.2
Peak oil and gas liquids, 2004 scenario

Essential minerals

It is possible that the world's businesses, especially the manufacturing sector, are sleepwalking into the future. In 2006, reports collated from some of the most respected international institutions, with expertise in materials and resources, indicated that supplies of some essential minerals would be depleted within a decade while others would last only for a generation.[37]

Land for food production

As the population increases, so does the demand for food and for land that can be converted to some form of agriculture. In addition to these demands there is a more recent demand for the growing of biofuels to replace fossil fuels and to meet carbon dioxide emission agreements that is putting additional strain on food production and tropical rainforest destruction. The United Nations' Food and Agriculture Organization (FAO) has examined how some of these issues are evolving in terms of food insecurity and the notion of paying farmers for looking after land to provide environmental, or ecosystem, services.[38] Add the phenomenon of peak oil into the equation and agriculture looks set to make a paradigm shift in its fundamental practices over the next 50 years. Organic farming, urban farming and permaculture-based systems with their low fossil fuel inputs (reduced oil and oil derivatives such as fertilizers and pesticides) already set the benchmark. Cuba's collective experiment over the past 20 years may provide a blueprint for new directions for agriculture to pursue.

Water for humans and agriculture

The pressures on the world's freshwater reserves are steadily increasing due to population growth, increased demand from consumers and industry, urbanization and changes to global hydrology systems. Since 1998, World Water has been tracking the state of global water reserves and consumption[39] and the increasing number of conflicts about these finite resources.[40] WWF reports a doubling of demand for world water between 1960 and 2000, with agriculture currently using 70 per cent and industry 20 per cent of available reserves.[41] Data on the withdrawals of water to availability ratio (wta ratio) show that 40 per cent of countries with a population over 1 million are showing severe water stress; 20–40 per cent moderate stress and 5–20 per cent mild stress. As the climate warms, the mid-latitudes in the Northern hemisphere will be subject to even more reduced water availability. It is therefore not surprising that well-known international aid agencies, like Christian Aid, are running media campaigns asking the 'over-consumers' to turn their thermostats down a degree.

Ecological Capacity and Biodiversity

The demands of anthropogenic activities are putting the world's ecosystems under stress. Nature is struggling to cope with the rate of consumption of its resources and its capacity to absorb the outputs of the global, regional and local economies. The MEA system was set up by the United Nations in 2000 to scientifically review the state of the world's ecosystems, assess what this may mean for human well-being and propose sensible policies to mitigate change and instigate improvements.[42] The first report by the MEA revealed that of the five main ecosystem types studied (agro-ecosystems, coastal systems, forest systems, freshwater, grasslands), the vast majority were showing a decline in ecosystem capacity to provide adequate food and fibre production, water quality and quantity, biodiversity and carbon storage.[43] In other words, the natural capital working to maintain the Earth's ecosystems is struggling to renew and regenerate itself

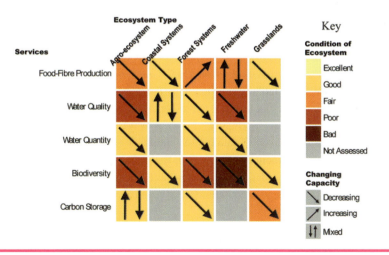

Figure 3.3
The condition of many global ecosystems has been declining

because humankind is extracting too much and/or polluting or disturbing the ecological balance of these systems (Figure 3.3).

The data on reductions of biodiversity and species in danger of extinction are even more disturbing. Over 41,500 species, including 12,000 plants, are currently listed on the International Union for Conservation of Nature and Natural Resources (IUCN) Red List, i.e. those under real threat of disappearing forever.[44] It is estimated that the list will grow to 50,000–60,000 species during 2008. Data going back 50 years indicate that the current state of affairs is part of a longer-term trend. Between 1950 and 1997, the world elephant population decreased by 90 per cent, as a result of habitat destruction, habitat alteration, restriction of population movements and illegal poaching, and the global rainforest cover decreased by 30 per cent.[45] Every choice a designer makes when specifying materials has an effect on the habitat of other living species, so knowing where materials come from is an essential design skill.

In an effort to examine just how much of natural capital different nation states were using, Rees and Wackernagel devised a model of accounting called 'ecological footprinting'.[46] At the core of the model is the idea that each country has a measurable ecological capacity, i.e. ecological productive land (and sea) and mineral wealth, and that it has a specific population in a given land area. The consumption of the citizens of each nation state is measured by examining data from within the country and data concerning exported and imported goods and products. An estimate can then be made as to whether citizens of a nation are living within their ecological capacity (and are in ecological credit) or are borrowing from other people's ecological capacity (and are in therefore in ecological debt). Figure 3.4 reveals that the majority of the developed countries – the 'North' – are in ecological debt; they are borrowing significant amounts of ecological capacity by importing food, raw materials, energy and goods. If ecological capacity were shared out equally between all the citizens of the world, we would each have about 1.8 global hectares (ha) per capita equivalent on which to survive. Typically, the citizens of developed nations of the North have footprints in excess of 4 and up to nearly 12 global ha per capita, whereas most citizens in the South have well below the global average. The New Economics Foundation (NEF) mapped the UK's global ecological footprint revealing just how extensive the reach of a developed nation for other nation's resources can be (Figure 3.5).[47] The WWF's *Living Planet Report* [48] reveals ecological footprint (EF) data for 148 countries. Seventeen of these countries have an EF of more than three times the global average, with North Americans (USA and Canada), two oil-rich Middle Eastern states (UAE and Kuwait) and two Scandinavian countries (Finland and Sweden) showing the highest EFs of all (Figure 3.6).

Ecological footprinting has its weaknesses as an ecological accounting model.[49] A key underlying assumption of the ecological footprinting methodology, and one the

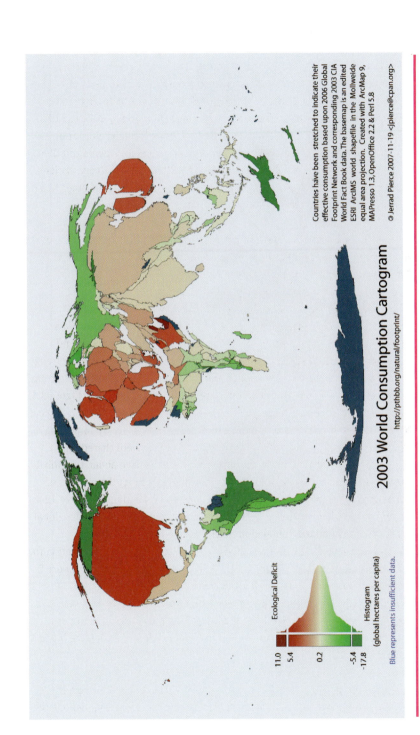

Countries have been stretched to indicate their effective consumption based upon 2006 Global Footprint Network and corresponding 2003 CIA World Fact Book data. The basemap is an edited ESRI ArcIMS world shapefile in the Mollweide equal area projection. Created with ArcMap 9, MAPresso 1.3, OpenOffice 2.2 & Perl 5.8

© Jerrad Pierce 2007-11-19 <jpierce@cpan.org>

2003 World Consumption Cartogram
http://pthbb.org/natural/footprint/

Ecological Deficit

Histogram
(global hectares per capita)

Blue represents insufficient data.

11.0
5.4
0.2
-5.4
-17.8

Figure 3.4
Countries in ecological deficit or credit

Figure 3.5
The UK's global ecological footprint

deep ecologists and biocentric thinkers do not subscribe to, is that only a very small percentage of the globe's biocapacity, 12.5–13.4 per cent, is allocated to all the other living species. This appears rather ungenerous and possibly is a dangerously low figure as we absolutely depend upon other living organisms to help regulate nature's support systems.

Add the inequity in use of our global ecological capacity to the anticipated changes in global climate, and its likely consequences on nature's ecosystems and food production hint at future problems for nations' food security. The fragility of global food production systems was further reinforced by perturbations of world food prices following the 'credit crunch' and oil price rises between mid-2007 and late 2008. Threats to the world's ecosystems directly impact on human welfare and survival, placing the poorest at most risk.

Unsustainable Consumption and Production

Whichever metric is applied – from ecological footprinting to environmental space[50] – it is abundantly clear that current rates of consumption of many resources are unsustainable. This is inextricably linked to our current systems of consumption and production. Climate change, resource depletion, the potential instability of ecosystems and our erosion of ecological capacity are some of the manifest symptoms of these consumption trends. The response by designers to the consumption and production agenda is diverse, ranging from discussions about systems change at a manufacturing level to notions of 'cradle-to-cradle', 'life cycle thinking' and 'industrial ecology' [51] to detailed design for the environment [52] or eco-design approaches in product design and manufacturing.[53] It also embraces ideas of dematerializing products by the provision of more product service systems (PSS).[54] Wider issues of consumption are covered in the green and ethical consumption debate and there is an emerging body of work re-examining the human motivational and economic drivers required for more sustainable consumption and production (SCP).[55]

The 'back story' to each product, what happens upstream of the product and its associated rucksack of environmental impacts, has encouraged a variety of approaches including light-weighting and materials intensity per unit service (MIPS).[56] Upstream and downstream impacts are covered for a variety of everyday products in the Worldwatch Institute's *Good Stuff* guide.[57]

Social Inequality, Poverty and Migration

At the heart of the sustainability prism (page 24) is a call for fairer distribution of economic, ecological, social and institutional capital between and within members of societies. Taking the economic dimension, statistics from the World Bank indicate

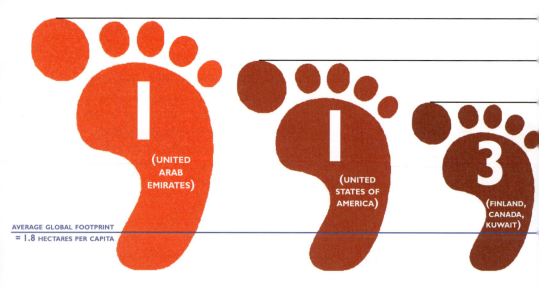

AVERAGE GLOBAL FOOTPRINT
= 1.8 HECTARES PER CAPITA

(UNITED ARAB EMIRATES)

(UNITED STATES OF AMERICA)

(FINLAND, CANADA, KUWAIT)

Figure 3.6
The ecological footprint of the 'over-consumers'

that poverty levels remain shockingly high for the vast majority of the world's citizens and the rich–poor income differential is widening.[58] The richest 20 per cent account for 75 per cent of world income, whereas the poorest 40 per cent account for only 5 per cent of world income. This economic inequality is matched by great disparities in a wide range of social indicators from poor provision for schools, low literacy levels, poor health (often linked with inadequate access to clean water and appropriate sanitation), malnourishment and poor life expectancy. While many of these disparities are recognized and specific goals have been set, for example, within the United Nations' Millennium Development Goals, progress is slow. Poverty, and its legion effects, remains one of the most shameful issues of the 21st century for all humankind. As does the issue of gender equality as recognition of women's rights is still woefully inadequate within many nation states.

With an increasing world population likely to rise from the current 6.7 billion to 8.9 billion by 2050,[59] social inequalities look set to increase unless there is a significant redistribution of wealth. The main population gains are going to be in the poorer countries, where the migration to urban centres coupled with a bulge in the demography towards the young could create significant future hardship.[60] To add to this pretty toxic mix of trends, it is predicted that climate change will force migrations unprecedented since the beginning of the Industrial Revolution. Current

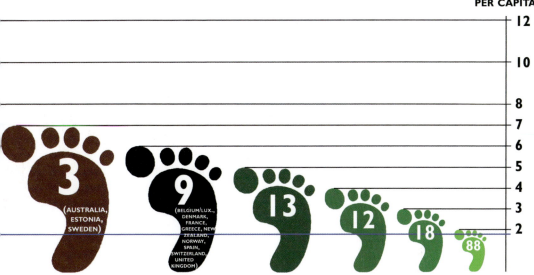

GLOBAL
HECTARES
PER CAPITA

12
10
8
7
6
5
4
3
2

THE NUMBER ON EACH FOOTPRINT INDICATES HOW MANY COUNTRIES HAVE AN 'ECOLOGICAL FOOTPRINT' OF THAT SIZE

migration trends reported by the United Nations show 13.5 million refugees in 2005;[61] and The Migration Policy Institute reveals a world on the move.[62] In our polyglot world there are numerous reasons for this migration, from economic necessity to political/ethnic persecution and refugees from hunger, war and, now, climate change; migration looks set to increase in the next 25–40 years.

Economic Inequity and New Visions of Enterprise

The global economy is still struggling to come to terms with the implications for finite limits of resources against a background of a rising global population, very high economic growth rates in two emerging nations, India and China (together accounting for more than one-third of world population) and the uncertainties introduced by climate change and peak oil. The financial world is also experiencing a collective shock as the ongoing 'credit crunch' of 2007 continues, reducing global cash available to banks and lenders alike and causing uncertainties around future employment and economic growth. However, this may be a blessing in disguise as Spangenberg[63] points out that, 'economic growth can only be environmentally sustainable if it is accompanied by resource productivity increases that are higher than the rate of growth'. This implies striving for and reaching much higher levels of eco-efficient production such as Factor 4 – a halving of resource use and a doubling of outputs[64] – and Factor 10 – a 90 per cent improvement on current efficiencies.[65] The current economic models of capitalism do not appear to be factoring these calculations into their immediate or long-term business plans, although some transnational businesses have adopted a downshifting view of resource use by applying The Natural Step model which accepts drastic future cuts in material resource flows.[66] PricewaterhouseCoopers, a leading global financial consultancy, think that sustainability is about creating new business value beyond the traditional view of assets, financial rewards, investors and customers (Figure 3.7). This involves a desire to include a wider range of stakeholders who will contribute to the creation of new values, including brand and intellectual value and also adding to human, social and environmental value, and so helping to expand or restore these capitals.

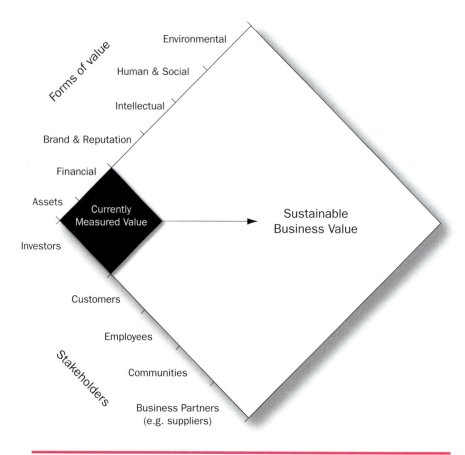

Figure 3.7
The future of 'sustainable business value'

The steady rise of the global economy, and its attendant benefits and woes, has also spawned visions of alternative economies, many being stimulated by a much earlier vision proposed by E. F. Schumacher in his 1973 book *Small is Beautiful: Economics as if People Mattered.*[67] Schumacher berated the materialism values of the dominant economic system and advocated a re-rationalization of resource use and diversification of regional economies, the application of intermediate (appropriate) technology, new patterns of ownership and a refocusing on the importance of local economies; all these themes still resonate today. The 1986 Towards Other Economic Systems (TOES) conference paralleled the G8 meeting of economic heads and generated a new but diverse movement of alternative economic thinking. One group, the New Economics Foundation[68] in London, a 'think-do' tank, emerged from TOES. NEF examines economic possibilities from the point of view of social welfare and environmentalism. It has examined ideas of happiness and wealth[69] and found that in Western societies life satisfaction has not increased significantly since the 1970s despite significant economic growth. NEF prefers to use the measure of domestic progress (MDP) as an indicator of economic growth. MDP is gross domestic product (GDP) minus the real (negative) costs of environmental damage and individual/social ill health associated with that economic growth. NEF feels this is a more realistic measure of economic progress and better mirrors people's perceptions of their happiness and general satisfaction with life.

As the 'haves' and 'have nots' of the global economy have emerged, new visions and models of enterprise are attracting more attention in order to improve the positive effects of economic growth without disastrous negative consequences being felt by others. These include models with a new range of stakeholders focused on local needs and circumstances (e.g. community interest companies); enterprises with a focus on a disadvantaged or under-represented group and/or those providing social/health services (e.g. social enterprises); and a diverse range of alternative economies from non-monetary systems (such as the Local Exchange Trading System (LETS), and the gift economy) to fairer trading schemes (e.g. Fairtrade) and to innovative 'micro-credit' schemes for the world's poor (such as the very successful Grameen Bank).[70] These alternative models recognize those left behind, those held in wage slavery and those not benefiting from the dominant capitalist economic model.

Other Significant Issues

The United Nations Millennium Development Goals, published in 2000, set targets for basic economic and social rights.[71] The base level was set at 1990 levels and minimum targets have to be reached by 2015. There are eight goals with 21 quantifiable targets that are measured by 60 indicators (see Appendix 2 for the details).

- Goal 1: Eradicate extreme poverty and hunger
- Goal 2: Achieve universal primary education
- Goal 3: Promote gender equality and empower women
- Goal 4: Reduce child mortality
- Goal 5: Improve maternal health
- Goal 6: Combat HIV/AIDS, malaria and other diseases
- Goal 7: Ensure environmental sustainability
- Goal 8: Develop a global partnership for development.

Progress is variable, but each goal encompasses a unique collection of problems, each of which becomes a design challenge.

Institutional change is happening in government, business and social sectors as legislation and regulation improves protection of the environment and encourages organizations to adopt corporate social responsibility measures. There are various portals offering an independent view of corporate progress in environmental and social issues. The European Union's record on environmental legislation has been exemplary and there is a growing raft of Directives covering a wide range of design-related activities from packaging, recycling, electronics and electrical equipment, and a growing number of energy-using products.

Technological change is a perennial key issue for sustainability and design. The internet, ICT developments and social networking platforms are changing the way everyday communication and collaboration is happening (see Chapter 6), opening up new ways of co-designing and more open-source and participatory design practices. Other technologies important to the sustainability journey include: technologies for renewable energy sources (solar, wind, wave, geothermal, biofuel); biomimetics and bionics; light-weighting; 'smart' materials, e.g. shape memory alloys and polymers, ultra-strong ceramics and fibres and 'eco' materials, e.g. biological materials easily recycled by nature, synthetic materials containing a high recycle fraction; and nanotechnologies, e.g. coatings for self-cleaning surfaces.

Having knowledge about all the issues above equips a designer with a broader awareness of how design decisions can have a significant knock-on effect to distant ecosystems, lands and peoples. It also opens up new opportunities to focus the lens of the design activist.

Notes

1 Lynas, M. (2008) *Six Degrees: Our Future on a Hotter Planet*, Harper Collins, London; Henson, R. (2006) *The Rough Guide to Climate Change*, Rough Guides, London.
2 Lynas, M. (2005) *High Tide: The Truth about our Climate Crisis*, Harper Perennial, London.

3   Shiva, V. (2002) *Water Wars: Privatisation, Pollution and Profit*, Pluto Press, London; Pearce, F. (2006) *When the Rivers Run Dry: Water – The Defining Crisis of the 21st Century*, The Eden Project, London.

4   Day, K. A. (2004) *China's Environment and the Challenge of Sustainable Development*, M. E. Sharpe, Armonk, NY.

5   Global Issues, www.globalissues.org/article/26/poverty-facts-and-stats

6   World Bank Development Indicators, 2008.

7   Fussler, C. with James, P. (1996) *Driving Eco-innovation: A Breakthrough Discipline for Innovation and Sustainability*, Pitman Publishing, London, p39.

8   Maslow, A. (1943) 'A theory of human motivation', *Psychological Review*, vol 50, pp370–396, http://psychclassics.yorku.ca/Maslow/motivation.htm, accessed September 2008; Huitt, W. (2004) 'Maslow's hierarchy of needs', *Educational Psychology Interactive*, Valdosta State University, Valdosta, GA, http://chiron.valdosta.edu/whuitt/col/regsys/ maslow.html, accessed September 2008; Max-Neef, M. A. (1991) *Human Scale Development: Conception, Application and Further Reflections*, Zed Books, London; Rainforest Information Centre, 'Max-Neef on human needs and human-scale development', www.rainforestinfo.org.au/background/ maxneef.htm, accessed September 2008.

9   See for example the Millennium Ecosystem Synthesis Assessment Report, 2005; Worldwatch Institute, 2000–2009.

10 World Wide Fund for Nature (2006) *The Living Planet 2006*, C. Hails (ed), WWF International, Gland, Switzerland. www.panda.org/news_facts/ publications/living_ planet_report/index.cfm

11 United Nations (2009) 'Stockholm 1972, Report on the United Nations Conference on the Human Environment' www.unep.org/Documents.Multilingual/Default.asp?documentID=97, accessed January 2009.

12 Wikipedia (2008) 'Earth Summit', http://en.wikipedia.org/wiki/Earth_Summit

13 World Commission on Environment and Development (1987) *Our Common Future*, Oxford University Press, Oxford. The WCED is often referred to as the 'Brundtland Commission' after the head of the commission, Gro Harland Brundtland.

14 Dresner, S. (2008) *The Principles of Sustainability*, 2nd edn, Earthscan, London, p54.

15 Ibid. p54.

16 Ibid. p63.

17 Lynas (2008), op. cit. Note 1, p255.

18 Intergovernmental Panel on Climate Change (2007) *Climate Change 2007*, Cambridge University Press, Cambridge, www.ipcc.ch/

19 Lynas (2008), op. cit. Note 1.

20 See for example Lomburg, B. (2001) *The Skeptical Environmentalist*, Cambridge University Press, Cambridge.

21 Lynas (2008), op. cit. Note 1.

22 Wikipedia (2008) 'Hurricane Katrina', http://en.wikipedia.org/wiki/Hurricane_ Katrina

23 Wikipedia (2008) 'Carteret Islands', http://en.wikipedia.org/wiki/Carteret_Islands

24 Gore, A. (2006) *An Inconvenient Truth: The Planetary Emergency of Global Warming and What We Can Do About It*, Bloomsbury Publishing, London.

25 Stern, N. (2006) *The Economics of Climate Change: The Stern Review*, Cambridge University Press, Cambridge, available from Her Majesty's Treasury, www.hm-treasury.gov.uk/independent_reviews/sertn_review_economics_climate_change/sertn_rev iew_ report.cfm

26 Henson (2006), op. cit. Note 1, p35.

27 Lynas (2008), op. cit. Note 1, pp276–277.

28 Henson, J. (2006) *The Rough Guide to Climate Change*, Rough Guides, London, Table 'Climate data: Insights and observations', data for the year 2000 as presented in the *2004 Pew Center Report*, p40.

29 FOE, www.foe.org

30 Plane Stupid, www.planestupid.com

31 The Carbon Trust, www.carbontrust.co.uk/about

32 Radford, T. (2005) 'Two-thirds of world's resources "used up"', *The Guardian*, 30 March 2005; Millennium Ecosystem Assessment Synthesis Report, 2005.

33 McLaren, D., Bullock, S. and Yousuf, N. (1998) *Tomorrow's World: Britain's Share in a Sustainable Future*, Earthscan, London.

34 Wikipedia (2008) 'M King Hubbert', http://en.wikipedia.org/wiki/M._King_Hubbert

35 Heinberg, R. (2007) *Peak Everything: Waking up to the Century of Decline in the Earth's Resources*, Clairview Books, Forest Row.

36 Hopkins, R. (2007) *The Transition Handbook: From Oil Dependency to Local Resilience*, Green Books, Dartington, Totnes.

37 Cohen, D. (2007) 'Earth's natural wealth: an audit', *New Scientist*, issue 2605, pp34–41.

38 FAO (2006) *The State of Food Insecurity in the World 2006*, Food and Agriculture Organization, Rome, ftp://ftp.fao.org/docrep/fao/009/a0750e/a0750e00.pdf, retrieved September 2008; FAO (2007) *The State of Food and Agriculture 2007: Paying Farmers for Environmental Services*, Food and Agriculture Organization, Rome, ftp://ftp.fao.org/docrep/fao/010/a1200e/a1200e00.pdf, retrieved September 2008.

39 World Water reports, 1998–2006, www.worldwater.org/books.html

40 Gleick, P. H. (2008) *Water Conflicts Chronology*, Pacific Institute for Studies in Development, Environment and Security, retrieved September 2008, www.worldwater.org/conflictchronology.pdf

41 WWF (2006), op. cit. Note 10.

42 Millennium Ecosystem Synthesis Assessment Report (2005) www.millennium assessment.org/en/Synthesis.aspx

43 Millennium Ecosystem Assessment Series (2003) *Eco-systems and Human Well-being*, Island Press and Millennium Ecosystem Assessment Series.

44 IUCN (2008) www.iucnredlist.org/

45 Curran, S. (1998) *The Environment Handbook*, The Stationery Office, London, pp5, 7.

46 Rees, W. and Wackernagel, M. (1995) *Our Ecological Footprint: Reducing Human Impact on Earth*, New Society Publishers, Philadelphia, PA.

47 New Economics Foundation (2006) *The UK Interdependence Report*, Mary Murfphy (ed), New Economics Foundation, London.

48 WWF (2006), op. cit. Note 10.

49 See the pros and cons at Wikipedia (2008) 'Ecological footprints', http://en.wikipedia.org/wiki/Ecological_footprints

50 Rees and Wackernagel (1995), op. cit. Note 46, for 'ecological footprinting' concept; McLaren et al (1998), op. cit. Note 33, for 'environmental space' concept.

51 See for example, McDonough, W. and Braungart, M. (2002) *Cradle to Cradle: Remaking the Way We Make Things*, North Point Press, New York.

52 Lewis, H. and Gertsakis, J. with Grant, T., Morelli, N. and Sweatman, A. (2001) *Design + Environment: A Global Guide to Designing Greener Goods*, Greenleaf Publishing, Sheffield.

53 Fuad-Luke, A. (2002, 2004) *The Eco-design Handbook*, Thames & Hudson, London; Datchefski, E. (2001) *The Total Beauty of Sustainable Products*, RotoVision, Crans-Près-Céligny, Switzerland.

54 SusProNET (2008), www.suspronet.org/, accessed September 2008.

55 Jackson, T. (ed) (2006) *The Earthscan Reader in Sustainable Consumption*, Earthscan, London.

56 Beukers, A. and van Hinte, E. (1999) *Lightness: The Inevitable Renaissance of Minimum Energy Structures*, 010 publishers, Rotterdam; see the Wuppertal Institute for more on MIPS, www.wupperinst.org/en/projects/topics_online/mips/index.html

57 Worldwatch Institute, www.worldwatch.org/taxonomy/term/44; Worldwatch Institute's 'State of the World' reports, 2000–2009, www.worldwatch.org/taxonomy/term/38

58 Global Issues, www.globalissues.org/article/26/poverty-facts-and-stats, World Bank Development Indicators.

59 UN (2004) www.un.org/esa/population/publications/sixbillion/sixbilpart1.pdf; Wikipedia (2008) 'World population', http://en.wikipedia.org/wiki/World_Population

60 UN (2002) United Nations Population Fund, www.unfpa.org/swp/2002/english/ch1/

61 UN (2005) http://esa.un.org/migration/

62 Migration Policy Institute, world migration map, www.migrationinformation.org/datahub/wmm.cfm

63 Spangenberg, J. H. (2001) 'Sustainable development: From catchwords to benchmarks and operational concepts', in M. Charter and U. Tischner (eds) *Sustainable Solutions: Developing Products and Services for the Future*, Greenleaf Publishing, Sheffield, pp24–47.

64 Von Weizsacker, E., Lovins, A. B. and Lovins, L. H. (1998) *Factor Four: Doubling Wealth, Halving Resource Use*, Earthscan, London.

65 Schmidt-Bleek, F. (2000) www.factor10-institute.org/files/MIPS.pdf; Factor 10 Manifesto, www.factor10-institute.org/files/F10_Manifesto_e.pdf, accessed September 2008.

66 The Natural Step, www.naturalstep.org/com/nyStart/, and Interface Flooring, www.interfaceinc.com/getting_there/natural.html

67 Schumacher, E. F. (1973) *Small is Beautiful: Economics as if People Mattered*, Harper & Row, London.

68 New Economics Foundation (NEF), www.neweconomics.org

69 NEF (2007) The European (Un)Happy Planet Index, www.neweconomics.org/gen/uploads/zeyhlcuhtfw0ge55lwnloi4520082007141551.pdf; NEF (2006) The (Un)Happy Planet Index, www.neweconomics.org/gen/uploads/dl44k145g5scuy453044gqbu11072006194758.pdf

70 LETS, www.letslinkuk.net/; Fairtrade, www.fairtrade.org.uk/; Grameen Bank, www.grameen-info.org/

71 United Nations Millennium Development Goals, www.undp.org/mdg/ and the latest report (2008) www.undp.org/publications/MDG_Report_2008_En.pdf

Contemporary Expressions: Design Activism, 2000 Onwards

'Never doubt that a small group of thoughtful, committed people can change the world. Indeed, it is the only thing that ever has.' Margaret Mead

It seems that the interest of the professional design community (practitioners, academics, researchers, theorists, critics and writers) in design activism is gathering fresh momentum. A number of new organizations were established between 1999 and 2008 with an activist agenda focusing on architecture, social design, slow design and/or interdisciplinary design (see Figure 6.2, p170). Authors have explicitly named and explored 'design activism',[1] while others have suggested new social dimensions for design practice[2] or for increased societal participation in the design process.[3] In 2005, a new biennale for social design was launched in the Netherlands – the Utrecht Manifest.[4] In 2008, there was a gathering of more than 300 design researchers, teachers and practitioners examining diverse sustainability issues at the Changing the Change conference in Turin, Italy.[5] Over the past few years, several design approaches are emerging to challenge the sustainability agenda and look beyond eco-efficiency. These include co-design, social design, slow design and metadesign (see Chapter 5, pp151–152). There are a number of new published works examining particular areas of design activism – in particular, architecture for humanitarian purposes,[6] graphic and communication design,[7] critical design,[8] design and feminism,[9] and the wider contemporary design and development agenda.[10] In 2007, the Cooper Hewitt National Design museum, New York, focused on design for the world's poor with an exhibition and publication entitled 'Design for the other 90%'.[11] So the design activism agenda appears to be in rude health, but how do we make sense of it?

The first part of this chapter looks at these activities and addresses a number of issues:

- How is theory informing action, and action informing theory?
- What are the contemporary expressions of design activism?
- Is there an emergent typology of design activism?
- What is the relationship between design practice, studies and explorations in design activism?
- What is the role of artefacts in design activism?

Figure 4.1
Sustainable Everyday – 'quick', 'slow' and 'co-operative' solutions

The second part of this chapter seeks to explore the range of expressions of contemporary design activism for two distinct audiences, the over-consumers (p86) and the under-consumers (p123). Why the distinction? The over-consumers must reduce their overall consumption by adopting new eco-efficient and positive behavioural strategies. To do this, designers need to educate by raising awareness of the real impacts of the over-consumers directly and indirectly on the global commons *and* on the under-consumers. Designers need to invoke new ideas about how to live a better life with reduced consumption. In contrast, the under-consumers are often struggling to meet basic physiological requirements for life. Yet they too need education and design solutions to gain access to appropriate levels of consumption that improve their quality of life.

The chapter predominantly addresses activism led by designers. This is design-led activism, although a few examples of designers collaborating with activist not-for-profit and other organizations are also given.

Thinking about Design Activism
'Socially active design': some emergent studies

There is a stream of consciousness and activity around what could be termed 'socially active design', where the focus of the design is society and its transition and/or transformation to a more sustainable way of living, working and producing. Ezio Manzini has long declared that sustainability is a societal journey, brought about by acquiring new awareness and perceptions, by generating new solutions, activating new behavioural patterns and, hence, cultural change.[12] This approach guided his work with Francois Jégou and their colleagues at the Faculty of Design at Milan Polytechnic, Italy, who linked 15 design schools from around the world to determine how design could help to enable everyday design solutions to help in the physical and social transition to sustainability in the project entitled Sustainable Everyday.[13] Each design school developed a range of scenarios for everyday living, looking at daily tasks and routines.[14] These were developed into an enabling

series of platforms based on whether the user required 'quick', 'slow' or 'co-op' (co-operative) solutions (Figure 4.1).[15] Another study coordinated by Milan Polytechnic – Emerging User Demands for Sustainable Solutions (EMUDE) – involved the collation of data on how creative communities in Europe use existing resources and social innovation to enable positive system change.[16] Each case study was subject to a qualitative social, economic and environmental evaluation in an attempt to define potential design research areas for products and PSSs that could be more efficient, widely accessible and easily diffused to other communities/ situations. In the UK, Guy Julier at Leeds Metropolitan University examined activism in the context of the social actors, stakeholders and structure of Leeds, a metropolitan UK city.[17] Julier makes a case that design activism builds on what already exists, on 'real-life processes from greening neighbourhoods to transforming communities through participatory design action',[18] rather than by advocating grandiose schemes which is the tendency of the urban planning process.

An emergent typology of contemporary design activism?

Mapping contemporary notions of design activism, Ann Thorpe of the Open University, UK, applies social sciences theory to examine the design literature in order to develop a conceptual framework.[19] She defines activism as 'taking intentional action to instigate change on behalf of a neglected group', indicating a strong focus on the social dimension of the sustainability prism, but adds a caveat that the Earth's ecosystems could also be regarded as a wronged group – so ecological design (and eco-design?) was a default representation of that group. She differentiated between designers as individual activists and designers as 'activists for hire', working for not-for-profit or public groups that espoused an environmental or social cause, but did not include cases of 'corporate design activism' such as greening of buildings or products. This perhaps creates an a priori judgement as to the efficacy of business versus the social and public sectors to deliver environmental or social positives. Nonetheless, the survey results were interesting.

Table 4.1
An initial typology of action for design activism

Action	% of total	Explanation
Demonstration artefacts	28	Demonstrating positive alternatives that are superior to the status quo
Info/ communication	27	Making information visual/tactile, devising rating systems, creating symbols, making physical links, etc.
Conventional actions	13	Proposing legislation, testifying at political meetings, writing polemics, conducting research, etc.
Competitions	10	
Service artefacts	10	Humanitarian aid
Events	9	Conferences, talks, installations or exhibitions
Protest artefacts	3	Confrontational, even offensive, prompting reflection on the morality of the status quo

Source: Thorpe (2008)[20]

Surveying the design press, using 'protest event analysis', a research methodology used by sociologists, Thorpe was looking for a typical 'repertoire of actions' (a term used by sociologists to talk about the activism of social movements) or what she calls a set of 'jazz standards' that design activists do/could adopt and modify. She coded about 15 per cent of 2000 identified cases in the design press and published some preliminary results detailing a typology of action (Table 4.1) and frequency of causes or focal issues (Table 4.2). A significant 41 per cent of actions were orientated around artefacts (subdivided as 'demonstration', 'protest' or 'service' artefacts) and 27 per cent around information/communication. The majority of design activist causes were of a human-centred orientation (63 per cent) rather than orientated to the cause of nature (38 per cent). In this survey, design activism tended to focus on the social and institutional dimensions of the sustainability prism, perhaps reflecting the bias in orientation of organizations in these recorded actions. However, this is a positive and welcome observation as it is the social–institutional axis of the prism that receives much less attention than the ecological–economic (eco-efficiency) axis.

Thorpe also noted that less than half of the cases studied (43 per cent) were instigated directly by designers themselves or by design-orientated non-profit organizations as opposed to other non-profits (schools, universities), public (government) and other organizations or partner-groups. Only about 15 per cent of the underlying activism strategies qualified as 'visionary', imagining or inventing new visions and actor/institution frameworks for the future (the remainder were reformist, i.e. building on what exists, or reactionary, i.e. taking past exemplars), although more than 65 per cent of these visionary strategies emanated from designers or design non-profits. This finding is perhaps not surprising given that design is fundamentally about creating and

Table 4.2
Frequency of design activism causes

Cause	% of total	Explanation
Nature	38	Reducing impact, preserving wilderness, regenerative
Community enabling	23	Education, user involvement, sense of place, relationships
Human rights	13	Justice, affordability, accessibility and democracy
Cultural diversity	11	Immigration, religious diversity, ethnic/racial diversity, time (memorial)
Disaster relief	9	
Range of causes	4	
Health	3	

Source: Thorpe (2008)[21]
Note: Biocentric or nature focus is 38 per cent of total, anthropocentric or social focus is 63 per cent of total.

giving new visions form. What this emergent typology does not reveal, and nor do the equivalent repertoire of actions typically cited by sociologists (marches, demonstrations, boycotts, strikes, bearing witness, pamphleteering, vigils, etc.), is anything about the intentions and motivations of the designers, the intended target audience(s), the intended scale or reach of the action, the relational fit of the particular activism to the wider activism and sustainability landscape, and, most importantly, its effectiveness. The typology of action in Table 4.1 lists 'competitions', 'events' and 'conventional actions'. These can potentially involve one or all of the other actions (artefacts and/or information/communication), so it is possible that the 'design action' and 'design outcome' are being blurred. Nonetheless, this is an interesting preliminary study and reveals that designers are definitely operating in activist mode.

Another approach to contextualizing design activism

There are a number of characteristics that could help define, orientate and contextualize the real focus and effectiveness of design activism (Tables 4.3, 4.4). The framework enables locating:

- the area of activism in the sustainability prism (Figure 1.11, p25)
- the area of activism from the maps of specific issues centred on the Five Capitals (Figures 1.1 to 1.8, pp3–15) plus 'man-made goods' capital model (see Figure 1.9, p16)
- the design project within a triangulation of design practice, studies and exploration domains – the latter is based upon the interaction design research triangle proposed by Fallman,[22] which is given schematically in Figure 4.2 and Table 4.5
- the specific design context and design project detail.

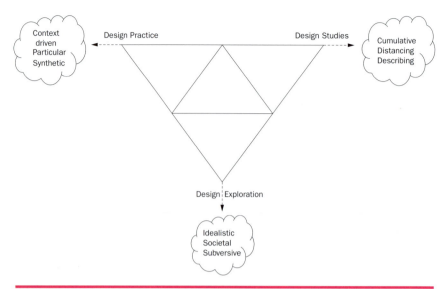

Figure 4.2
Fallman's triangle of design practice, studies and explorations

Table 4.3
A checklist for characterizing design activism

Orientation	Parameter	Characteristics
Sustainability	Sustainability prism (see Figure 1.11, p25)	Economic, ecological, social and/or institutional dimensions
	Key sustainability issues	Climate change, resource depletion, food, water, ecological capacity, biodiversity, consumption and production, social injustice, poverty, new enterprise, technology and/or 'other' (specify)
Activist	Activist domains – based on the Five Capitals plus 'man-made goods' capital (see Figures 1.4–1.9)	Economics, technology, natural environment, institutions, individual (human perception, activity and behaviour)
	Activist subdomains	See Figures 1.4–1.9 to determine the relevant subdomains
Design context	Boundaries to context	Define boundaries, e.g. physical location, timeframe, cultural conditions, any constraints, etc.
Design project detail	Design mode	Practice, studies and/or exploration (see Figure 4.2, Fallman's triangle, and Table 4.5)
	Design actions and/or output(s)	Information/communication, concept, artefact*, built artefact/environment*, process, action, other – please specify

Intention and dynamic of the artefact*	**Intention of artefact:** *Propositional artefacts* explore or embody theory or practice expressing something that actually demonstrates its sustainability,[23] suggesting visions for changing the status quo. *Demonstration artefacts* 'demonstrate positive alternatives that are superior to the status quo'[24] – perhaps only prototypes or small batch production. *Service artefacts* provided for 'humanitarian purposes'.[25] *Protest artefacts* 'are confrontational, even offensive, prompting reflection on the morality of the status quo'.[26] *Entrepreneurial artefacts* are designed and produced to challenge the status quo of the marketplace and are produced in small batches or are mass manufactured. **Dynamic of a design artefact:** The *dynamic* of a design artefact refers to whether it is closed, open or hybrid design. 'Closed' is complete, static, finished. 'Open' means it is intended that the user complete the design or is invited to modify it (a halfway design or artefact, see p95). 'Hybrid' is a design artefact with 'closed' and 'open' elements or characteristics.
Intention of project	Define purpose and goal(s)
Target beneficiary(-ies)	Define primary, secondary and/or other
Target audience(s)	Define primary, secondary and/or other

Note: * Artefacts – construed here as a man-made 2D or 3D physical object ranging from hand-held objects to buildings or landscapes. There are two dimensions to artefacts, their intention and their dynamic in relation to the end-users.

Table 4.4
Parameters for interrogating the effectiveness, or reaching the goals/aims of the design activism

Score: Level 0 = ineffective, Level 10 = highly effective

Parameter	Effectiveness assessment
Reaching the beneficiary or beneficiaries	
Reaching the target audience(s)	
Achievement of goals/aims	
Effectiveness (impact on positive change)	

Table 4.5

Fallman's typical characteristics showing the differences of tradition and perspective between design practice, studies and explorations

Design practice	Design exploration	Design studies
Real	The possible	True
Judgement intuitive and taste	Show alternatives	Logic
Competence	Ideals	Knowledge
Particular and contextual	Transcend	Universal
Client	Provoke	Peers
Create	Experiment	Explain
Change	Aesthetics	Understand
Involving and synthetic	Productive Societal, 'now' orientated Critique Political	Distancing and analytical

This framework provides a means of understanding the circumstances of any case study in design activism.

The natural candidate in Fallman's triangle for design activism seems to be the category 'design exploration', which is referred to as design critique, art and humanities driven by the 'idealistic, societal and subversive'. Fallman refers to Ehn's ideas of 'transcendence', the exploration of possibilities outside of the current paradigms of style, use, technology or economics – which seems to fit the notion of a counter-narrative. Furthermore, design explorations are seen as imagined futures, or scenarios, to show alternatives, to critique the existing, or to provoke, such as the 'critical design' of Dunne and Raby.[27] However, the characteristics assigned by Fallman to design exploration (Table 4.5) can be extended to areas of design practice and design studies. Stuart Walker has recently proposed that pure design research should have the licence to create provocative experiments that step outside the boundary constraints of real-world economics (and current trends in higher education design research) by actively seeking to extend the role of design studies in examining the transition towards sustainability,[28] aiming somewhere to the right of Fallman's triangle. A coming together of the global design research community focused on sustainability in Turin in July 2008 at the Changing the Change conference indicates that design explorations can be central to encouraging the social learning journey required to move towards more sustainable ways of living and working, but that advances in design practice and design studies are equally important.[29] The evidence of a growing practical canon of work for design for sustainability (DfS)[30] indicates that there are many proactive designers already addressing the eco-efficiency axis of the sustainability prism through practice, i.e. they are effectively engaged in giving form to new *practical* outputs that are exploratory, since they contest market norms, and could be denoted as eco- or socio-preneurial. It seems reasonable to create a fifth category of artefacts (to accompany protest, service, propositional, demonstration, as proposed by Thorpe and Walker) that is overtly activist – the entrepreneurial artefact.

Design activism can be considered as something that can be an outcome of practice or explorations in real-life situations and/or academia. However, there is an implicit difference in the intended target audience and beneficiaries between practice and academia. The implication of the 'practice' context is that the outcomes are aimed at positive change in a real-life situation involving the wider culture and fabric of society. The implication of the academic-orientated 'design studies' context is that the target is predominantly, although not exclusively, the design culture of academia.

A critical facet of any activism is to have an understanding of the beneficiaries of the activist act(s) and its effectiveness in terms of scale and degree of impact on positive change (Table 4.4). Whether qualitative or quantitative, this feedback or assessment will help determine if this kind of activism is worth continuing, or if a change of strategy and tactics is needed.

The critical role of artefacts in design activism

As has already been noted above, artefacts can assume an activist role. 'Activism' artefacts can be for demonstration, service or protest[31] or to present a proposition.[32] Thorpe sees a *protest artefact* as being deliberately confrontational in order to prompt reflection on the morality of the status quo. Frequently these are one-offs and meet the criteria cited by Fallman's 'design explorations'. A *demonstration artefact* reveals positive alternatives that are superior to the status quo. These can occupy any part of Fallman's triangle, design practice, research or explorations. A *service artefact* is one intended to provide humanitarian aid or aid for a needy group or population, for example in the event of a natural or man-made disaster. The service artefact clearly operates in design practice. Walker's *propositional artefact* is a vehicle for the exploration of theoretical ideas (design research/studies), an embodiment of the ideas (design exploration) and an important element in advancing 'sustainable design' thinking and thus extending design practice. The idea of entrepreneurial artefacts as vehicles for activism in the market has also been suggested above.

Artefacts also embed ideas of inclusion or exclusion of individuals or particular social groups. So it is possible to talk about an 'including artefact' and an 'excluding artefact'. Universal or inclusive design aims to minimize exclusion by ensuring the design can be used by most people most of the time. Left-handed people, on average about 15 per cent of the population, will certainly experience exclusion almost every day as most manufacturers minimize market risk by specifying right-handed options if a 'universal' orientation isn't possible. A potential design activist strategy could involve positive discrimination by favouring the original excluded social group with a design intended only for them.

It seems that the typology of artefacts for activism needs further study. Many purposes can be ascribed to, and communicated by, an artefact. Knowing your purpose or intention will help determine what kind of artefact will achieve the specified goal. Reaching that goal depends upon communicating the correct message through the desired form and aesthetics. A good starting point is Susann Vilma's *Products as Representations* and having a good understanding of the 'aesthetic sign function' which addresses cognitive and emotive messaging simultanteously.[33]

Activism Targeting the Over-consumers

If there is a critical mass population that can minimize future risk around the big global issues then it is the rich 20 per cent of the global population whose total mass and flow of consumption is causing most of the problems (see Chapter 3, p56). The need for change is clear, it is often a question of how to change.[34] The arrangement in the following sections is an attempt to reveal some interesting projects, cross-cutting themes and approaches in the contemporary design activism landscape. It is to be hoped that the examples below show some fruitful areas for exploring potential actions and directions for change; here are some 'designerly ways' of being an activist. This should be seen as a curatorial collection of design activism expressions rather than an attempt to define a classification or typology. Some of the selected examples appear in one subsection, but could equally well illustrate principles in other subsections too.

Raising awareness, changing perceptions, changing behaviour

Sustainability is learning about living well but consuming (much) less; it is a social learning process and will involve moving from a 'product-based well-being' to thinking about products, dematerialized products, services and enabling solutions to satisfy our needs.[35] A personal and collective realization of the importance of adopting cyclic rather than linear consumption and production is also implicit in achieving long-term sustainability. Frederich Schmidt-Bleek and his colleagues at the Wuppertal Institute and Factor 10 club suggest that a 90 per cent increase in efficiencies of resource use is required to ensure that an increasing global human population can be maintained within stable environmental and social systems.[36] Heinberg suggests that the rate at which resources are being consumed makes resource use efficiency and avoidance of resource depletion the key challenges of the early 21st century.[37] An intertwined strategy is required: the strategy to *directly* improve the eco-efficiencies of the product or service throughout its life cycle; and the strategy to deliver eco-efficiencies *indirectly* by changing behaviours. To make this strategy effective also means engaging with academic, social, political and commercial agendas.

Redirective theory and practice

The first group of people that urgently need to change their behaviour are the designers themselves. Various design theorists and critics have been touching on the sustainability theme since Richard Neutra's 1954 book, *Survival through Design*,[38] but it was not until the early 1990s that the discourse on the environmental impacts of design came of age (see pp47–48) and only in the past five years or so that attention refocused on design in the social arena (see pp152–153). Concurrently, there have been a number of emergent new design approaches that have gathered within the sustainability canon. These receive more attention below (Chapter 5) but include critical design,[39] slow design,[40] co-design[41] and metadesign.[42] Such approaches are an attempt to reframe design theory and practice. Anne-Marie Willis talks about 'redirective practice' which requires a deep understanding of what we currently design that is unsustainable, in order that design as 'preconfiguration and directionality' can move towards more sustainable solutions.[43] Design's preconfiguration and directionality echoes the sentiments of Tony Fry who noted that 'design designs'.[44] The objective of redirective practice is 'sustainment', a complex concept that eludes one explicit meaning but gathers around the idea of 'sustaining that which sustains'.[45] Transforming thoughts and perceptions of the culture of design about sustainability seems a crucial undertaking for the design activist that is now gathering significant attention in design research, studies and practice in Europe and worldwide.[46]

Communication by information

Organizations such as Adbusters have long raised the spectre of over-consumption and its promulgation by the multinational corporations and the media, although Janet Wolff is cautionary about how effective this kind of culture jamming is compared with genuine critical political debate.[47] Others are now finding ways of engaging people to question their own responsibilities in the way they consume. Giraffe Innovation's Changing Habbits project with the Royal Society of Arts, UK, enables individuals to enter specific consumption criteria about their use of energy, water, food, electrical goods and waste generation in the home, plus transport patterns, in order to calculate their consumer 'habit'.[48] The data from this habit are converted into a 3D rendered image of an androgynous human being whose head, body and limbs are distorted from the 'ideal habit' to graphically show where the consumer's maximum environmental impacts, in terms of tonnes of carbon dioxide per annum, are being made (Figure 4.3). Another project that utilizes familiar images in new configurations is Worldmapper comprising several hundred cartograms, where land mass from a standard world projection is distorted for each country according to the metric being measured (Figure 4.4). These maps transmit

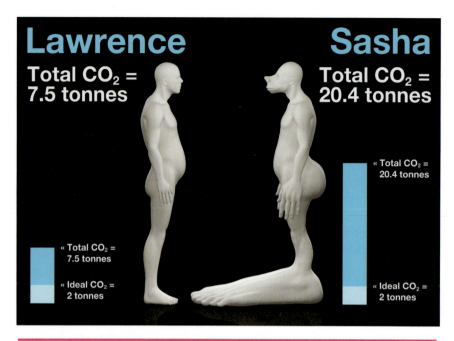

Figure 4.3
Changing Habbits, Giraffe Innovation/Royal Society of Arts

strong visual messages that are more easily assimilated than the mass of statistical data that creates them. Simplifying the message seems an important challenge. Timm Kerkeritz's Virtual Water poster graphically illustrates the consumption of water associated with everyday food and drink, and on the flip side reveals the water footprint of consumers in countries around the world (Figure 4.5). A recently initiated project called 192021 focuses on the challenges that are facing the world's global cities in a looped slide show (Figure 4.6). One slide shows a real-time counter of world population growth – the world population clock – which illustrates the net increase of newborns minus deaths each second, adding to future consumption demands. *The Story of Stuff* by Annie Leonard also uses the web to deliver a 20-minute video, using clever graphics and a riveting storyline.[49]

Finding new ways to communicate requires imaginative use of design to penetrate beyond the 'white noise' (many random signals of equal intensity) of contemporary life.

Communication by concept, prototype or artefact
Concept designs are frequently deployed to challenge an existing canon or imagine future possibilities. They often emerge as the result of design competitions, as explorations for clients, from research projects, and/or from the development of a personal design ethos, portfolio or body of work. The MIT Smart Cities project is a

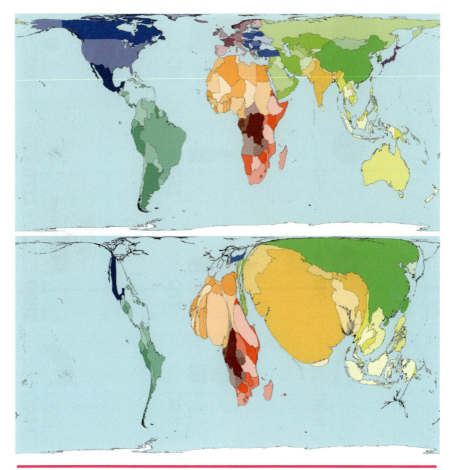

Figure 4.4
Worldmapper cartograms: Standard projection (top) and 'absolute poverty' (bottom)

concept generation laboratory, imagining everything from growing your own house (Fab Tree Hab) to stackable electric cars for dense urban areas (CityCar).[50] The strength of these designs is to ask 'what if', a central question to any design exploration.[51] It is most important to ask 'what is the intention of the designer of these concepts and to which audience is he/she reaching?'

Danish designer, Mads Hagstroem, created the brand FLOWmarket to generate 'thought awakening' by taking ubiquitous products, such as bottled water, and interrogating their existence in our lives (Figure 4.7). FLOWmarket is a global brand crossing cultural boundaries. Hagstroem's nonchalant arrangement of facts and texts in his 'scarcity goods collection' reveals the relationship between flows of the individual, the collective and the environment. Arranged in a shop, his products reveal the vacuity of their supermarket cousins and contest their right to exist.

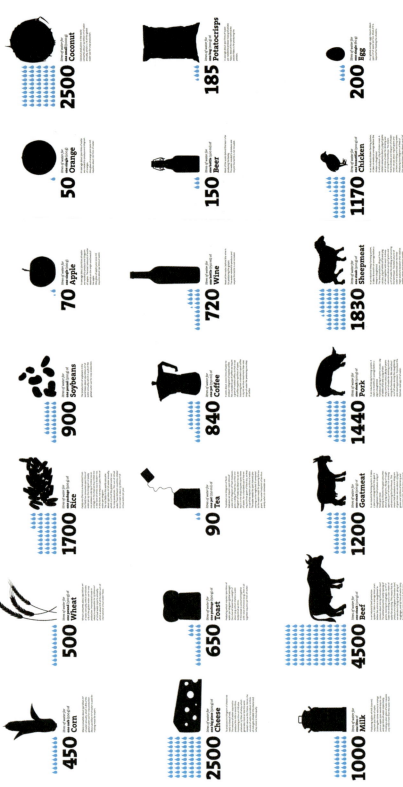

Figure 4.5
Virtual Water poster by Timm Kerkeritz

VIRTUAL **WATER** *inside products*

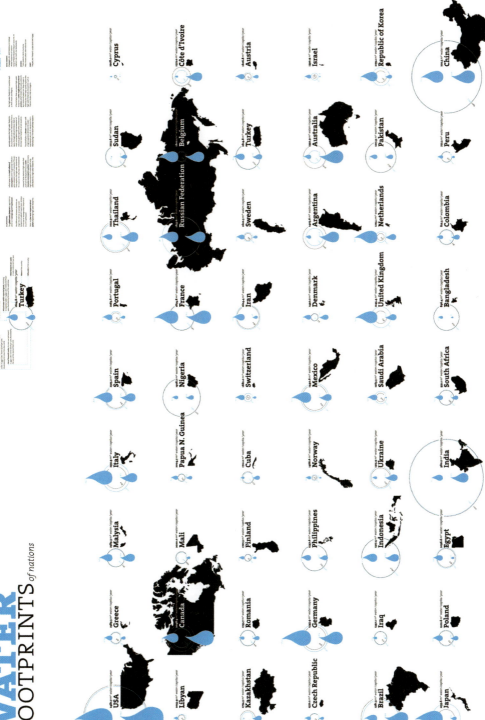

WATER
FOOTPRINTS *of nations*

192021

6,743,470,362
World Population Clock

Figure 4.6
Project 192021 world population clock

clean
tap
water
330ml

Figure 4.7
Clean tap water by Mads Hagstroem, FLOWmarket

Figure 4.8
Lunchbox Laboratory by Futurefarmers and National Renewable Energy Laboratory

Since 1995, Futurefarmers in San Francisco have consistently promoted public projects to raise awareness around issues of growing local food, permaculture systems and biofuel production (Figure 4.8). Their quirky prototypes and experimental artefacts drive home consistent messages of autonomy, self-help, DIY culture and downshifting. Their DIY Algae/Hydrogen Bioreactor, 2004, explored the feasibility of making hydrogen from algae at home, using easily obtainable components. A follow-up project called Lunchbox Laboratory, 2008, in collaboration with the National Renewable Energy Lab, was exhibited at the Museum of Modern Art, New York. It is a portable laboratory that enables schoolchildren to collect local algae strains, culture them and test how much hydrogen each strain can produce. It creates the potentiality of finding more efficient strains faster and is analogous to distributed computing networks, where the power of many individual networked computers is brought together, for example, for climate modeling.[52]

Communication by event, story or scenario

An event by a professional activist group provides a challenge for the commissioned designers. Thomas Matthews highlighted International Buy Nothing Day for its client, Friends of the Earth, UK, by creating 'No Shop' in central London. It sold nothing but was a repository for information about the campaign (Figure 4.9). In another example, the UK government commissioned an illustrator to show four possible scenarios for sustainable travel in 2020 (Figure 4.10). Powerful visual communications not only tell stories but elicit strong cognitive and emotive responses, engaging the viewer.

Figure 4.9
No Shop by Thomas Matthews

Sustainable Everyday – an international design project, led by Milan Polytechnic – deployed scenarios and storytelling to reveal possibilities for quick, slow and co-operative enabling solutions for urban dwellers to meet their needs (see Figure 4.1). Scenarios, built by using a participatory approach in design workshops around the world, focused on aspects of everyday life in the city from moving around, getting and cooking food/water/energy, leisure activities and work/family life. The objective was to create a range of solutions that were enabled or facilitated individually or collectively using existing resources as much as possible. Central to the project was the idea of elevating the well-being *and* capability of the people involved. Some common principles and features emerged from the scenarios (Table 4.6). These reflect many of the characteristics defined earlier by the Postmodern ecologists (see p42) but also introduce a transformational shift from individually owned products to collectively organized products and PSS coordinated by increasing system/social connections and networks.

Communication by project

RED, a design group with the Design Council, UK, ran a number of projects aimed at involving the public in design-led projects by an approach called 'transformation design'.[53] One project, called Future Currents, examined how households could be made aware of their impact on global warming and be encouraged to reduce their carbon footprints. Four top-level behavioural strategies emerged from the series of workshops: home monitoring, rank and reward, peer power and hot products (Figure 4.11). The diversity of the strategy outcomes testified to the importance of the participatory design approach (see Chapter 5) and revealed the limitations of products and services alone to promulgate a significant change in behaviour. Cay Green came to a similar conclusion in a postgraduate study focusing on changing energy consumption in domestic households. She designed a tool for consumers in the form of a booklet called *Grow Fur* that showed how households could run their own 'workshops' to co-create and co-design their own solutions to fit their lives (Figure 4.12).

Ways of making and producing

The global economy enables transnational corporations to manufacture their brands anywhere that competitive labour prices and raw or manufactured materials can be readily brought together. This 'distributed' manufacturing relies entirely on fossil fuels to move raw materials, components and finished products around the globe. Peak oil will challenge this model of manufacturing as the proportional cost of oil rises in each part of the supply and distribution chains. The growth of the green, ethical and 'organic' consumer markets since the mid-1980s[54] and more recent attention to 'localization'[55] is also affecting what, where and when products are made. This trend appears set to continue.

Other more fuzzy trends are contesting the way things are made. Demands for products that are more easily personalized or customizable, tend to offer the promise of more durable emotional relationships.[56] The inextricable rise of the internet in everyday life is leading to much experimentation in ways of making and the emergence of co-created, co-designed and replicable designs is a plausible reality (see Chapter 5, 'Designing Together'). In the search for more meaning there may be a shift in the balance between what is made by manufacturers, designed by professionals, and what is self-made, designed by non(professional)-designers[57] (Figure 4.13).

Halfway products

In a 'halfway' product, the designer/maker/manufacturer only takes the product so far, leaving a space for the user to complete the making.[58] The user embeds their

Narinder Sagoo / Foster and Partners

Narinder Sagoo / Foster and Partners

Figure 4.10
UK government's future transport scenarios

Table 4.6
The orientations and guidelines for the Sustainable Everyday project

General principles
Think before doing. Weigh up objectives and ethical considerations
Promote variety. Biological, socio-cultural and technical diversity
Use what already exists. Reduce the need for the new. Minimize intervention. Enhance what is there
Quality of context
Give space to nature. Protect natural environments and promote 'symbiotic nature'
Re-naturalize food. Cultivate naturally
Bring people and things together. Reduce demand for transport
Share tools and equipment. Reduce the demand for products. Foster new forms of socialization
System intelligence
Empower people. Increase participation
Develop networks. Promote decentralized, flexible forms of organization. Develop learning systems with feedback that can be reorientated
Use the sun, wind and biomass. Reduce dependence on oil. Alternative energy systems minimizing CO_2 emissions
Produce at zero waste. Promote forms of industrial ecology. Closed loops of materials and cascade energy

Source: Manzini and Jégou (2003)[59]

Narinder Sagoo / Foster and Partners

Narinder Sagoo / Foster and Partners

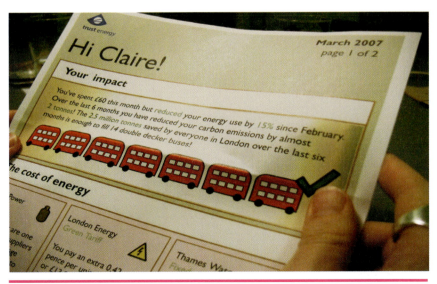

Figure 4.11
Future Currents project, RED, the Design Council, UK

own creativity, stories and mistakes in the process of finishing the product, thereby cementing a personal narrative, memory and associations that differentiate this product from others manufactured at the same time. Halfway products differ from examples of car customization where the user has taken a standard production car, removed elements and added their own 'customized' element. They also differ from 'mass customization' or 'mass personalization', i.e. manufacturers offering a range of colours or model types, or offering a standard model with variable elements, e.g. the mobile phone with clip-on external casing.

Tache Naturelle by Martin Ruiz de Azúa builds on commercial ideas of pottery painting in cafés by encouraging the user to take a biscuit-fired vase and complete its decoration, but de Azúa suggests that the user secrets it in the urban or rural landscape and lets nature provide the final serendipitous markings (Figure 4.14). This involves the user imagining stories, trying out different locations and retrieving it after varying time periods elapsing; in short, each user creates a different set of circumstances for 'finishing' the vase. In a more direct and obvious challenge, Natalie Schaap confronts the user with a real and symbolic chair, An Affair with a Chair. She offers a chair frame which the user must complete to obtain the final use-value and full functionality

Figure 4.12
Grow Fur by Cay Green

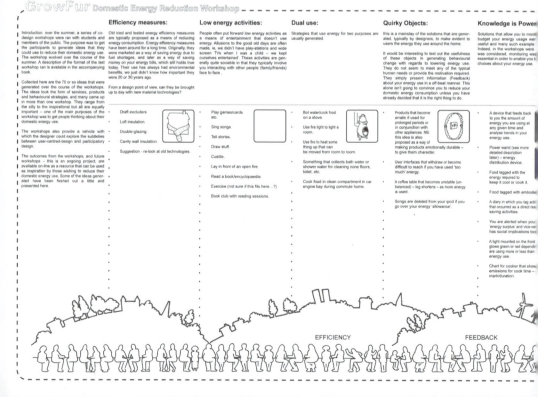

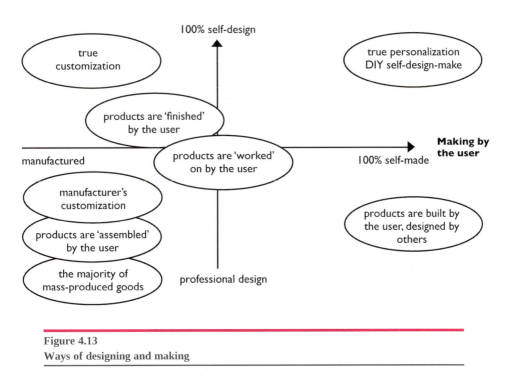

Figure 4.13
Ways of designing and making

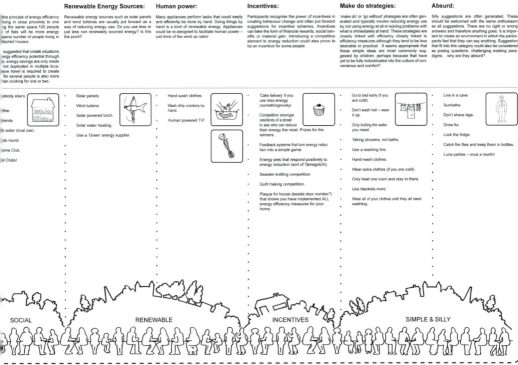

Figure 4.14
Tache Naturelle by Martin Ruiz de Azúa

of a chair (Figure 4.15). As the name of her product suggests this product 'elopes' with its user and a relationship begins. Both these approaches attempt to create added layers of meaning for the user by involving them tangibly in completion of the form giving. In doing so, the aesthetic is made personal.

A fictional new brand, 'do' was created by Kesselskramer, a Dutch publicity agency which engaged the Droog Design collective to interpret the brand. Ten

Figure 4.15
An Affair with a Chair by Natalie Schaap

designers exhibited in Milan in 2000 under the banner 'do Create', demonstrating new possibilities for creating new objects in our lives, objects embedded with new meaning by the user finishing the product.[60] Examples include Marijn van der Poll's 'do Hit' metal cube that the user shapes into an armchair by using a sledge hammer (Figure 4.16); Martí Guixé's 'do Scratch' a transparent box coated in black paint that the user scratches to permit the light rays to escape. An emotional mortar with the brand is forged by the user becoming an active participant in the final creation.

Modular evolved products

Traditional ways of organizing and managing mass industrial production have largely been uncontested since the mid-19th century, because they support a well-understood and risk-limited business model. This model also generates huge quantities of stuff, much of it on a rather short-lived journey to a landfill site. A study by the Dutch Eternally Yours Foundation revealed that 20–90 per cent of discarded domestic electrical products were still working and offered the original functionality.[61] If functionality had not broken, then the relationship between user and product clearly had. In this super-saturated world of stuff, the 'real world' for the over-consumers, Walker[62] suggested that a radical new design and manufacturing approach is required. His design of a digital clock separates the functional components from a 'chassis', the latter being a white armature or

Figure 4.16
do Hit chair for Droog by Marijn van der Poll

canvas (Figure 4.17). Over time, the functional components can be replaced, repaired and upgraded as required. In Three White Canvas Clocks, the user has control over the final form, through modification of a number of variables. Function and utility can literally be mixed in a visual palette chosen by the user. The symbolic meanings are therefore at the control of the user. The user even has to 'tend' his/her clock by supplanting fresh fruit to provide the living battery. Such a system confers some psychological advantages to the user, allowing them to evolve and extend the relationship with the product. This type of product may require new business models and manufacturing systems to deliver commercial viability.

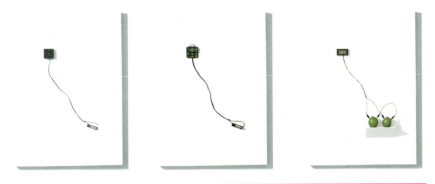

Figure 4.17
Three White Canvas Clocks by Stuart Walker

Ethical products

The history of ethical product manufacturing for the consumer economy commences in the 1970s with the Body Shop cosmetics chain and Ben & Jerry ice cream that pioneered brands with strong ethical values as a means to differentiate these companies from their competitors. Wider consumer market demand did not emerge until the late 1980s in Britain, when magazines such as *Ethical Consumer* examined the credentials and products of companies espousing to be ethical.[63] Since then new labels and certification schemes have emerged to give the consumer information on a wide variety of ethical concerns. The Fairtrade label that ensures a fairer percentage of profits goes to the primary grower, is perhaps the best known. Industries have adopted their own methods of communicating their ethical standards. For example, in the fashion and clothing industry there is a number of campaign groups that have highlighted sweat shop labour issues, such as Labour Behind the Label and the Clean Clothes Campaign, and even large commercial companies promote their ethical stance, for example, American Apparel lists its credentials with a label that notes 'Made in Downtown LA, Sweatshop Free'.[64] Are these initiatives activist? Yes, as they look after the interests of neglected and minority groups and prevent their exploitation. Yet, most of the above examples are generally not led by designers. For design-led activism around ethical products we have to turn to the likes of Adbuster, with its campaign around Blackspot sneakers and boots made from organic hemp in a Portuguese union shop,[65] or to individual designer-makers determined to forge new models of production. In 2000, Natalie Chanin set up a cottage industry making bespoke garments under an initiative called Alabama Chanin.[66] She revived many crafts skills beginning to dwindle in the local community and encouraged the women to come together in circles to stitch, quilt and embroider, often using reused materials.

Replicating machines, brokered manufacturing, downloadable designs

The 'information age', facilitated by the inextricable rise of the internet, is generating new visions of manufacturing. RepRap (Replicating Rapid Prototyper), designed by Adrian Bowyer and Vik Oliver at Bath University, is a self-copying 3D printer that

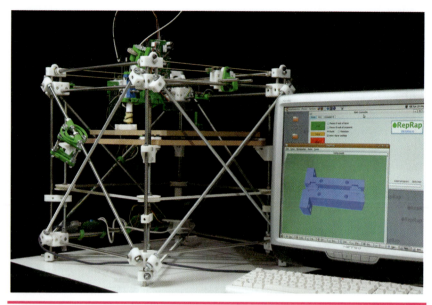

Figure 4.18
RepRap by Adrian Bowyer and Vik Oliver

builds components by building up layers of plastic (Figure 4.18). Once one RepRap
has been built, it can then replicate itself, as indeed happened in the laboratory at
Bath on 29 May 2008. As the designs for the machine are available under the GNU
General Public License, anyone can build and upgrade one. This potentially opens up
radical new ways of organizing manufacturing, servicing and maintenance for
elements, components or whole products (see more in Chapter 6, pp174–175). An
alternative system is being offered by Ponoko, New Zealand. The company will
receive designers' flatpack designs, find the buyers and get specific manufacturers to
cut and deliver them. Ponoko also offers an online space for co-creation. This
personalized manufacturing platform permits make-on-demand. Taking it one stage
further there are a number of platforms offering downloadable designs via the
internet. Kith-Kin has a shop of downloadable designs for chairs, paper objects and
diverse creative 'inventions'.[67] Paper Critters offers a web platform and software
tools for creating paper toys.[68] The cutting plans can be downloaded by the users. To
date, more than 5000 contributors have unleashed their creativity using this facility.

Bonding with the workers – meaningful production
While the workers are largely forgotten in the manufacturing process, some
designers have taken an interest in these unsung labourers. Connecting Lines by
Judith van den Boom is an ongoing collaboration, commenced in 2007, with
workers in a bone china factory in Jingdezhen, China (Figure 4.19). She is a
catalyst, facilitator and designer running workshops and poetry readings with the
workers. The intention is to humanize processes and encourage collective

Figure 4.19
Connecting Lines, a project with factory workers in Jingdezhen, China,
by Judith van den Boom

intelligence to create a 'smart factory' where designers and employees co-create, co-design and co-make. How workers are engaged with the act of making seems of paramount importance in a society focused on the good life (at work and at home). Proto Gardening Bench by Jurgen Bey for Droog was the output from a larger project, Couleur Locale, examining the revitalization of the communities of the town of Oranienbaum, Germany (Figure 4.20). This ephemeral seating is a

Figure 4.20
Proto Gardening Bench by Jurgen Bey for the Oranienbaum project for Droog

conceptual design made from garden waste harvested at different times of the year by the local community. Waste is compressed and bonded in a resin matrix. As the seating weathers, it is slowly returned to nature and the cycle begins again.

Experiments in bio- and techno-cyclicity

Closing the loop by seeing waste as food is an important principle in realizing eco-efficiency improvements. McDonough and Braungart refer to biological and technological materials as nutrients that can nourish new generations of products.[69] The possibilities of growing furniture in-situ are being investigated by everyone from arboriculturalists to designers. Yael Stav of Innivo Design works with Plantware in Israel to create living plants that are functional household and office objects (Figure 4.21). Christopher Cattle of the UK's Grown-Furniture promotes the skills and simple technology of training and grafting plants to grow your own stool, taking about five years for a three-legged stool of sycamore.[70]

Recycling synthetic plastics is fraught with difficulties because of a recalcitrant plastic industry protecting its virgin markets, supply–demand and perceived issues of the quality of recyclates and because the plastic waste is highly distributed once it enters the retail chain. However, recycling can make good business sense and has attracted attention from

Figure 4.21
Plantware, living functional plant structures, by Yael Stav of Innivo Design

Figure 4.22
Codha chair by Richard Liddle,
Codha Design

Figure 4.23
REEE chair by Sprout Design
for Pli Design

designer-makers to international manufacturers. Richard Liddle of Codha Design is
experimenting with ways of using recycled high density polyethylene (HDPE) to
create new domestic seating (Figure 4.22). A continuous ribbon of re-pigmented
HDPE extrusion is applied manually to a mould creating one-offs. This celebratory
use of plastic recyclate contrasts with other examples, such as the REEE chair by
Sprout Design (Figure 4.23) where the recyclable (in this case Sony PlayStation
cases) is invisible, invoking a 'sustainability by stealth' approach. Since Herman
Miller, the international office furniture manufacturer, launched its classic Aeron
chair in 1991 using components from recyclate, the company has continued to
refine its designs. Its latest design, the Celle chair is 99 per cent recyclable at end-
of-life and includes 33 per cent of its components from recyclate.[71] These
approaches position the cultural acceptability of their design outcomes in different
ways. Codha Design make a significant aesthetic statement about 'closing the
loop' by creating a practical yet 'propositional or demonstration' artefact (see
pp83, 85) deliberately trying to go beyond what the great US industrial designer
Raymond Loewy called 'most advanced yet acceptable' (MAYA),[72] while Sprout
Design and Herman Miller demonstrate recycling as a sensible business proposition,
and so tacitly acknowledge MAYA's boundaries, which are determined by reducing
capital risk while maximizing potential profit per unit production.

Eco-efficiency improvements

Improving the eco-efficiency of any design artefact or service is an act of activism
to reduce impacts on the world's ecosystems (and humankind). While this is clearly

Figure 4.24
MP3 eco-player by Trevor Baylis

different from an activist who takes action to protect a habitat, ecosystem or specific species, reducing the impacts of our production and consumption is of great importance. Since the turn of the millennium, a significant body of work has been published on design that aims for improved eco-efficiencies in order to lighten our impact on the Earth's resources, habitats and ecosystems (see pp47–48). There are legion examples showing that designers of all persuasions, and some enlightened clients and manufacturers too, are striving to turn rhetoric into new eco-design or ecological design practice.[73] While these examples are many, and growing, many have not achieved critical mass in the markets. A good analogy is to walk around a typical Western supermarket and see the proportion of organic food in relation to all the rest of the food being sold. Organic food is present but the vast bulk of food produced, bought and consumed, originates from inorganic systems requiring high oil energy inputs and oil-dependent derivatives (oil-based fertilizers, pesticides). This same picture emerges scanning across other consumables (cleaning products, cosmetics and paints) to durables (from houses to cars to electrical/electronic goods and fashion). With housing, transportation and food governing almost 70 per cent of total environmental impacts in the 2006 in the (then) 25 countries comprising the European Union,[74] the eco-efficiency challenge remains daunting. Recalcitrant industries, housing developers and governments (what we may call the 'business-as-usual' majority) need to be shown that there is a strong business case for eco-efficient designs. The evidence is just starting to show in the latest trends predicting that eco-products will be an emergent area for many manufacturing sectors in the next few years.[75] Any designer prepared to take on this role, and enlist the silent client of the environment – nature – is a default activist. There is a growing cadre of e-zines dedicated to celebrating these eco-design activists, including *Treehugger*, *Inhabitat* and *Worldchanging*.[76] Many eco-efficient products utilize materials with an inherently lower impact (recycled, biological origin materials) and reduce energy during the manufacturing and/or during the use phase of the product. The thinking behind these products uses existing technological approaches, for example, Trevor Baylis's MP3 player (Figure 4.24), utilizing proven wind-up energy technology to

Figure 4.25
Flamp by Martí Guixé

more tangential solutions, such as Martí Guixé's Flamp, a wooden table lamp coated in phosphorescent paint that absorbs UV light and re-emits it when darkness falls (Figure 4.25). While the innovations are many, few products are designed to be taken back by the manufacturers at end-of-life, so there is still significant progress required in this area to 'close the loop' and ensure eco-efficient recycling of valuable materials. That these manufacturers and designers are actively striving to make their products more efficient is laudable, but measuring their true eco-effectiveness remains problematic, especially since studies show that eco-efficient products can generate a negative rebound effect – that is when the users spend the money or energy saved from these products in other areas in their lives.[77] In a worst case scenario, the successful sale of millions of eco-efficient products into new markets has the potential to actually increase overall energy consumption.

Design concepts

Smart Cities is a range of diverse mini-projects at Massachusetts Institute of Technology (MIT), US, united under a research focus on 'intelligent, sustainable buildings, mobility systems and cities' that is not constrained by traditional boundaries.[78] While techno-centric thinking dominates most of the Smart Cities concepts, other MIT-initiated projects show plausible biocentric tendencies, such as the Fab Tree Hab, a growing house of living trees grafted onto on computer numeric controlled (CNC) reusable structures (Figure 4.26) designed by the Human Ecology Design team (now Terreform 1). This is blue sky thinking about using existing and new technologies with networked intelligence, as illustrated in the CityCar, a stackable two-seater electric vehicle for one-way journeys from Vehicle Stacks at suitable nodes in the city (Figure 4.27). The analogy is the stackable supermarket or airport trolley – to be used when needed. Given the international profile of MIT, the primary intention of these exploratory Smart

Figure 4.26
Fab Tree Hab by Terreform 1

Cities projects may be to encourage further R&D funding to convert the concepts into reality, but the huge media attention also ensures elevating general awareness among research communities and the general public.

Prototypes

At the Amsterdam AutoRAI show in January 2007, yet another prototype car was launched. However, this one was remarkably different. It did not emerge from the R&D department of the global car manufacturing industry, it was the outcome of a collaborative open source design project involving the Netherlands Society for Nature and the Environment, the Technical Universities at Delft, Eindhoven and Enschede. The technical drawings and other design details for 'c,mm,n', the zero-emission hydrogen engine car (Figure 4.28), are available for download on the internet allowing others to participate in refining the design.[79] While the merits and eco-efficacy of hydrogen fuel is still open to debate, the process of open source design is to be lauded.

Figure 4.27
CityCar by MIT Smart Cities

Figure 4.28
c,mm,n open source car, the Netherlands

New builds

A young Danish architecture practice, Force4, teamed up with KHRAS to win the Home of the Future Competition organized by the Danish Building Research Institute and RealDania in 2001 (Figure 4.29). Their first-prize concept, Boase,[80] provided affordable housing on stilts over a contaminated post-industrial site planted with trees for phyto-remediation of the toxins in the soil. With more than 150 of these brownfield sites identified in Copenhagen, the land area is substantial, yet housing development is not normally approved on these types of sites by the authorities. Phase two of the project ensued in 2005 with a 1:1 scale mock-up examining the basic technologies required for site decontamination, development of solar membranes and the energy-gathering potential of the facade, plus optimization of the spatial organization of each dwelling. In early 2009, Boase is scheduled to be applied to the first site in Copenhagen, demonstrating just how much persistence is required to activate more radical ideas. This project steps beyond eco-efficiency and aims to build new communities while regenerating the biological capacity of the site, something advocated by Janis Birkeland in her call for 'positive development' not 'sustainable development'.[81]

Contesting meaning and consumption

'Green', 'ethical' and 'sustainable' consumption received consistent attention from the late 1980s onwards but these approaches gather around abstract notions of causing less damage to the environment. In the design debate, the human, and hence social, imperatives of consumption received less attention. The real question rests on how we can consume to improve well-being and quality of life *and* simultaneously reduce our environmental footprint. Understanding what motivates us to consume *differently* seems to be important. Researchers turned towards needs theory to understand the physiological, psychological and social functionings that contribute to well-being.[82] Others examined how design can offer substantive improvements to deepening our relationship with products in order to extend the lives of products while enriching the users' lives;[83] how a new model of well-being posited on balancing the individual against economic, environmental and social factors could refocus designers and manufacturers;[84] and the role that design can play in cementing powerful emotional and experiential relationships with objects.[85]

Ways of deepening and extending relationships throughout the lifetime of a product, the introduction of new rhythms and experiences, and shifting consumers from products to dematerialized services form the bedrock of designers searching to deliver new meanings to artefacts and hence to the act of consumption.

Figure 4.29 (opposite)
Boase housing development, Copenhagen, by Force4 and KHRAS

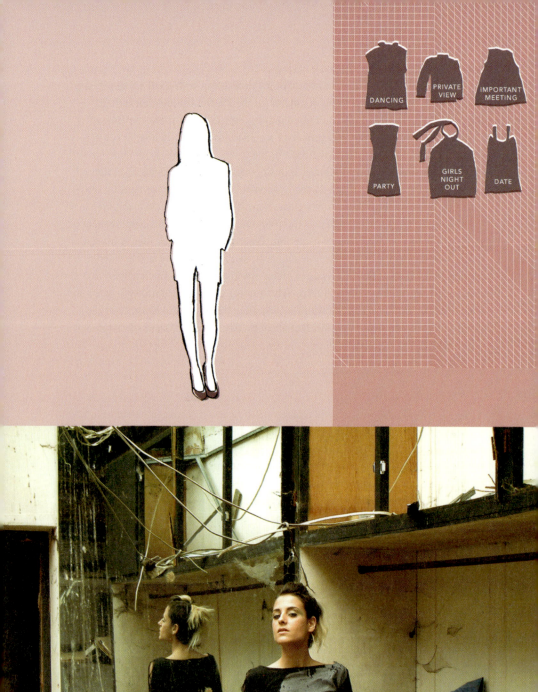

DANCING

PRIVATE
VIEW

IMPORTANT
MEETING

PARTY

GIRLS
NIGHT
OUT

DATE

Improving human–product relationships

Two design research projects examining our relationship with textiles and clothing reveal the nuances of design detail and their considerable ramifications for environmental impacts throughout the life cycle of the clothing. The Lifetimes Project[86] and the 5 Ways Project[87] think about how ecological values are embedded in the various components/elements of a fashion design and how they enable new notions of washability, locally made, multi-life designs and offer options for updatability (Figure 4.30). Other strategies to make the consumer look afresh at the products that surround them include a direct approach by Dick van Hoff whose ambition, via his project Tyranny of the Plug (Figure 4.31), is to liberate us from having to plug into the domestic electricity supply by creating high-specification engineered kitchen products that reinstate the joy of manual methods of food preparation. Simon Heijdens aims for a slow dawning and realization by the user that the product is evolving, growing. The minute cracks in the glaze of Broken White reveal themselves more and 'grow' as the plate is used more (Figure 4.32). Monika Hoinkis finds ways of reintroducing us to objects we no longer see by removing vital components that force us to become intimate with the object in a new way, to find new poetry in the mutual existence of person–object, to renew the vigour of the relationship (Figure 4.33).

Focusing on experiences not objects

Life's experiences and the social relationships we develop tend to be a forceful arbiter of what we make of life. Lawrence and Nohria[88] observed that we are 'hardwired' with four innate, universal, independent yet inter-connected drives:

- to acquire objects and experiences that improve our status relative to others
- to establish long-term bonds with others based on reciprocity, of mutual caring commitment
- to learn about and makes sense of our world, which is largely our own social creation, and of ourselves
- to defend ourselves, our families and friends, our beliefs, and our resources from harm.

The acquisition of objects is an important drive that the design of artefacts can help satiate, but the other drives are orientated around experiential, social, existential and survival factors. Moving beyond form and function, some designers use the object as a conduit to an experience 'beyond the object'. Swedish design agency Front, created a wallpaper that absorbs ultraviolet light, emitting mood altering glows as darkness falls. Front also initiated Tensta Konsthall, an interior design project where change is deliberately built into the design elements (Figure 4.34). As time

Figure 4.30 (opposite)
One-Night Wonder, The Lifetimes Project and No Wash Top, 5 Ways Project

Figure 4.31
Tyranny of the Plug by Dick van Hoff

progresses the elements fade, providing a slowly evolving time marker to change we tend not to see. Playing with the emotions of time was a key aim of Thorunn Arnadottir's Clock, comprising an electric cogwheel on which a string of coloured beads sits (Figure 4.35). As the clock turns, the beads change position. Blue beads represent five minutes, orange and red the hour points, gold for midday and silver for midnight. In a powerful emotional and symbolic moment, removing the beads

Figure 4.32
Broken White by Simon Heijdens

Figure 4.33
Living with Things by Monika Hoinkis

Figure 4.34
Tensta Konsthall by Front

Figure 4.35
Clock by Thorunn Arnadottir

from the clockface and using them as a necklace liberates the wearer from the 'clock time' to your own 'free time'. Arnadottir's invocation of a different sense of time is a central theme to many designers working within the 'slow design' approach (see Chapter 5, p157).

Another time-enabled experience is initiated by CuteCircuit's The Hug Shirt™, where electronic circuitry includes sensors that measure touch, skin warmth and the heartbeat of the sender and actuators that recreate those sensations in the recipient's shirt (Figure 4.36). All this is achieved by the shirt having Bluetooth technology embedded in it, the signal being transmitted from a Java-enabled mobile phone. Sending a 'hug', actually a bit of HugMe™ Java-enabled software script, is just as easy as sending an SMS message. The shirt is washable and complies with latest Restriction of Hazardous Substances (RoHS) regulations for electronic equipment.

Figure 4.36
The Hug Shirt™ by CuteCircuit

Remote sensory experiences may seem rather an indulgence but given that contemporary work patterns often entail time away from loved ones, The Hug Shirt™ potentially offers some solace.

Invisible forces

Inextricably linked to our very visible world of electronics and ICT are the invisible electromagnetic fields created by these gadgets and systems. Design researchers and theorists, Antony Dunne and Fiona Raby at the Royal College of Art, London, refer to the radiating electromagnetic fields as a physical environment and call it 'hertzian' space.[89] Their work, under the rubric of 'critical design', design that does not affirm the industrial agendas but challenges and questions it, focuses on the 'interaction between devices, hertzian space and the imagination'.[90] Their design is the opposite of the Hollywood blockbuster, it is Design Noir, fusing complex narratives in the context of everyday life. Critical design's purpose is to 'stimulate discussion and debate among designers, industry and the public about the aesthetic quality of our electronically mediated existence'[91]; it is not for the purpose of commercialization or exploitation by industry. In this sense it is not research and development but research and exploration, more closely allied to Walker's propositional artefact (p83). It is concerned with the 'lived experience not the medium' which was aptly demonstrated in their experiment called the Placebo Project (Figure 4.37). Eight prototypes of semi-familiar domestic objects made of medium-density fibreboard (MDF) were given to individuals to introduce into their domestic environments who were later interviewed about their

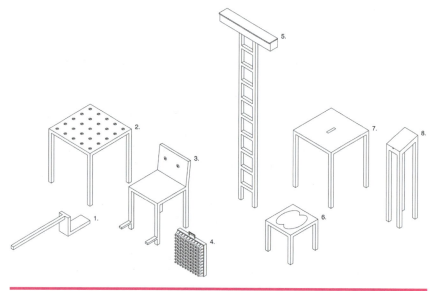

Figure 4.37
The Placebo Project by Antony Dunne and Fiona Raby

experiences with these objects. Electronic circuitry was embedded in some of the objects enabling specific functions as the electromagnetic fields from other electronic products in the home were encountered. Some objects did not have this capability. Each prototype was effectively a cultural probe[92] providing an interface for learning about the lives of the individuals, the lives of the objects and their rich interactions. One of the more revealing facets of this study was the power of the ambiguity of the 'placebo' designs to stimulate the imagination of the users while simultaneously raising their awareness as to the invisible landscape and territories of electromagnetic radiation, a topic rarely touched upon in social discourse.

The purpose of Dunne and Raby's experimental work was clear. Less easy to establish, as is common with much research-focused 'design activism', is how effective it was in communicating with and influencing its key audiences and its effectiveness in our transition to sustainable ways of living. The debate requires much wider currency to elicit positive transformative actions or for products to emerge in the marketplace or public domain.

Social cohesion and community building

'Sustainable communities' became a catchphrase for the New Labour government in the UK in the early 2000s,[93] although defining a sustainable community remains problematic. Manfred Max-Neef's framework for Universal Human-Scale Development[94] attests to our genuine need for participatory, social and collective experiences, so the idea of using design to help generate improvements in social cohesion, to repair existing communities, or build new ones, seems to offer some promise. The ability for green interventions in the urban landscape to reconfigure and reorientate communities was positively demonstrated by the Home Zones project in 1996 in the Methleys neighbourhood of inner-city Leeds, in the north of England.[95] A total of 800m^2 of turf were laid for a weekend to given pedestrian priority to a busy urban street and host the Methleys Olympics. This story is embedded in the urban mythology of the area but even more importantly the event led to the official recognition of Methleys as a Home Zone by the local authority in 2002 – reward indeed to the champions in the local community, Heads Together, a creative agency, and architect Eddy Walker.

Catalysing positive social and environmental change is the founding premise of the Designs of the time 2007 (Dott 07) Project, an initiative funded by the UK's Design Council and One NorthEast, in the north-east of England in 2007.[96] Dott 07 was an exploration of how design could help society explore 'what life in a sustainable region could be like', through a year of community projects, events and exhibitions. The project focused on five aspects of daily life: movement, energy, school, health and food. One project that encouraged significant participation through design was Urban Farming (Figure 4.38). Consumer concerns over food miles, the carbon

Figure 4.38
The Urban Farming Project by Dott 07

footprint or emissions, and contaminations with toxins coupled with the separation of food production from the city, has led UK planners and architects to ask how the urban landscape can be more ecologically productive and socially cohesive. Dott 07 enlisted a range of local partners in the project location, the town of Middlesbrough, with national partners with an interest in bio-regional systems of food production, and artist/blogger Debra Solomon who promotes food culture through Culiblog.[97] In May 2007, containers of varying sizes (1m^2 to 4m^2) were delivered to locations across the town and more than 1000 people began producing fruit and vegetables culminating in a banquet for 1500 people in the town square in September 2007. The next phase of the project involves scaling up the operation by identifying new locations for urban farming. This task was completed by designers Andre Viljoen and Katrina Bohn, who have both investigated how urban landscapes can be more biologically productive and socially inclusive.[98] The map generated represents a blueprint for a more sustainable local food economy. Other approaches to re-examining the ecological productivity of the urban or suburban landscape can be found in projects like Edible Estates,[99] Edible Campus[100] and the High Line Project in New York to utilize an abandoned elevated railway line for various landscape uses.[101] Dott 07's Urban Farming Project and other projects with ambitions to change our urban landscapes, clearly illustrate the catalytic potential of design to encourage communities to take action.

Miscellaneous activism

Activism finds expressions around a multitude of causes and issues (see Chapter 1, Figures 1.4–1.9) and activists will mobilize around emergent issues as they arise. The focus is on the present with a view to changing the near future. However, there are a handful of design activists who demand that we pause to examine rather more different timeframes. Long-term horizons are invoked by the sustainability debate but rarely given form or substance.

Time and design

These activists are mavericks by the very nature of their philosophical real-life manifestations. Here, the use of the word philosophical is applied in the old Greek sense of a way of living a life through practical realizations. They use profound design principles built on the disciplines of architecture, science and engineering, although they may not describe themselves as designers. Louis Le Roy's Eco-cathedral near Mildam in the Netherlands contests our very notion of man-made works and their explicit man-defined design lives[102] (Figure 4.39). Le Roy's hand-built monument of recycled brick and stone, constructed over 30 years, is just the beginning of a 1000-year project where time and space interweave in a mutually evolving, synergistic design.

Stewart Brand proposes a corrective project to deal with civilization's dangerously short attention span.[103] Brand's Clock of the Long Now encourages long-term thinking; his clock is very big, very slow and is a strictly notional 'instrument for thinking about time in a different way'.[104] Founded in 1998, The Long Now Foundation is working on the practicalities of the clock and what it may mean to maintain something for 10,000 years. Lastly, we have the slow-burn project Roden Crater, the work of artist James Turrell, to turn an extinct crater in the Painted Desert, northern Arizona, US, into a place where the human spirit can seek a deeper relationship with the Earth and the universe through sensory synaesthesia and by being exposed to experiences whose depth is magnified by the manipulation of natural light.[105] Famous for his 'skyspaces', Turrell has excavated inside the crater and created apertures through which the light of the sun, moon, distant planets, galaxies and even light beyond our galaxy (light that is 3.5 billion years old) can be experienced. In this place, examination of the word 'sustainability' takes an entirely new trajectory.

Activism Targeting the Under-consumers

The 'under-consumers' may seem a strange term in a world where current levels of consumption seem unsustainable, the more so with the population due to increase to somewhere between 7.3 billion and 10.5 billion by 2050.[106] The reality is that significant numbers of people go hungry every day, many do not have access to potable water, earn less than US$2 per day and/or live in temporary shelter

Figure 4.39
Eco-cathedral by Louis Le Roy

(see Chapter 3, p55). These under-consumers exist in the affluent societies of the North as well as the societies of the South. Under these conditions, quality of life remains an abstract expression; these people are focused on survival, striving to meet basic physiological needs, permanently stuck on the bottom of Maslow's hierarchy of needs.[107] These people actually need to have access to appropriate technologies and resources; they need to consume *more* resources. Resources may be available locally or regionally but unequal distribution and/or consumption of these resources by distant others able to pay a higher price, compounds local problems. A recent WWF report detailed the consumption of real and 'virtual' water for UK consumers.[108] While the average UK consumer takes 150 litres a day from the water supply system, their 'virtual' water footprint (in food, textiles for clothing and other goods) is 30 times this amount, a total of 4645 litres per day per capita. This includes the water essential to food and other crop growth, plus water used in the manufacturing and processing industries. The latter is extensive as supermarket vegetables tend to be washed using very high volumes of water.[109] One litre of water, sold in a PET plastic bottle can take up to nine litres of water in its production. A New Economics Foundation study in 2006 revealed the tentacles of the 'UK plc' supply chain feeding the UK's high ecological footprint[110] (see Figure 3.5). For the UK, this is about 5.8 global ha equivalent per capita (if shared around the world equably, the average footprint would be 1.8 global ha equivalent).[111]

Depending on the various statistics that can be invoked, the 'under-consumers' represent between a sixth and a third of the global human population. Most of the design outputs addressing the under-consumers are predominantly 'service artefacts' (p85), services, and information and communication projects to raise awareness/education and/or provide new skills. Designs primarily focus on affordability, practicality, functionality and utility; other qualities, such as aesthetics, cultural fit and the generation of pleasure, are of secondary consideration and are often inadequately addressed. The drivers for this are diverse but may hint at a continuing underlying paternalism from the North, a lower order of priorities for this type of design, and lack of funds for designers keen to work with the under-consumers. Might there also be a lack of ambition by many designers to work in this arena? Papanek[112] called upon designers to give just 10 per cent of their time to design for real needs. His clarion call seems worth reiterating today.

There are some positive signs that more designers are taking up the task of addressing their more global, as opposed to just commercial, responsibilities. In 1999, Architecture for Humanity (AfH) was established,[113] out of which emerged the Open Architecture Network giving an opportunity for architects to donate design days to ongoing projects. In 2005, Denmark's not-for-profit organization INDEX launched its Index: Design to Improve Life awards. Today INDEX is now operated and owned by the Danish Design Centre, Copenhagen, an original founding partner. These awards have undoubtedly helped call attention to and encouraged greater involvement of the global design community in targeting the over-consumers *and* the under-consumers.[114] In 2007, a total of 337 design institutions nominated specific designs for the awards. Unfortunately, only a relatively small proportion of the designs of the nominated winners in 2007 would be affordable to those earning a few US dollars a day, and the cultural acceptability of some of the designs remains a moot point. A recent exhibition held at the Cooper Hewitt Museum, entitled 'Design for the other 90%', reveals varying standards of aesthetics, technology and production.[115] In fact, some designs seem stuck in a time-warp, progressing little beyond the achievements illustrated in Papanek's book 37 years ago. The conundrum expressed then is still valid today – how can we create useful, affordable, life-enhancing and *beautiful* design for the under-consumers? Nonetheless, all designers working to improve the lives of the under-consumers rightly deserve the moniker 'design activists', as they are genuinely intent on lifting people's lives beyond a litany of daily tasks just to survive.

Shelter, water, food

Shelter

The provision of shelter for the needy reflects the stresses and strains evident on populations affected by economies that magnify the rich–poor divide, by global geopolitics and economics, by political regimes that result in inequality and persecution, and by disruptive man-made and natural disasters. AfH categorizes housing shelter driven by reasons of emergency, transition, permanence and homelessness, and addresses issues of community under 'gathering spaces' and 'women specific places'.[116] Tens of examples reveal inputs from international and local designers actively striving to meet the shelter needs of diverse populations. There always seems to be a delicate balance between imposed solutions from non-locals and the enablement of local creativity, skills and desires. A project called Siyathemba provides an excellent example of getting the correct balance. Siyathemba, meaning 'we hope' in Zulu, originated as a community-driven project in KwaZulu-Natal, South Africa, to address the very high incidence of HIV/AIDS in young people. It is both a community shelter and point of healthcare (Figure 4.40). A competition was hosted by AfH in 2004, the brief being to design a youth care centre located and integral to a football/soccer field, the latter acting as a focal attraction to youth. Hundreds of designs were submitted by the international design community, were whittled down to a shortlist of nine and the winner chosen by young people in KwaZulu-Natal schools. The winner, designer Swee Hong Ng then travelled to the project collaborator's Africa Centre for Health and Population Studies in rural Somkhele to refine the designs with local people. The resultant design provides Somkhele with a FIFA grade football pitch, a facility that combines healthcare services and football facilities and the first girls' soccer league.

Figure 4.40
Siyathemba by Swee Hong Ng, Architecture for Humanity

The under-consumers in the US have received consistent attention from a variety of sources. Since its inception in 1993, Auburn University's Rural Studio founded by Samuel Mockbee and D. K. Ruth has encouraged generations of students to work in collaboration with Alabama's rural poor to improve housing stock and the well-being of its occupants.[117] A recent project by graduates is the $20,000 house (Figure 4.41) offering a variety of configurations and aesthetics to meet real needs.

The diversity of needs of specific communities is being recognized by designers who create interventions, resources and concepts as a response. ParaSITE by Michael Rakowitz appropriates the waste heat/cooling from buildings' heating/ventilation/air-conditioning (HVAC) systems by attaching inflatable structures that provide temporary accommodation for the homeless (Figure 4.42). One Small Project[118] has multi-contributors that collate diverse solutions and creativity by slum dwellers to provide their own shelter. The Day Labor Station by Public Architecture examines the needs of the estimated 120,000 labourers that seek temporary day-by-day work[119] and suggests a conceptual multi-functional space where labourers can up-skill and share peer-to-peer experiences.

Water and food

Many rural and urban poor require robust, affordable solutions that can be locally made. The tradition of ceramic making continues in many communities and provides a means to meet basic water and cooking needs with an appropriate level of technology. Examples include the Kenya Ceramic Jiko, a portable charcoal stove (Figure 4.43) and the Ceramic Water Filter deployed in Cambodia

$20K House - Roundwood House
Greensboro, AL
2007-2008 Thesis/Outreach Project
Student Team. Mackenzie Stagg, Matt Mueller, Laurienne Uguen, Ryan Coleman

www.cadc.auburn.edu/soa/rural-studio/20k/index.php/roundwood/

MISSION
MOCKBEE
PROGRAMS
PROJECTS
PEOPLE
PLACE
MAKING
MEDIA
AWARDS
EVENTS
EXHIBITS
ALUMNI
GIVE
VISIT
CONTACT
HOME

rural studio
projects.

SEARCH BY TYPE
SEARCH BY YEAR

Continuing exploration into the 20K house project, the Roundwood house examines the viability of using locally sourced forest thinnings as a building material. The loblolly pine thinnings, often cut down and left to rot in the forest, were acquired for fifty cents per tree from the Talladega National Forest. The four team members were responsible for pulling the cut thinnings out of the forest and debarking them by hand.

Early design decisions led to the creation of a truss, as the logs' strength lies in tension and compression. Protecting the roundwood from rot and insects was also a main priority. Conceptually, the roundwood provides the structure of the house, while a dimensional lumber shell, or curtain wall, covers and protects the truss.

One of the biggest challenges of the project was to use the logs while they were still green, meaning that the logs were subject to shrinking and twisting over time. Adjustable joints made of threaded rod and circular steel tube provided a solution that allowed the logs to twist as they dried and also created nodal points from which to hang the exterior curtain wall.

Figure 4.41
The US$20,000 house by Rural Studio graduates

Figure 4.42
ParaSITE by Michael Rakowitz

128

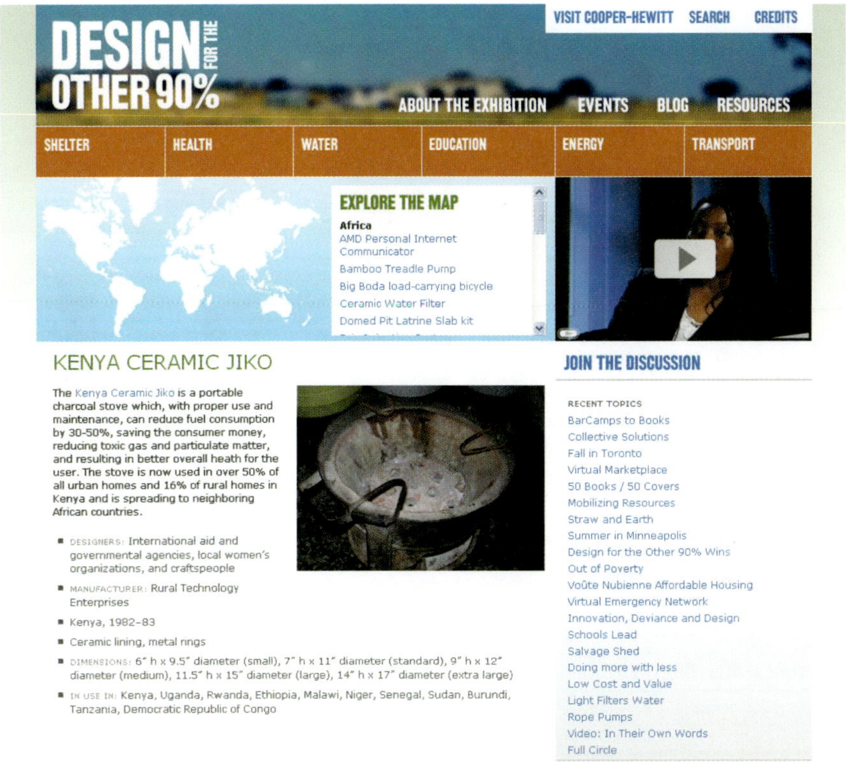
DESIGN FOR THE OTHER 90%
VISIT COOPER-HEWITT
SEARCH
CREDITS
ABOUT THE EXHIBITION
EVENTS
BLOG
RESOURCES
SHELTER
HEALTH
WATER
EDUCATION
ENERGY
TRANSPORT
EXPLORE THE MAP
Africa
AMD Personal Internet Communicator
Bamboo Treadle Pump
Big Boda load-carrying bicycle
Ceramic Water Filter
Domed Pit Latrine Slab kit
KENYA CERAMIC JIKO
The Kenya Ceramic Jiko is a portable charcoal stove which, with proper use and maintenance, can reduce fuel consumption by 30-50%, saving the consumer money, reducing toxic gas and particulate matter, and resulting in better overall heath for the user. The stove is now used in over 50% of all urban homes and 16% of rural homes in Kenya and is spreading to neighboring African countries.
DESIGNERS: International aid and governmental agencies, local women's organizations, and craftspeople
MANUFACTURER: Rural Technology Enterprises
Kenya, 1982–83
Ceramic lining, metal rings
DIMENSIONS: 6" h x 9.5" diameter (small), 7" h x 11" diameter (standard), 9" h x 12" diameter (medium), 11.5" h x 15" diameter (large), 14" h x 17" diameter (extra large)
IN USE IN: Kenya, Uganda, Rwanda, Ethiopia, Malawi, Niger, Senegal, Sudan, Burundi, Tanzania, Democratic Republic of Congo
JOIN THE DISCUSSION
RECENT TOPICS
BarCamps to Books
Collective Solutions
Fall in Toronto
Virtual Marketplace
50 Books / 50 Covers
Mobilizing Resources
Straw and Earth
Summer in Minneapolis
Design for the Other 90% Wins
Out of Poverty
Voûte Nubienne Affordable Housing
Virtual Emergency Network
Innovation, Deviance and Design
Schools Lead
Salvage Shed
Doing more with less
Low Cost and Value
Light Filters Water
Rope Pumps
Video: In Their Own Words
Full Circle

Figure 4.43
Kenya Ceramic Jiko portable charcoal stove, Design for the Other 90%

(Figure 4.44). Often these designs experience iterations over time with input by a wide variety of 'designers'. By contrast, other devices are a specific outcome of a conventional design process driven by individual designers or a design team, such as the Q Drum water transporter, Oxfam bucket and Watercone® (Figures 4.45 to 4.47). The true test of the effectiveness of such designs is their availability, affordability and cultural acceptability.

Raising awareness by education

Access to resources is an integral part of raising awareness and educational standards. Inventor and designer Trevor Baylis recognized the vital role that radio can play in giving whole communities access to information. His 1996 Baygen Clockwork radio, powered by a wind-up generator became an emblem of empowerment and led to the founding of Baygen Power Industries in South Africa. This company evolved into Freeplay Energy plc which now serves African and European markets, but has gone the classic route of 'product differentiation' to service the green consumers and compete in the markets of the North.

Figure 4.44
Ceramic water filter, Cambodia

Figure 4.45
Q Drum water transporter

Figure 4.46
Oxfam bucket

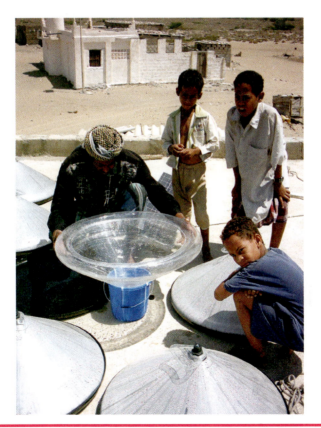

Figure 4.47
Watercone® by Stephan Augustin

Figure 4.48
One Laptop per Child (OLPC)

The One Laptop per Child (OLPC) project, originated by Nicholas Negroponte with Yves Béhar, fuseproject and Design Continuum, has created a very eco-efficient, light-weight laptop and an intuitive PC interface to help address the digital divide and provide internet access to poor children, especially in the South (Figure 4.48). The much vaunted $100 laptop is a bold experiment that elicited a protectionist and competitive response from key players in the micro-chip and Windows open source (OS) industry. OLPC obviously touched some raw nerves as it actively contests the current global transnationals controlling ICT technologies.

Tackling health issues

A Danish/Swiss company, Vestergaard Frandsen, specializes in products that provide immediate healthcare benefits ranging from malaria protection (PermaNet®, ZeroFly®) and personal ceramic filters for obtaining clean water (LifeStraw®) (Figure 4.49). These fit the market-driven philosophy of most product design and undoubtedly provide immediate help, but are more probably most effective in combination with more holistic and systemic provisions at the local level. The balance between product interventions and the creation of systems of self-reliance is another tough challenge for those wanting to make a difference for the under-consumers. Yet another challenge is to apply the same high standards of design that the over-consumers take for granted. The Solar Aid designed and manufactured by Godisa Technologies in Botswana is making a positive difference to the lives of those with impaired hearing with its solar panel battery recharger (Figure 4.50), but how can further improvements be made?

Figure 4.49
LifeStraw® by Vestergaard Frandsen

Figure 4.50
Solar Aid by Godisa Technologies

Miscellaneous activism

There are legion opportunities for those involved in graphic and communications design to help raise awareness, communicate vital information to engage people in activities to raise their understanding, improve access to services and elevate the capacity for self-help. This often requires a deep understanding of the target audiences, their culture and constraints, or good design intentions may go adrift.[120]

The scope for addressing a wider range of issues affecting the under-consumers is clear. This section has covered only some of the basic activities being carried out under the auspices of design. Volunteering or pro bono work provide a means for designers to contribute their creativity while learning on the job about the realities facing the under-consumers within their own and distant societies.

Notes

1 Julier, G. (2008) 'Design activism as a tool for creating new urban narratives', a paper presented at *Changing the Change*, Turin, July, www.changingthechange.org, paper available at www.allemandi.com/cp/ctc/book.php?id=57; Thorpe, A. (2008) 'Design as activism: A conceptual tool', a paper presented at *Changing the Change*, Turin, July, www.changingthechange.org, paper available at www.allemandi.com/cp/ctc/book.php?id=115

2 Margolin, V. and Margolin, S. (2002) 'A "social model" of design: Issues of practice and research,' *Design Issues*, vol 18, no 4, pp24–30; Kirkbride, R. (2008) 'Proposals for a good life: Senior thesis projects from Parsons Product Design 2003–2008', a paper presented at *Changing the Change*, Turin, July, www.changingthechange.org, paper available at www.allemandi.com/cp/ ctc/book.php?id=59

3 See Chapter 5, section 'Co-design'.

4 Utrecht Manifest, www.utrechtmanifest.nl

5 Changing the Change, www.changingthechange.org

6 See for example, Bell, B. (2004) *Good Deeds, Good Design: Community Service through Architecture*, Princeton Architectural Press, New York; Sinclair, C., Stohr, K. and Architecture for Humanity (2006) *Design Like You Give a Damn: Architectural Responses to Humanitarian Crises*, Thames & Hudson, London.

7 See for example, Cranmer, J. and Zappaterra, Y. (2004) *Conscientious Objectives: Designing for an Ethical Message*, RotoVision, Mies, Switzerland, pp10–29; Heller, S. and Vienne, V. (eds) (2003) *Citizen Designer: Perspectives on Design Responsibility*, Allworth Press, New York; Heller, S. and Kushner, T. (2005) *The Design of Dissent: Socially and Politically Driven Graphics*, Rockport Publishers Inc, Massachusetts; cover design by Milton Glaser and M. Ilic.

8 Dunne, A. and Raby, F. (2001) *Design Noir: The Secret Life of Electronic Objects*, Birkhäuser, Basel.

9 Rothschild, J. and Cheng, A. (1999) *Design and Feminism: Re-visioning Spaces, Places, and Everyday Things*, Rutgers University Press, New Brunswick, NJ.

10 Mau, B. (2004) *Massive Change*, Phaidon Press, London; Steffen, A. (ed) (2006) *World Changing: A User's Guide for the 21st Century*, Abrams, New York.

11 Smith, C. E. and Cooper-Hewitt Museum (2007) *Design for the Other 90%*, Editions Assouline, Paris, with online exhibition at http://other90.cooperhewitt.org/, accessed September 2008.

12 Manzini, E. (1997) 'Leapfrog – designing sustainability', *Domus*, January 1997, pp43–51.

13 Manzini, E. and Jégou, F. (2003a) *Sustainable Everyday: Scenarios of Urban Life*, Edizioni Ambiente, Milan, pp45–60.

14 Manzini, E. and Jégou, F. (2003b) 'Album: A catalogue of promising solutions', workshops of the research *Sustainable Everyday*, Edizioni Ambiente, Milan, p94.

15 Manzini and Jegou (2003a), op. cit. Note 13, pp165–213.

16 EMUDE, www.sustainable-everyday.net/EMUDE/?page_id=85

17 Julier (2008), op. cit. Note 1.

18 Ibid. p2.

19 Thorpe (2008), op. cit. Note 1.

20 Thorpe (2008), op. cit. Note 1, www.allemandi.com/cp/ctc/book.php? id=115&p=1

21 Ibid.

22 Fallman, D. (2008) 'The Interaction design research triangle of design practice, design studies and design exploration', *Design Issues*, vol 24, no 3, MIT Press Journals, Cambridge, MA, pp4–18.

23 Walker, S. (2008) 'Following will-o'-the-wisps and chasing ghosts: Design-centred research, sustainability and the bottom line', *The Design Journal*, vol 11, no 1, pp51–64.

24 Thorpe (2008), op. cit. Note 1.

25 Ibid.

26 Ibid.

27 Dunne and Raby (2001), op. cit. Note 8.

28 Walker (2008), op. cit. Note 23.

29 Changing the Change, July 2008, www.changingthechange.org

30 See for example, products: Fuad-Luke, A. (2002, 2004) *The Eco-design Handbook*, Thames & Hudson, London; Datchefski, E. (2001) *The Total Beauty of Sustainable Products*, RotoVision, Cran-Près-Céligny.

31 Thorpe (2008), op. cit. Note 1.

32 Walker (2008), op. cit. Note 23.

33 Vilma, S. (1995) *Products as Representations*, University of Helsinki Press, Helsinki.

34 Walker, S. (2006) *Sustainable by Design: Explorations in Theory and Practice*, Earthscan, London, p199.

35 Manzini and Jégou (2003a), op. cit. Note 13.

36 Schmidt-Bleek, F. (2000) www.factor10-institute.org/files/MIPS.pdf and Factor 10 Manifesto, www.factor10-institute.org/files/F10_Manifesto_e.pdf

37 Heinburg, R. (2007) *Peak Everything: Waking up to the Century of Decline in Earth's Resources*, Clairview, Forest Row.

38 Neutra, R. (1954) *Survival through Design*, Oxford University Press, Oxford.

39 Dunne and Raby (2001), op. cit. Note 8.

40 See Fuad-Luke, A. (2002) 'Slow design – a paradigm shift in design philosophy?', a paper presented at *Development by Design*, Bangalore, India, November; Fuad-Luke, A. (2004) 'Slow design: A paradigm for living sustainably', published by Slow, www.slowdesign.org; Fuad-Luke, A. (2008) 'Slow design', in M. Erlhoff and T. Marshall (eds) *Design Dictionary: Perspectives on Design Terminology*, Birkhäuser-Verlag, Basel/Boston/Berlin, pp361–363; Strauss, C. and Fuad-Luke, A. (2008) 'The slow design principles: A new interrogative and reflexive tool for design research and practice', a paper presented at *Changing the Change*, Turin, July, www.changingthechange.org, available at www.allemandi.com/cp/ctc/book.php?id=109

41 Fuad-Luke, A. (2007) 'Re-defining the purpose of (sustainable) design: Enter the design enablers, catalysts in co-design', in J. Chapman and N. Gant (eds) *Designers, Visionaries + Other Stories*, Earthscan, London, pp18–52; Burns, C., Cottam, H., Vanstone, C. and Winhall, J. (2006) *RED Paper 02 Transformation Design*, Design Council, London.

42 Giaccardi, E. and Fisher, G. (2005) 'Creativity and evolution: A metadesign perspective', in *Sixth International Conference of the European Academy of Design (EAD06) on Design>System>Evolution*, Bremen, University of the Arts, March, 2005, 16pp; Wood, J. (2008) 'Changing the change: A fractal framework for metadesign', a paper presented

at *Changing the Change*, Turin, July, www.changingthechange.org, available at www.allemandi.com/cp/ ctc/book.php?id=129

43 Willis, A.-M. (2008) 'Design, redirective practice and sustainment', a keynote address at *360 Degrees*, a conference organized by University of Brighton and the DEEDS project, Brighton, UK, September.

44 Fry, T. (1994) *Remakings: Ecology, Design, Philosophy*, Envirobook, Sydney.

45 Willis (2008), op. cit. Note 43.

46 See *Changing the Change* (2008) www.changingthechange.org; the DEEDS (Design Education & Sustainability) project sponsored by the Leonardo da Vinci programme of the European Union, www.deedsproject.org

47 See Adbusters, www.adbusters.org/about/adbusters; Wolff, J. (1993) *The Social Production of Art*, 2nd edn, New York University Press, New York, p85, cited in Soar, M. (2003) 'Culture jamming or something like it', in S. Heller and V. Vienne (eds) *Citizen Designer: Perspectives on Design Responsibility*, Allworth Press, New York, pp210–211.

48 Royal Society of Arts, Changing Habbits project, www.rsachanginghabbits.org/, accessed 8 August 2008.

49 The Story of Stuff, www.storyofstuff.com/

50 MIT Smart Cities project, http://cities.media.mit.edu/

51 Fuad-Luke, A. (2006) 'Reflection, consciousness, progress: Creatively slow designing the present', a keynote address given to the conference *Reflections on Creativity*, University of Dundee, UK, April, http://imaging.dundee.ac.uk/reflections/

52 For example, the BBC's Climate prediction project, www.climateprediction.net/ commenced in 2006.

53 Burns et al (2006), op. cit. Note 41.

54 Elkington, J. and Hailes, J. (1988) *The Green Consumer*, Gollancz, London; revised and updated in Hailes, J. (2007) *The New Green Consumer Guide*, Simon & Schuster, London; Hickman, L. (2005) *A Good Life: The Guide to Ethical Living*, Transworld Publishers, London.

55 Hines, C. (2000) *Localization: A Global Manifesto*, Earthscan, London.

56 Chapman, J. (2005) *Emotionally Durable Design: Objects, Experiences, Empathy*, Earthscan, London.

57 Fuad-Luke, A. (2006) 'Reflective consumption: Slowness and nourishing rituals of delay in anticipation of a post-consumer age', a paper presented at *Design for Durability*, seminar at the Design Council, UK, April, organized by the EPSRC Product Lifespan Network, University of Sheffield, UK, available at http://extra.shu.ac.uk/productlife/ 2%20Alistair%20Faud-LukeXX.ppt

58 Ibid.

59 Manzini and Jégou (2003a), op. cit. Note 13, pp56–59.

60 The 'do Create' project by Dutch co-operative, Droog Design, www.droog.com/ creativeagency/do-create/

61 Eternally Yours Foundation (1999) cited in White et al (2004) *Okala: Learning Ecological Design*, Industrial Designers Society of America (IDSA), Portland, Oregon, p40.

62 Walker (2006), op. cit. Note 34, pp149–166.

63 Whiteley, N. (1993) *Design for Society*, Reaktion Books, London, p126.

64 Fletcher, K. (2007) *Sustainable Fashion & Textiles: Design Journeys*, Earthscan, London, pp57–59, 69.

65 Blackspot shoes by Adbuster, www.adbusters.org/campaigns/blackspot

66 Alabama Chanin via SlowLab, www.slowlab.org/, see 'Projects' Participate/Evolve, Alabama Chanin.

67 Kith-Kin downloadable designs, www.kith-kin.co.uk

68 Paper Critters downloadable paper designs, www.papercritters.com/

69 McDonough, W. and Braungart, M. (2002) *Cradle to Cradle*, North Point Press, New York.

70 Christopher Cattle's grown sycamore stools, www.grown-furniture.co.uk/ index.html

71 Herman Miller's 'Celle' chair, 99 per cent recyclable, www.hermanmiller.com/

72 Loewy, R. (2002) *Never Leave Well Enough Alone*, John Hopkins University Press, new edition, 31 December 2002, first published in 1951.

73 See for example, Fuad-Luke (2002, 2004), op. cit. Note 30.

74 Tukker, A. and Jansen, B. (2006) 'Environmental impacts of products: A detailed review of studies', *Journal of Industrial Ecology*, vol 10, no 3, pp159–182.

75 Trendwatching, June 2008, 'Eco-iconic', available at http://trendwatching.com/ trends/ecoiconic.htm

76 *Treehugger*, www.treehugger.com, *Inhabitat*, www.inhabitat.com, *Worldchanging*, www.worldchanging.com

77 The 'rebound effect' is described here – UNEP, www.unep.fr/shared/publications/other/ WEBx0008xPA/ecodesign.pdf

78 MIT Smart Cities, http://cities.media.mit.edu/

79 c,mm,n open source car design, www.cmmn.org

80 Boase project, www.force4.dk

81 Birkeland, J. (2008) *Positive Development*, Earthscan, London.

82 Jackson, T. (2004) *Chasing Progress: Beyond Measuring Economic Growth*, New Economics Foundation, London; Jackson, T. (2006) *The Earthscan Reader in Sustainable Consumption*, Earthscan, London.

83 The Eternally Yours Foundation in the Netherlands, www.eternallyyours.nl; van Hinte, E. (2004) *Eternally Yours, Time in Design*, 010 Publishers, Rotterdam; Cooper, T. (ed) (in press) *Longer Lasting Solutions*, publication due November 2009 from Gower Publishing, London.

84 Fuad-Luke, A. (2005) 'A new model of well-being to design "products" that sustain people, environments and profits', in *Towards Sustainable Product Design 10*, Centre for Sustainable Design, Farnham Castle, Farnham, UK, 24–25 October 2005.

85 Chapman (2005), op. cit. Note 56.

86 Fletcher, K. and Tham, M. (2004–present) *The Lifetimes Project*, www.lifetimes.info, accessed August 2008.

87 The 5 Ways Project, www.5ways.info, accessed August 2008.

88 Lawrence, P. R. and Nohria, N. (2002) *Driven: How Human Nature Shapes Our Choices*, Jossey-Bass, San Francisco.

89 Dunne and Raby (2001), op. cit. Note 8, p8.

90 Ibid. p13.

91 Ibid. p58.

92 Gaver, W., Boucher, A., Pennington, S. and Walker, B. (2004) 'Cultural probes and the value of uncertainty', *Interactions*, vol XL5, pp53–56; Gaffney, G. (2006) 'Cultural probes', www.infodesign.com.au/ftp/CulturalProbes.pdf

93 UK government's sustainable development strategy, www.sustainable-development.gov.uk/ publications/pdf/strategy/Chap%206.pdf

94 Max-Neef, M. (1991) *Human Scale Development, Conception Application and Further Reflections*, Apex Press, NY and London.

95 Julier, G. (2008) *The Culture of Design*, 2nd edn, Sage Publications, London, pp204–208.

96 Thackara, J. (2007) 'Wouldn't it be great if … we could live sustainably – by design?', *Dott 07 Manual*, Dott 07 and Design Council, London.

97 Debra Solomon's Culiblog, www.culiblog.com

98 See Viljoen, A. (2005) *Continuous Productive Urban Landscapes: Designing Urban Agriculture for Sustainable Cities*, Architectural Press, London.

99   Edible Estates, www.fritzhaeg.com/garden/initiatives/edibleestates/main.html

100 Edible Campus, www.mcgill.ca/files/mchg/MakingtheEdibleCampus.pdf

101 The High Line Project, New York, www.thehighline.org

102 Vollaard, P., Rosenheinreich, H. and Overbeek, G. (2002) *Louis Le Roy: Nature-Culture-Fusion*, Netherlands Institute Architecture (NAi), Uitgevers, bilingual edition.

103 Brand, S. (1999) *Clock of the Long Now: Time and Responsibility*, Phoenix, London.

104 Ibid. p2.

105 Roden Crater by James Turrell, www.pbs.org/art21/artists/turrell/clip1.html

106 United Nations Population Division, www.un.org/esa/population/unpop.htm

107 Abraham Maslow, a humanistic psychologist, proposed a theory for classifying human needs in an original paper published in 1943, 'A Theory of Human Motivation', *Psychological Review* vol 50, no 4, pp370–396. Maslow's work is often depicted graphically as a 'hierarchy of needs' in a pyramid or triangle with five levels, the base representing basic physiological needs, followed by safety, love/belonging, esteem and self-actualization/self-transcendence needs. The latter four levels represent growth needs and are deemed only to be sought when basic physiological needs have been met. It is just one reference framework for studying human needs, personality and motivation. See a brief description at Wikipedia, 'Maslow's hierarchy of needs', http://en.wikipedia.org/wiki/Maslow_hierarchy_of_needs, accessed September 2008.

108 WWF (2008) *UK Water Footprint*, vol 1, www.wwf.org.uk/filelibrary/pdf/water_footprint_uk.pdf

109 Lawrence, F. (2008) 'UK adds to drain on global water resources', *The Guardian*, 20 August 2008, p9.

110 Simms, A., Moran, D. and Chowla, P. (2006) *The UK Interdependence Report: How the World Sustains the Nation's Lifestyle and the Price it Pays*, New Economics Foundation, London.

111 World Wide Fund for Nature (2006) *The Living Planet 2006*, C. Hails (ed), WWF International, Gland, Switzerland, www.panda.org/news_facts/publications/living_planet_report/index.cfm

112 Papanek, V. (1974) *Design for the Real World*, Paladin, London.

113 See Architecture for Humanity, www.architectureforhumanity.org/, accessed September 2008.

114 Index Awards, Denmark, www.indexaward.dk/2007/default.asp?id=706&Article=867&Folder=867

115 Cooper-Hewitt Museum (2007), op. cit. Note 11.

116 Sinclair and Stohr with Architecture for Humanity (2006), op. cit. Note 6.

117 Mockbee, S. (2000) in Bell, B. (2004) *Good Deeds, Good Design: Community Service through Architecture*, Princeton Architectural Press, New York; see also Rural Studio website, www.cadc.auburn.edu/soa/rural-studio/

118 One Small Project, www.onesmallproject.com

119 Public Architecture, www.publicarchitecture.org/design_campaigns.htm

120 Bush, A. (2003) 'Beyond pro bono: Graphic design's social work', in S. Heller and V. Vienne (eds) *Citizen Designer, Perspectives on Design Responsibility*, Allworth Press, New York, pp25–31.

5

Designing Together:
The Power of 'We Think',
'We Design', 'We Make'

'The purpose of (co-)design is the creation of new societal values to balance human happiness with ecological truths. In doing so design contests the notion of material and economic progress, and its inherent ecological untruths.'

Alastair Fuad-Luke

The phenomenon of globalization[1] has produced a profound shift in societal perceptions and behaviour, especially in the current 1.4 billon internet users. Since the 1970s, a redrawing of the distribution of industrial, post-industrial and recently industrialized societies has occurred. The past ten years have seen even more radical shifts in this distribution. European politicians gradually acknowledged that the centre of gravity of the industrialized world had moved from Europe to East Asia, towards China in particular. This shift in the global industrial axis is permissible because of cheap labour in certain parts of the world and the ability for rapid flows of people, money, raw materials, finished products, information and ideas. Technology, especially ICT, has added new facets to the Postmodern space–time compression articulated by Charles Jencks.[2] Simultaneous conferencing, chatting, trading, gambling, blogging and sex are 365/24/7 everyday internet pastimes. Telephony networks intensify their geographic reach worldwide enabling a leapfrogging from 'no landline phone' to 'mobile phone'. Under these circumstances there should be little wonder that the notions of designing and manufacturing established in the 19th century, honed in the 20th century and taken as the norm a mere decade ago, are facing a period of 'massive change', a phrase coined by Bruce Mau.[3] The speed of the transition is remarkable and hardly permits time to catch breath. There's no time to experience the phenomenon that Alvin Toffler observed in 1965, called 'future shock' – 'the shattering stress and disorientation that we induce in individuals by subjecting them to too much change in too short a time'.[4] We become desensitized to change as a new manifestation of globalization is joined, hybridized or is superseded by yet another manifestation. Change has been normalized and so has the rapid tempo of daily life. The reaction to this real and perceived speed of contemporary life is the ebullient rise of a 'slow' counter-movement,[5] the aforementioned flows of the real and intangible are also generating fresh opportunities, exchanges, alliances, social phenomena and genuine philanthropic positive change. People and ideas are blending, and clashing, in

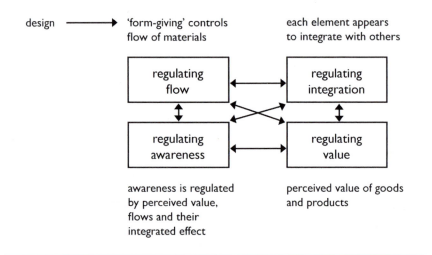

design   ⟶   'form-giving' controls flow of materials

each element appears to integrate with others

| regulating flow | regulating integration |

| regulating awareness | regulating value |

awareness is regulated by perceived value, flows and their integrated effect

perceived value of goods and products

Figure 5.1
Design, the wise regulation of dynamic elements

unpredictable ways. The flows are fast, furious and diverse. Design has a pivotal role in controlling the metabolism of these flows, as noted by John Wood (Figure 5.1).[6] Design mediates the flows of natural, financial, manufactured, man-made, symbolic and cultural capitals. Intervening to rechannel the amount and direction of these flows provides fertile ground for any design activist.

Dealing with 'Wicked Problems'

Sustainability could be defined as a 'wicked problem', a problem first characterized by Horst Rittel in the 1960s as 'a class of social system problems which are ill-formulated, where the information is confusing, where there are many clients and decision makers with conflicting values, and where the ramifications of the whole system are thoroughly confusing'.[7] Rittel's thinking has recently, and deservedly, been re-examined.[8] Problem definition is itself subjective as it originates from a point of view, therefore all stakeholders' points of view are equally knowledgeable (or unknowledgeable) whether they are experts, designers or other actors.[9] Rittel is an advocate of designing together because people have to dialogue, agree on how to frame the problem, agree goals and actions, and this argumentative process is inherently political, in fact design is political,[10] a view supported by Guy Bonsiepe, who defines political in the sense of a societal way of living rather than narrow party politics.[11] If sustainability is the most challenging wicked problem of the current era, then participation in design, as a means to effect deep, transformative, socio-political change, seems essential. This suggests a significant new direction for design to seize.

The Rise of Co-creation, Co-innovation and Co-design

Since the 1980s there has been a shift in attitude of certain business sectors towards its customers. The realization that the creative potential of these very same customers can help business create better services and products has encouraged the development of a range of methodologies to tap this potential. The language has shifted, as noted by Liz Sanders of US design agency SonicRim, who was an early pioneer in revitalizing participatory design approaches[12] from designing *for* users to designing *with* users, from customer to user to co-creator (Figure 5.2). This shift has been paralleled with a resurgent debate about the social dimensions of design,[13] the role of the internet in opening up new opportunities for design/designing,[14] a widening of ecological reform to embrace technocratic to strong democratic approaches,[15] and the shifting canvas of design praxis.[16] Now that the participatory genie is out of the bottle, designers need to get a firm grip on what it means for the design profession and how it can be engaged effectively for design activism. One particularly important dimension is how intellectual property (IP) is protected in this participatory culture. A balance needs to be struck between commercial appropriation and the creation of a genuine *commons of knowledge and know-how*.

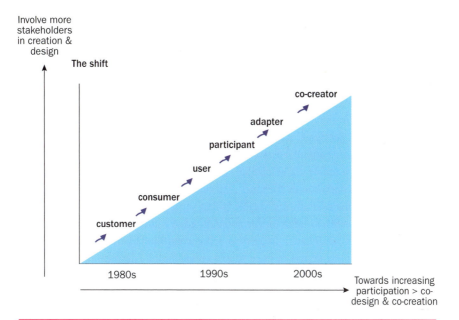

Figure 5.2
The shift from customers to co-creators

The open source and open design movements

Academics, science and technology specialists have long held the principles of openness, peer review and co-operation as essential to advancing a particular canon(s) of philosophy, thought and action. It was this desire that originated ARPANET, the first ICT network to enable communication between University College Los Angeles (UCLA) and Stanford Research Institute International in California in 1969.[17] ARPANET is a key ancestor of the internet as we know it today. The arrival of personal computers (PCs) on the office desktop in the 1980s gave significant impetus to improving connectivity and communication between PC users, locally and globally to facilitate collaboration and exchange of information. The development of appropriate communication protocols enabling computers to 'talk' to each other more easily moved rapidly and, by the late 1980s, the Transmission Control Protocol/Internet Protocol (TCP/IP) was firmly established. This encouraged the joining together of more networks. By the early 1990s these networks had gained a new public interface, the World Wide Web, based on web browsers and hypertext mark-up language (html) developed by Tim Berners-Lee.[18] The possibilities for the dissemination of information and collaboration made a step-change. More recent emergence of internet technologies such as chat rooms, blogs and wikis has provided further opportunities for collaboration.

Parallel to the development of the internet in the 1980s was the development and sharing of free software. This software is frequently developed by collaboration within a group or groups of people, freely committing their time, knowledge and skills to build and test the software then offer it for free usage (usually with specific or general conditions attached). A general definition of 'open source' refers to a 'product' comprising source code, design documents and/or content that users have permission to use.[19] Open source has a variety of expressions being applied to 'products' such as software (e.g. operating systems such as Linux; internet browsers such as Mozilla Firefox; content management systems such as Moodle for educational uses), hardware, games and, more recently, music, but it is also extended to embrace particular expressions of democracy – open source content (e.g. Wikipedia the online encyclopedia), governance, government and politics.[20] Where there is an open source 'product', various licences may specify the exact terms of use, but the overriding principle is that some or all of the knowledge within the 'product' is made available for the common good and is not retained as closed source, proprietary intellectual property which is controlled by the owners. Two of the most successful examples of open source collaboration comprise the worldwide communities that have developed, and continue to develop, and support Linux – an operating system software whose development started with Linus Torvalds in Helsinki in 1991[21] – and Wikipedia founded by Larry Sanger and Jimmy Wales in 2001.[22]

The World Wide Web is a socio-cultural project whose ramifications are still unfolding, but advocates of its ability to democratize the sharing of knowledge and creativity, indeed to significantly alter the way we collaborate, make and shape the world,[23] see nascent opportunities for mass collaboration, innovation and production. The term 'open design' has recently joined the internet lexicon as 'the investigation and potential of open source and the collaborative nature of the internet to create physical objects'.[24] The success of open source is now stimulating not-for-profit '.orgs' and commercial companies to foster collaboration to tackle global problems. Diverse organizations from the global design diaspora are seeing the potential of web-led technologies for donative, altruistic design work (see Chapter 6, pp169–175). The internet facilitates interdisciplinary ways of working. For example, Designbreak is an advocacy group for open design bringing together scientists and engineers to tackle environmental degradation and raise standards of living and access to medicines for the poor in developing countries.[25]

The intellectual commons

Earning a living as a designer, especially for the typical European design practice which aptly fits the descriptor of 'micro-enterprise' (one or two people) or 'small and medium-sized enterprise' (SME), which for the average European company comprises eight to ten people, is difficult if the IP of a design cannot be given some protection in a competitive global marketplace. However, there are advantages in not protecting all of one's creative work. Computer scientists, hardware engineers and software writers have long enjoyed gainful employment, working under strict IP environments, while enjoying parallel working with more altruistic goals and more open IP environments. The latter provide collaboration in open source projects and help build essential skills that enhance the professional in his/her 'employed' positions. The emergence of Linux as a commercially viable operating system for computers is a successful example of how open IP environments can actually challenge and win business from the closed IP environments of transnationals. Charles Leadbeater notes that Linux and Wikipedia, which are challenging the established copyright paradigms, rely on a core or kernel of active experts, a large interested cohort of active participants, and an even larger audience of passive recipients.[26]

There is a fundamentally more important reason as to why we should look after and improve the health of the open source IP environments – sustainability is such a complex mix of connected problématiques that it can only succeed with extensive local, regional, national and international co-operation using the knowledge and know-how embedded in different geographies and cultures. This requires an openness and willingness to share knowledge, experience and wisdom. This condition is recognized by a number of organizations that have invested much effort and attention to modernize the debate on IP in the 'information age'.

Contestation of modern IP law goes back to the 1970s cultural Zeitgeist of sharing, openness and collaboration. In October 1976, Li-Chen Wang and Roger Rauskolb issued a software program in BASIC computer language for the Palo Alto Tiny BASIC with an Intel 8080 microprocessor ('chip') with the following copyright statement, '@Copyleft. All Wrongs Reserved', a complete reversal of the legally enshrined, '©Copyright. All Rights Reserved'.[27] Today there are a number of copyleft licences, some with stronger copyleft tendencies than others. GNU General Public License is a popular free software licence[28] and the Design Science License is suitable for non-software works including art, music, photography and video.[29] Copyleft licences require that all subsequent and derived works are copyleft too, and in doing so there is a concern to prevent the re-appropriation of copyleft work by private interests that wish to gain proprietary control over the IP. The copyleft movement has been joined by a sophisticated operator in recent years: Creative Commons, a not-for-profit organization founded in 2001 by Molly van Houweling, the then president, and a board of directors including Lawrence Lessig, published its first set of Creative Commons licenses in December 2002.[30] Since then Creative Commons has developed and published a wide variety of licences some of which recognize the different needs of the scientific, educational and other communities.

> Creative Commons 'defines the spectrum of possibilities between full copyright – all rights reserved – and the public domain – no rights reserved. Our licenses help you keep your copyright while inviting certain uses of your work – a "some rights reserved" copyright.'   Creative Commons, September 2008

The debate around Creative Commons is fast and furious, with some critics arguing that it facilitates corporate co-option of creativity[31] and others noting that the licensed Creative Commons is not an autonomous, productive commons owned by the people for the people.[32] Pasquinelli also includes his and others' observations about Copyfarleft, a system that only allows commercial use of public domain works by other workers and small co-operatives that do not exploit wage labour.[33]

The message is clear, any designer considering a work of design altruism needs to think carefully about the target beneficiaries and how they may have access to use (or be denied use of or have restricted access to) the designer's IP. It is advisable to inform oneself of the appropriate IP framework and licences prior to proceeding to design using a participatory approach, although the final decision on IP protection (by individuals, groups, organizations or the commons) may need to be made during the design process by the participants.

Design Approaches that Encourage Participation

The inherent nature of design as a human activity is that it is, in general, deeply socially orientated,[34] involving a variety of actors in the chain of events from contextualization of the problématique, ideation, conceptualization, detailed design, making or construction, operation or use, and after-life or reuse. Moreover, participation emancipates people by making them active contributors rather than passive recipients. It is therefore a form of design humanism aimed at reducing domination.[35] Participation in design meets the human ideal of mutual support or altruism, a collective instinct of humanity.[36] There is an upsurge of interest in participatory design approaches, perhaps in part due to the increasing complexity of problems that all organizations face. While Nigel Whiteley[37] noted over a decade ago that participation in design decision-making in consumer culture is token and effectively reduced to participation by affirmative purchasing only, there is evidence that the way the consumer/user is now being involved in the design process is subtly changing.[38] There are some well-developed and emerging approaches to design that place particular emphasis on participation by diverse stakeholders and actors. The term 'approach' is used here to denote a combination of elements of an underlying design philosophy, processes, methodologies and tools. The level to which these elements are developed does vary.

Co-design

'Co-design' is a catch-all term to embrace participatory design, metadesign, social design and other design approaches that encourage participation.[39] The prefix 'co-' is the short form of 'com' meaning 'with', and is applied to verbs, e.g. co-operate, nouns, e.g. co-operation and adjectives, e.g. co-operative. The term 'co-design' is used to denote 'designing with (others)'. The underlying premise of co-design is that it is an approach 'predicated on the concept that people who ultimately use a designed artefact are entitled to have a voice in determining how that artefact is designed'.[40] Another fundamental premise is that co-design offers an opportunity for multi-stakeholders and actors to collectively define the context and problem and in doing so improve the chances of a design outcome being *effective*. Co-design is a commitment regarding inclusion and power, as it contests dominant hierarchically orientated top-down power structures; it requires *mutual learning* between the stakeholders/actors; and invokes many of the soft system methodologies described by Broadbent:[41]

- being an iterative, non-linear, interactive process
- being 'action-based' research
- involving 'top-down' and 'bottom-up' approaches
- simulating the real world
- being useful for complex systems or problems
- being situation driven, especially by common human situations
- satisfying pluralistic outcomes
- being internalized by the system.

Co-design is at the core of a more democratic, open and porous design process and is finding expression in the business and not-for-profit sectors.[42] As a design approach it can potentially generate new affordances and new values but demands a new skill set and underlying philosophical approach from designers.

Early formative steps in the co-design process led to the mutual agreement of the design context, boundaries and problem definition, and collective definition of the required design brief (Figure 5.3). Once the brief is agreed then stakeholders and actors can be central to or more peripheral to the design process – they can deliver ideation, conceptualization, prototyping or proposals, prototype or proposal selection, design specification and, finally, the detailing, implementing, construction or making of the design outcome/solution. The final phases of the co-design process involve using and experiencing the design outcome/solution, learning from the experience, and noting and giving feedback to the stakeholders and actors to enable continuous learning and redesigning.

Co-design can be initiated and led by those with professional design experience, such as architects, planners, design managers and designers, but may also be organized and facilitated by other consultants or experts, and by businesses, governmental or non-governmental organizations.[43] Presently, the practice of co-design among design professionals is more advanced in architecture, especially community architecture[44] and urban design planning,[45] than in other design fields, although new design initiatives are emerging such as Dott 07 and System Reload.[46]

Co-design is imbued with political ambitions regarding power and inclusion because it invokes notions of *direct, anticipatory and deep democracy,*[47] whereby the participants have a voice and that voice informs the design process. Co-design embraces a number of historical and emerging design approaches.

Participatory design

The early history of participatory design (PD) is shaped by its application by co-determination laws in Scandinavia and US labour laws in the 1950s aimed at empowering workers to participate in decision-making in the workplace.[48] PD fitted the Zeitgeist of the 1970s when openness and collaboration were welcomed. PD was a central tenet of the writings of Ivan Illich:

> '*People need not only to obtain things, they need above all the freedom to make things among which they can live, to give shape to them according to their own tastes, and to put them to use in caring for and about others.*'[49]

PD contests top-down only decision-making and attempts to democratize it by ensuring, 'people destined to use the system play a critical role in designing it'.[50] The emphasis here is on a systemic view of design to redesign or design systems, and a means to use the design process to mediate conflicting interests arising from different perspectives (of actors or stakeholders). The PD approach specifically

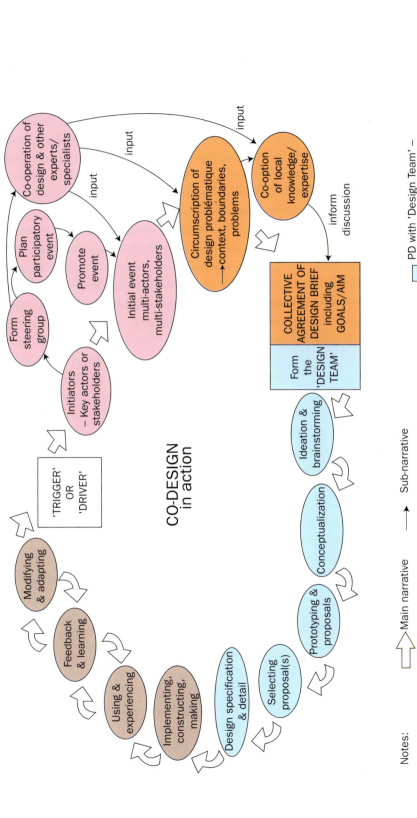

Figure 5.3

An idealized schematic for the co-design process

facilitates the design of systems, which perhaps explains its consistent use in collaboration between scientists and computer software and hardware developers and human computer interaction,[51] but it has also been applied to artefacts and built environments generated by architectural and other design practice.[52] PD is not a single and integral design method but according to Carroll[53] involves the following dimensions:

- domains of human activity
- roles of stakeholders in a design
- types of shared design representations
- the scope and duration of participatory interactions
- the relationship of users to design activity with respect to changes in their knowledge and skill.

The latter dimension indicates that participation in PD leads to transformation of the participants (see below).

Modified versions of PD, such as user-centred design (see below), have been co-opted by product designers to minimize risk by maximizing 'user fit' and hence the market reach of new manufactured goods. However, PD is not simply about the application of methodologies to achieve a design result, it is about 'a mindset and attitude about people' and a belief that everyone has something to offer the design process.[54] As Sanders notes, 'Today it is not "business as usual" anymore. The rules have changed and continue to change. The new rules are the rules of networks, not hierarchies.' This attitude mirrors a shift from the product to beyond the product, and to designing meaningful product–user relationships and experiences.[55]

A variant of PD is 'transformation design', a term coined by the now defunct RED group at the UK's Design Council[56] to describe a nascent but growing community of practice that is applying user-centred design principles to large-scale systems and services to invoke new patterns of understanding context, new methods to deal with complex problems, teams involving the core skills of product, communication, interaction and spatial designers, and an emergent philosophy. Projects where transformation design was applied demonstrate six characteristics and signal a real challenge to the notion of the designer as auteur:

- defining and redefining the brief – by understanding the scope of the issue and defining the right problem to tackle upstream of the brief
- collaborating between disciplines – by creating a neutral interdisciplinary space
- employing participatory design techniques – by making the design process more accessible to 'non-designers'
- building capacity, not dependency – by not only shaping a solution but leaving behind the tools, skills and capacity for ongoing change

- designing beyond traditional solutions – by applying design skills in non-traditional territories giving rise to the creation of new roles, new organizations, new systems and new policies, i.e. requiring a high level of 'systems thinking'
- creating fundamental change – by aiming high and at transforming a national system or company's culture.

Transformation design shares certain characteristics with PD and with metadesign (see below) in that it is about encouraging, shaping and catalysing rather than directing and controlling. It is open-ended, welcomes diversity and encourages a pro-am (professional-amateur) community of designers.

Metadesign

In the 1980s, the concept of metadesign, or meta-design, emerged with the use of information technologies in the practices of art, cultural theories and design. The expansion of networking information technologies, particularly the internet, led to a revival of interest in metadesign in the late 1990s and it is now an emergent design approach beyond that of user-centred and participatory design.[57] According to Fischer, 'Meta-design characterizes objective techniques and processes for creating new media and environments that allow the owners of problems to act as designers.' The aim is to empower users to engage in 'informed participation'[58] – where participants from lay and professional backgrounds transcend beyond the acquisition of information to acquire ownership in problems and contribute to their solutions. Metadesign is particularly suited to dealing with complex problems and enabling knowledge sharing to encourage *social creativity*.[59] Metadesign actually offers a process model for designing that sets up a conceptual framework of seeding followed by evolutionary growth and reseeding of the process model (SER Process Model).[60] In this sense the designed environment for metadesign to take place is under-designed to create spaces for others to add their creativity and design, and to permit the system to evolve. This process contrasts with PD processes where there tends to be an end-point when the design outcome/solution is designed and can no longer be evolved by users.[61] Metadesign is seen as co-creative and co-evolutionary, encouraging an 'unselfconscious (or spontaneous) culture of design'.[62]

John Wood sees metadesign as a way to create beneficial affordances by offering a more holarchic, consensual and transdisciplinary approach – i.e. a superset of design.[63] Metadesign teams would include *entredonneurs* (innovative altruists who broker new connections) and entrepreneurs (similar, but motivated by personal gain). Offering ten characteristics of metadesign, Wood believes this approach to be one of the few ways that (meta)designers might change the paradigm.[64] In a colloquium on metadesign hosted by Attainable Utopias at Goldsmiths, University of London in June 2007, a wide range of contributors from the culture of design voiced their thoughts.[65] Metadesign could:

- be a vision of 'creative democracy' (John Chris Jones)
- encourage autopoiesis (any organism – whether it be a social institution or a cellular life form – maintains its survival by self-balancing its self-identity with its external identity) and self-regulation (Otto van Nieuwenhuijze)
- facilitate an increase in virtually inexhaustible resources – ideas and happiness (Richard Douthwaite)
- encourage more self-reflexive, co-creative tasks and teams that regulate themselves (Rachel Cooper and Daniela Sangiorgi)
- raise the expectations of the ultimate potential of organizations and hence society (Ken Fairclough)
- inspire a new design approach in which participants work together in a social, cultural and ecological interdependence (Batel Dinur)
- create a society with a focus on the human-centred experience and new 'qualities of life' (Ian Grout)
- generate increased levels of synergy, i.e. better accord between different parts of the whole, where synergy is defined as the sharing of data, the sharing of information, integration of experience and skill in knowledge-sharing synergies, and the complex idea of wisdom-sharing synergies (John Wood)
- redefine designers to include not only the professionals, but also all participants in the extended designing network (Ezio Manzini).

A handbook of 21 metadesign tools to be published in 2010[66] will show real-world examples and offer a conceptual framework. In the meantime an outline of 21 metadesign tools is given in Appendix 3. It appears that metadesign offers an adaptive space for redirective practice to encourage designers to find innovative ways of addressing situations for the over-consumers and under-consumers.

Social design

All design is social, as design is the enactment of human instinct and a construct that facilitates the materialization of our world.[67] The idea that design is instinctive is supported by Alexander's notion of an *unselfconscious* culture of design where it is natural to fix or redesign something that results from a failure or inadequacy of form[68] and given further credence by Herbert Simon's observation that we all tend to design by changing existing situations into preferred ones.[69] The term 'social design' has diverse meanings,[70] but here it refers to the development of a social model of design,[71] and a design process intended to contribute to improving human well-being and livelihood.[72] While 'the primary purpose of design for the market is creating products for sale … the foremost intent of social design is the satisfaction of human needs'.[73] Social work theory (and practice) examines the interaction between client systems and environmental domains (Figure 5.4). Improvements in

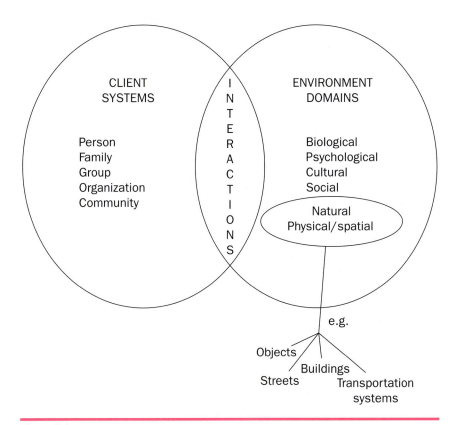

CLIENT SYSTEMS

Person
Family
Group
Organization
Community

INTERACTIONS

ENVIRONMENT DOMAINS

Biological
Psychological
Cultural
Social

Natural
Physical/spatial

e.g.

Objects
Buildings
Streets
Transportation systems

Figure 5.4
Interactions examined in social theory

any of the environmental domains would generate an improved satisfaction of human needs. Social workers bring in additional professional support for the client system, as required, to the collaborative social worker–client space. Clients are then taken through a step-by-step process of problem solving involving engagement, assessment, planning, implementation, evaluation and termination (Figure 5.5). There are some obvious parallels between the social worker's and designer's roles in PD and the skill set required by a designer applying social design requires a deepened ability to listen and holistically explore the environment domains.

The broad objective of social design is to improve 'social quality', defined by De Leonardis as 'the measure of citizens' capability of participating in the social and economic life of their community in conditions that improve both their individual wealth and the conditions of their community'.[74] Morelli suggests that the identification of actors and their motivations, and the use of mapping tools used in social construction studies, is an essential step in realizing innovation at the local

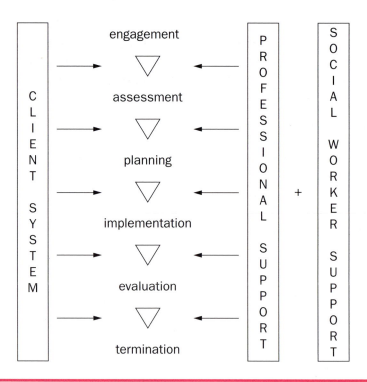

Figure 5.5
Social workers' generalist practice of problem solving

level.[75] This also establishes how the existing context provides products and services that are intended to improve our well-being. In the project Sustainable Everyday, organized and coordinated by Milan Polytechnic, access to *result-orientated networks* in a particular context offer people a series of potential *functionings* (a set of solutions people have access to) and *capability* is defined as the possibility of a person achieving a satisfying result from these functionings.[76] Here, designing new functionings to elevate individual and community capability, focuses the designer on the social dimensions of the outcomes but encourages the provision of *enabling solutions*, solutions that genuinely empower and extend the capability of the user. This strategy contrasts with the provision of yet more products and services, which can produce passive rather than active citizens. As the transition towards sustainability is seen as a social learning process,[77] then the further development of a theory of social design seems an imperative. This is being recognized under new programmes such as the Utrecht Manifest,[78] the emergence of a number of organizations collating and disseminating efforts in social design[79] and educational programmes, such as The Good Life Project at Parsons School of Design, New York.[80]

Other approaches

Co-design is expressed to varying degrees in other design approaches – some with an extensive history and well-developed methodologies (user-centred design, inclusive/universal design) and others that are emergent (user-innovation, mass collaboration, slow design).

User-centred design

The involvement of users, i.e. the end-users, of the design artefact, service or outcome, in the (professionally guided) design process presents a continuum from no involvement to some expression of co-design. User-centred design (UCD) can be applied at any stage in the design process and aims to interrogate the needs, wants and limitations of users in the design context. UCD emerged in the 1980s as a tool to assist in new product development (NPD) where particular user groups would be invited or selected to participate in focus groups commenting on certain stages in the design process, especially the testing of early concepts and prototypes.[81] Gathering user-based intelligence through lead-user innovators and user-innovation was later introduced as a new UCD approach to assist NPD.[82] This was in addition to information on users supplied by market research (again, often relying on focus groups) and was a means to get feedback on the emergent designs prior to committing further financial investment. UCD in the context of the design of software systems is a well-prescribed methodology and even has its own ISO standard for human-centred design processes for interactive systems.[83] UCD often requires particular adaptations to fit the particular design discipline or is dovetailed to another design approach.[84] Other user-research methods can extend UCD intelligence, such as ethnographic research and cultural probes.[85] Today, the use of distributed networking technologies, especially the internet, is enabling a new evolution of UCD with more participatory methods involving user-innovation and even mass collaboration (see below).

Inclusive/universal design

The terms 'inclusive' and 'universal' are often interchangeable but imply that the intention of this kind of design approach is that no one is excluded from access or use of a design product, service or outcome.[86] Inclusive design invites inclusion of all members of society, while universal design is readily accessible and usable by all members of society. Other terms are invoked, such as 'design for all', 'transgenerational design' and 'barrier-free design'.[87] Designing to be inclusive or universal aligns with contemporary political thought about an inclusive society, adopted by government, commercial and not-for-profit sectors.

As the proportion of elderly increases in many societies in the North, their exclusion from access to products, services and public places by poor design remains a problem. Making design more inclusive is part of being a responsible socially orientated designer. There are a wide range of techniques and methodologies to support inclusive design practice, some recently developed by the Helen Hamlyn Research Institute.[88] The degree of participation required of the users, stakeholders and actors is under the direction of the designers relevant to the context in hand.

Mass collaboration and user-innovation design
A diverse and fluxing group of participatory design approaches, many poorly defined as yet, are associated with the emergence of Web 2.0 technologies, such as wikis, blogs, etc.[89] which facilitate communication, discussion and collective working on distributed networks. The main thrust of these emergent mass collaboration and user-innovation approaches is that they tend to be driven from the internet community at large rather than from specific commercial or government organizations. The term 'mass collaboration' is defined as 'a form of collective action that occurs when large numbers of people work independently on a single project, often modular in its nature'.[90] The emergent phenomenon is seen as heralding a paradigm shift in how existing and future business will be conducted.[91] Charles Leadbeater coined the term 'we-think', suggesting that current experiments in we-think are creating new possibilities for 'we-make',[92] and suggests these new trends may also spread to the provision of public services. Mass collaboration is closely linked with other internet phenomena such as 'smart mobs' – a form of intelligent self-structuring social organization and coordination through technology-mediated networks and communication – a term coined by Rheingold,[93] and 'crowdsourcing' – a form of PD enabled through distributed networks that is predominantly being tested by businesses to outsource certain services and skills.[94]

The societal and economic value of these forms of PD is yet to be fully realized, but the success of building content-based text resources, such as Wikipedia, or software, such as the Linux operating system and OS software, suggests these approaches will be tested further for their application to design projects. As one of the founders of Wikipedia, Jimmy Wales, has noted, its success is down to a mix of five constituents held in the kind of productive tension that traditional organizations may find difficult to adopt:

- one part anarchy (anything goes)
- one part democracy (people can vote on a disagreement)
- one part aristocracy (people who have been around for a long time get listened to)
- one part meritocracy (the best ideas win out), and
- one part monarchy (on rare occasions the buck has to stop somewhere).

This suggests that any designer entering such a process has to simultaneously respect the inherent design abilities of other participants while bringing their special design skills to bear.

Slow design

Another emergent design approach is slow design, a term initially coined as a rhetorical query of the default 'fast design' paradigm with its uncontested and unsustainable flows of resources, and as a means of reframing eco- and sustainable design.[95] Slow design requires stepping outside the existing mental construct of capitalism, where metabolism is driven entirely by economic imperatives, to consider other metabolisms and in doing so generate fresh awareness, possibilities and subsequently help create new societal values. Initial areas of focus posited for slow design included ritual, tradition, experiential, evolved, slowness, eco-efficiency, open-source knowledge and (slow) technology,[96] and proposed some guiding principles, processes and outcomes (Appendix 4).

Slow design contributes to an emergent slow movement, inspired originally by the Italian organization, Slow Food, founded by Carlo Petrini in 1989,[97] encompassing a diverse range of slow activists (Table 5.1). This reveals an increasing public consciousness about the positive impacts of slowness[98] and a potential role for design in eliciting transition towards slower societal metabolisms.[99] In 2006, SlowLab posited six principles of slow design[100] as follows:

- Principle 1: Reveal: Slow design reveals experiences in everyday life that are often missed or forgotten, including the materials and processes that can be easily overlooked in an artefact's existence or creation.
- Principle 2: Expand: Slow design considers the real and potential 'expressions' of artefacts and environments beyond their perceived functionalities, physical attributes and lifespans.
- Principle 3: Reflect: Slow design artefacts/environments/experiences induce contemplation and what SlowLab has coined 'reflective consumption'.

Table 5.1
Expressions of activism in a diverse 'slow movement'

Type	Subtype	Examples
'Anti'-activists	Anti-globalization Anti-car culture Anti-consumerist	A diverse coalition of groups Reclaim the streets, critical mass Buy nothing day – Adbusters
Slow positivism	Slow localism Slow environmentalism Slow design	Slow Food, slow cities, Transition Towns The Sloth Club Slow, SlowLab
Green or eco-lifestyle	Organic food Consumerism Transportation Tourist	Soil Association Green Map, Global Eco-label Network (GEN) Sustrans, Human Powered Vehicle Association (HPVA) The International Ecotourism Society

Source: Fuad-Luke (2007)[101]

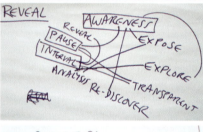

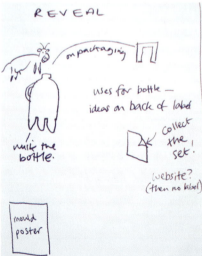

Figure 5.6
Ideation of new concepts in a workshop
by using the 'slow design' principles

- Principle 4: Engage: Slow design processes are 'open source' and collaborative, relying on sharing, co-operation and transparency of information so that designs may continue to evolve into the future.
- Principle 5: Participate: Slow design encourages users to become active participants in the design process, embracing ideas of conviviality and exchange to foster social accountability and enhance communities.
- Principle 6: Evolve: Slow design recognizes that richer experiences can emerge from the dynamic maturation of artefacts, environments and systems over time. Looking beyond the needs and circumstances of the present day, slow designs are (behavioural) change agents.

These principles can be used by individual designers as a guide to developing their practice and for collaborative, participatory workshops. The principles are useful for interrogating the sustainability prism and have potential to generate new products, product-services and business models as revealed in the Milkota local, organic, milk sales system, generated during a participatory slow design workshop (Figures 5.6 to 5.8). SlowLab reveals an eclectic output of work from 'slow designers' that indicates transformation in the way designers work and how they come together and participate with others to encourage social cohesion.[102] Slow design's full potential remains to be explored.

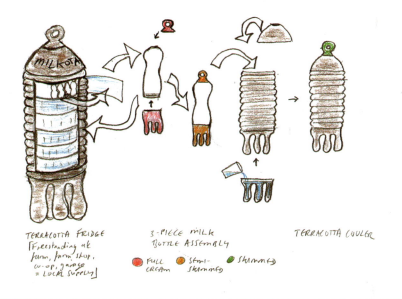

Figure 5.7
Concept design for a local, organic, cyclic milk system – 'Milkota'

Figure 5.8
'Milkota' – concept renders for a milk bottle and cooler system

Notes

1   Globalization is defined here as 'the connecting of individuals, communities, companies, non-profits and governments within networks of economic, technical, socio-cultural and political functionality'.

2   Jencks, C. (1996) *What is Post-Modernism?*, Academy Editions, London.

3   Mau, B. with Leonard, J. and the Institute without Boundaries (2004) *Massive Change*, Phaidon, London.

4   Toffler, A. (1971) *Future Shock*, Pan Books, London, p12.

5   See Honoré C. (2004) *In Praise of Slow*, Orion Books, London; Petrini, C. (2007) *Slow Food Nation: Why Our Food Should Be Good, Clean and Fair*, Rizzoli, New York.

6   Wood, J. (2003) 'The wisdom of nature = the nature of wisdom. Could design bring human society closer to an attainable form of utopia?', paper presented at 5th European Design Academy conference, April, Barcelona.

7   Buchanan, R. (1995) 'Wicked problems in design thinking', in V. Margolin and R. Buchanan (eds) *The Idea of Design*, The MIT Press, Cambridge, MA, p14.

8   See several articles in *Design Issues*, vol 23.

9   Rith, C. and Dubberly, H. (2007) 'Why Horst W. J. Rittel matters', *Design Issues*, vol 23, no 2, p73.

10 Ibid.

11 Bonsiepe, G. (1997) 'Design – the blind spot of theory, or, theory – the blind spot of design', conference paper for a semi-public event at the Jan van Eyk Academy, Maastricht, April 1997.

12 Liz Sanders and G. K. van Patter in conversation, 'Science in the making: Understanding generative research now!', NextDesign Leadership Institute (NextD), 2004, www.nestd.org/02/05/01/contents.htm, accessed September 2008.

13 Margolin, V. and Margolin, S. (2002) 'A "social model" of design: Issues of practice and research', *Design Issues*, vol 18, no 4, pp24–30; Morelli, N. (2007) 'Social innovation and new industrial contexts: Can designers "Industrialize" socially responsible solutions?', *Design Issues*, vol 23, no 4, pp3–21.

14 Leadbeater, C. (2008) *We Think: Mass Innovation, Not Mass Production*, Profile Books, London.

15 Howard, J. (2004) 'Toward participatory ecological design of technological systems', *Design Issues*, vol 20, no 3, pp40–53.

16 Thackara, J. (2005) *In the Bubble: Designing in a Complex World*, The MIT Press, Cambridge, MA.

17 Wikipedia (2008) 'ARPANET', http://en.wikipedia.org/wiki/ARPANET

18 Wikipedia (2008) 'World Wide Web', http://en.wikipedia.org/wiki/World_wide_web; Wikipedia (2008) 'Tim Berners-Lee', http://en.wikipedia.org/wiki/Tim_Berners-Lee

19 Wikipedia (2008) 'Open source definition' http://en.wikipedia.org/wiki/Open_source_definition

20 Wikipedia (2008) 'Open source', http://en.wikipedia.org/wiki/Open_source_content

21 Wikipedia (2008) 'Linux', http://en.wikipedia.org/wiki/LINUX

22 Wikipedia (2008) 'Wikipedia', http://en.wikipedia.org/wiki/Wikipedia

23 Leadbeater (2008), op. cit. Note 14; Tapscott, D. and Williams, A. D. (2007) *Wikinomics: How Mass Collaboration Changes Everything*, Atlantic Books, London.

24 Wikipedia (2008) 'Open design', http://en.wikipedia.org/wiki/Open_design

25 Designbreak, www.designbreak.org

26 Leadbeater (2008), op. cit. Note 14.

27 Wikipedia (2008) 'Copyleft', http://en.wikipedia.org/wiki/Copyleft

28   Wikipedia (2008) 'GNU General Public License', http://en.wikipedia.org/wiki/GNU_General_Public_License; and the GNU Project, www.gnu.org

29   Wikipedia (2008) 'Design Science License', http://en.wikipedia.org/wiki/Design_Science_License

30   Creative Commons, www.creativecommons.org; Wikipedia (2008) 'Creative Commons', http://en.wikipedia.org/wiki/Creative_Commons

31   Hardie, M. (2007) 'Creative License Fetishism', available at http://summit.keiin.org/node/308

32   Pasquinelli, M. (2008) 'The ideology of free culture and the grammar of sabotage', available at http://rekombinant.org/docs/Ideology-of-Free-Culture.pdf, NAi Publishers, Rotterdam.

33   See also Wikipedia (2008) 'Copyfarleft', http://p2pfoundation.net/Copyfarleft

34   Woodhouse, E. and Patton, J. W. (2004) 'Design by society: Science and technology studies and the social shaping of design', *Design Issues*, vol 20, no 3, pp1–12.

35   Bonsiepe, G. (2006) 'Design and democracy', *Design Issues*, vol 22, no 2, pp27–34.

36   Stairs, D. (2005) 'Altruism as design methodology', *Design Issues*, vol 21, no 2, pp3–12.

37   Whiteley, N. (2003) *Design for Society*, Reaktion Books, London.

38   See for example, Rocchi, S. (2005) 'Enhancing sustainable innovation by design: An approach to the co-creation of economic, social and environmental value', PhD thesis for Erasmus University, Centre for Environmental Studies, Rotterdam; Morelli (2007), op. cit. Note 13; Thackara (2005), op. cit. Note 16; Howard (2004), op. cit. Note 15.

39   Fuad-Luke, A. (2007) 'Re-defining the purpose of (sustainable) design: Enter the design enablers, catalysts in co-design', in J. Chapman and N. Gant (eds) *Designers, Visionaries + Other Stories*, Earthscan, London, pp18–52.

40   Carroll, J. M. (2006) 'Dimensions of participation in Simon's design', *Design Issues*, vol 22, no 2, pp3–18.

41   Broadbent, J. (2003) 'Generations in design methodology', *The Design Journal*, vol 6, no 1, pp2–13.

42   Fuad-Luke (2007), op. cit. Note 39, pp37–47.

43   See for example, Transition Towns, www.transitiontowns.org/, described in Hopkins R. (2008) *The Transition Handbook: From Oil Dependency to Local Resilience*, Green Books, Totnes.

44   See for example, Bell, B. (2004) *Good Deeds, Good Design: Community Service through Architecture*, Princeton Architectural Press, New York.

45   See for example, Wates, N. (ed) (2008) *The Community Planning Event Manual*, Earthscan, London.

46   See for example, Designs of the Time 07, Dott 07, www.dott07.com/, and described in Thackara, J. (2007) 'Wouldn't it be great if … we could live sustainably – by design?', *Dott 07 Manual*, Dott 07 and Design Council, London; System Reload, www.systemreload.org/

47   Wikipedia (2008) 'Direct democracy', http://en.wikipedia.org/wiki/Direct_democracy; 'anticipatory democracy', http://en.wikipedia.org/wiki/Anticipatory_democracy; and 'deep democracy', http://en.wikipedia.org/wiki/Deep_democracy

48   Nieusma, D. (2004) 'Alternative design scholarship: Working towards appropriate design', *Design Issues*, vol 20, no 3, p16.

49   Illich, I. (1973) *Tools for Conviviality*, Harper & Row Publishers, New York.

50   Schuler, D. and Naimioka, A. (1993) *Participatory Design: Principles and Practices*, Erlbaum Associates, Hillsdale, New Jersey, pXI, quoted in Nieusma (2004), op. cit. Note 48, p16.

51   Faiola, A. (2007) 'The design enterprise: Rethinking the HCI education paradigm', *Design Issues*, vol 23, no 3, pp30–45.

52 Bell (2004), op. cit. Note 44; Wates (2008), op. cit. Note 45.

53 Carroll (2006), op. cit. Note 40.

54 Sanders (2002), op. cit. Note 12.

55 See for example the Italian design agency Experientia, and its blog, 'Putting people first', www.experientia.com/blog/

56 Burns, C., Cottam, H., Vanstone, C. and Winhall, J. (2006) *RED Paper 02 Transformation Design*, Design Council, London.

57 Fischer, G. (2003) 'Meta-design: Beyond user-centered and participatory design', available at http://l3d.cs.colorado.edu/~gerhard/papes/hci2003-meta-design.pdf

58 Brown, J. S. and Duguid, P. (2000) *The Social Life of Information*, Harvard Business School Press, Boston, MA, cited in Fischer (2003), op. cit. Note 57.

59 Arias, E. G., Eden, H., Fischer, G., Gorman, A. and Scharff, E. (2000) 'Transcending the individual human mind – creating shared understanding through collaborative design', *ACM Transactions on Computer Human Interaction*, vol 7, no 1, pp84–113, cited in Fischer (2003), op. cit. Note 57.

60 Fischer, G. and Oswald, J. (2002) 'Seeding, evolutionary growth, and reseeding: Enriching participatory design with informed participation', *Proceedings of the Participatory Design Conference (PDC'02)*, Malmö University, Sweden, pp135–143, cited in Fischer (2003), op. cit. Note 57.

61 Giaccardi, E. and Fischer, G. (2005) 'Creativity and evolution: A metadesign perspective', in *Sixth International Conference of the European Academy of Design (EAD06) on Design>System>Evolution*, Bremen, University of the Arts, March.

62 Alexander, C. (1964) *The Synthesis of Form*, Harvard University Press, Cambridge, MA, cited in Giaccardi and Fischer (2005), op. cit. Note 61.

63 See John Wood in the June 2007 colloquium, 'The Idea of Metadesign, Attainable Utopias', http://attainable-utopias.org/tiki/tiki-index.php?page=MetadesignColloquiumOverview

64 Wood, J. (2008) 'Changing the change: A fractal framework for metadesign', a paper presented at *Changing the Change* conference, Turin, July, available at www.allemandi.com/cp/ctc/book.php?id=129

65 See the various contributors in the June 2007 colloquium, 'The Idea of Metadesign, Attainable Utopias', http://attainable-utopias.org/tiki/tiki-index.php?page=MetadesignColloquium Overview

66 Wood, J. (forthcoming) *21 Metadesign Tools for the 21st Century*.

67 See forexample, Papanek, V. (1971) *Design for the Real World*, Paladin, St Albans; Papanek, V. (1995) *The Green Imperative*, Thames & Hudson, London; Neutra, R. (1954) *Survival through Design*, Oxford University Press, Oxford, p314.

68 Alexander (1964), op. cit. Note 62.

69 Simon, H. (1996) *Sciences of the Artificial*, MIT Press, Cambridge, MA, originally published 1969.

70 Wikipedia (2008) 'Social design', http://en.wikipedia.org/wiki/Social_design

71 Margolin and Margolin (2002), op. cit. Note 13.

72 Holm, I. (2006) *Ideas and Beliefs in Architecture and Industrial Design: How Attitudes, Orientations and Underlying Assumptions Shape the Built Environment*, Oslo School of Architecture and Design, Oslo.

73 Margolin and Margolin (2002), op. cit. Note 13, p25.

74 De Leonardis cited in Morelli (2007), op. cit. Note 13.

75 Morelli (2007), op. cit. Note 13, p11.

76 Manzini, E. and F. Jégou (2003) Sustainable Everyday: Scenarios of Urban Life, Edizioni Ambiente, Milan; Sustainable Everyday website 2003–2008, www.sustainable-everyday.net/SEPhome/home.html#scenarios

77 Manzini and Jégou (2003), op. cit. Note 76, p45.

78 Utrecht Manifest, www.utrechtmanifest.nl/en/

79 For example, Social Design Site, www.socialdesignsite.com/ and Design 21, the Social Design Network in partnership with UNESCO, www.design21sdn.com/

80 Kirkbride, R. (2008) 'Proposals for a good life: Senior thesis projects from Parsons Product Design 2003–2008', a paper presented at *Changing the Change* conference, Turin, July, www.changingthechange.org, paper available at www.allemandi.com/cp/ctc/book.php?id=59

81 See for example, Norman, D. A. (1988) *The Design of Everyday Things*, Basic Books, New York.

82 von Hippel, E. (2005) *Democratising Innovation*, MIT Press, Cambridge, MA.

83 International Organization for Standardization (1999) ISO 13407 model.

84 For example, inclusive design through 'critical user forums', Dong, H., Clarkson, P. J., Cassim, J. and Keates, S. (2005) 'Critical user forums – An effective user research method for inclusive design', *The Design Journal*, vol 8, no 2 pp49–59.

85 Gaver, W., Dunne, A., and Pascenti, E. (1999) 'Cultural probes', *Interactions*, vol vi, no 1, pp21–29; Gaver, W., Boucher, A., Pennington, S. and Walker, B. (2004) 'Cultural probes and the value of uncertainty', *Interactions*, vol XL5, pp53–56.

86 See for example, inclusive design – Clarkson, P.J., Coleman, R., Keates, S. and Lebbon, C. (eds) (2003) *Inclusive Design: Design for the Whole Population*, Springer-Verlag, London; universal design – Preiser, W. E. F. and Ostroff, E. (eds) (2001) *Universal Design Handbook*, McGraw-Hill, New York.

87 Dong et al (2005), op. cit. Note 84.

88 See for example, Helen Hamlyn Research Institute, www.hhc.rca.ac.uk/archive/hhrc/ resources/index.html; Clarkson et al (2003), op. cit. Note 86; Keates, S. and Clarkson, P. J. (2003) *Countering Design Exclusion: An Introduction to Inclusive Design*, Springer, London.

89 Wikipedia (2008) 'Web 2.0', http://en.wikipedia.org/wiki/Web_2.0

90 Wikipedia (2008) 'Mass collaboration', http://en.wikipedia.org/wiki/Mass_collaboration

91 Tapscott and Williams (2007), op. cit. Note 23; Leadbeater (2008), op. cit. Note 14.

92 Ibid. Leadbeater (2008), pp133–141.

93 Rheingold, H. (2002) *Smart Mobs: The Next Social Revolution*, Perseus Books, New York.

94 Wikipedia (2008) 'Crowdsourcing', http://en.wikipedia.org/wiki/Crowdsourcing

95 Fuad-Luke, A. (2002) '"Slow design" – a paradigm shift in design philosophy?', a paper presented at *Development by Design*, Bangalore, India, November 2002.

96 Fuad-Luke, A. (2004) 'Slow design: A paradigm for living sustainably', available at Slow, www.slowdesign.org

97 Slow Food, www.slowfood.com/

98 Honoré, C. (2004) *In Praise of Slow*, Orion Books, London; also see SlowPlanet, www.slowplanet.com

99 'Slow + design: Slow approach to distributed economy and sustainable sensoriality', international seminar, Milan, 6 October 2006, www.agranelli.net/DIR_rassegna/convegno_Slow+Design.pdf, accessed 17 January 2008.

100 Fuad-Luke, A. (2008) 'Slow design', in Erlhoff, M. and Marshall, T. (eds) *Design Dictionary: Perspectives on Design Terminology*, Birkhäuser-Verlag, Basel/Boston/Berlin, pp361–363; Strauss, C. and Fuad-Luke, A. (2008) 'The slow design principles: A new interrogative and reflexive tool for design research and practice', a paper presented at *Changing the Change* conference, Turin, July, www.changingthechange.org, available at www.allemandi.com/cp/ctc/book .php?id=109

101 Fuad-Luke, A. (2007) 'Reflection, consciousness, progress: Creatively slow designing the present', http://imaging.dundee.ac.uk/reflections/pdfs/AlastairFuad-Luke.pdf, accessed September 2008. A keynote presentation made at the conference *Reflections on Creativity: Exploring the Role of Theory in Creative Practice*, University of Dundee, April 2006, published 2007.

102 SlowLab, www.slowlab.net

6

Activist Frameworks and Tools: Nodes, Networks and Technology

'Imagine a better future. Find your allies. Share tools. Build it. Start now.'

Alex Steffan, Worldchanging[1]

People, People, People

Activism is about motivating, activating and transforming people. This means connecting with people, using networks and organizing face-to-face meetings. It is also about the activists themselves, their motivations and intentions. A clear vision of the intention, purpose, strategies and goal of the activism, and the sustainability issues involved, will help identify the people that could contribute to the design process. One way to do this is to identify the primary, secondary and key actors and stakeholders (Figure 6.1). Here an actor is defined as a person or organization that will remain centre stage and is essential to the main storyline of the design project. A stakeholder is any person or organization that will have an effect on, and/or be affected by the design project. A stakeholder may or may not be an actor, depending upon their interests in the design project. An initial mapping of actors and stakeholders may evolve over the lifetime of the design project. Typically, stakeholder mapping in the business or commercial world is defined on an adversarial basis, i.e. those for and those against, and those who are neutral. This can be an additional layer of information added to the stakeholder map. Co-design processes are underlaid with strong participatory democratic principles encouraging equal representation, so positive and negative voices are seen as equally valuable because they help interrogate the problématique(s) more thoroughly.

Once the people are identified there is a broad array of techniques and technologies to bring them together and create a productive environment. The rise of the internet and Web 2.0 technologies, with the rapid expansion of hosted web services including social networking, video sharing, wikis, blogs and folksonomies,[2] have enhanced our ability to communicate and coordinate with distributed networks. The rapid expansion of what is collectively called *social software*[3] over the past few years offers a bewildering choice. Making an appropriate choice depends upon the intention and purpose of the (design) activist(s), the target audience and intended

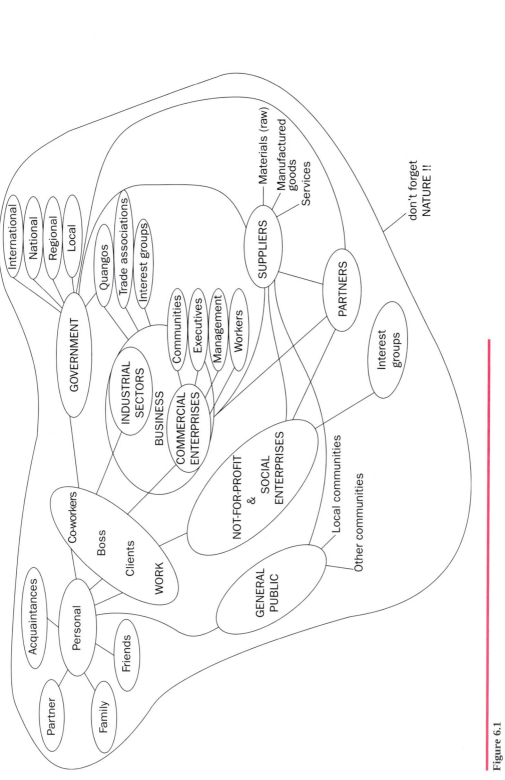

Figure 6.1
Identifying key actors and stakeholders

beneficiaries. The tools for connecting potential design collaborators may, or may not, be different from those used to help action the work and/or publicize it.

Whether old media or 'new media' are deployed to engage people, at some point people will need to get together. When this happens, how is this process facilitated to create maximum synergy and the best design outcomes/solutions? This section illustrates existing nodes, networks, technology and tools that help the design activist to be more strategically and practically focused. There is an a priori assumption that involving a wider range of people in the early appraisal of the problématique and early concept generation will tend to generate a more enabling design solution.

Toolbox for Online World

Existing design activism networks

The networks featured here are founded by and organized by designers. The complex demands of dealing with sustainability issues means that many design networks are multidisciplinary and/or experiment with emergent design approaches (Figure 6.2, Appendix 6). There are a significant number that gather around architecture for the poor (in the South and the North) and for disaster relief or general humanitarian work. A number of networks that have been around since the 1980s – Adbusters, Architects/Designers/Planners for Social Responsibility, Architects for Peace, and the O2 network[4] – but many more have emerged over the past decade and some, such as The Designers Accord and Design Can Change, are very recently established.[5] This indicates a resurgent interest from the design profession in local and global issues, and confirms a belief in the potential contribution that designers can make, and are already making, towards positive change.[6]

Distributed collaboration

Today the range of online collaboration options, beyond the ubiquitous email and telephone, is extensive and involves choices around the use of particular social, communications, and open source (OS) software (Figure 6.3). The 'best fit' choice depends on the task(s) in hand, the access to ICT and physical resources by the people involved, and their ability to use them. Although some of the dominant proprietary software brands are often the easiest option to use for a project, there is a diverse platform of OS software to help with setting up and running servers (e.g. Apache), operating systems (e.g. Linux) and applications (e.g. OpenOffice). These require some technical skill to set up but there are services to help with this task (e.g. Redhat, a commercial company, or Ubantu, a not-for-profit, for setting up Linux operating systems). Conferencing between multi-actors requires synchronous,

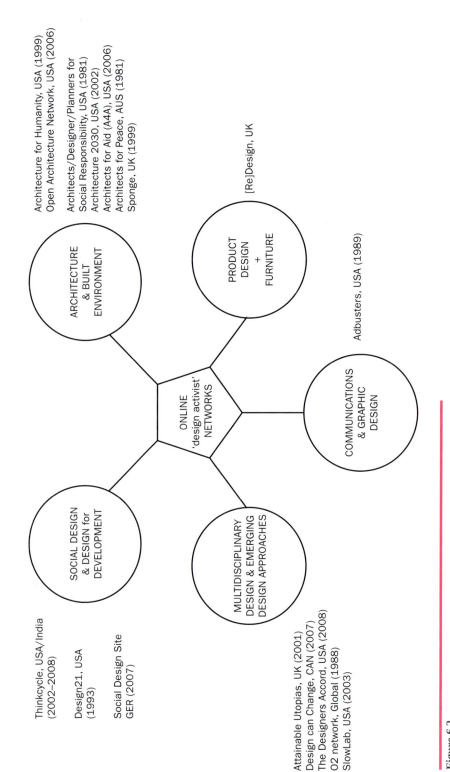

Architecture for Humanity, USA (1999)
Open Architecture Network, USA (2006)

Architects/Designer/Planners for
Social Responsibility, USA (1981)
Architecture 2030, USA (2002)
Architects for Aid (A4A), USA (2006)
Architects for Peace, AUS (1981)
Sponge, UK (1999)

[Re]Design, UK

Adbusters, USA (1989)

ARCHITECTURE
& BUILT
ENVIRONMENT

PRODUCT
DESIGN
+
FURNITURE

ONLINE
'design activist'
NETWORKS

COMMUNICATIONS
& GRAPHIC
DESIGN

SOCIAL DESIGN
& DESIGN for
DEVELOPMENT

MULTIDISCIPLINARY
DESIGN & EMERGING
DESIGN APPROACHES

Thinkcycle, USA/India
(2002–2008)

Design21, USA
(1993)

Social Design Site
GER (2007)

Attainable Utopias, UK (2001)
Design can Change, CAN (2007)
The Designers Accord, USA (2008)
O2 network, Global (1988)
SlowLab, USA (2003)

Figure 6.2
Contemporary design activist networks

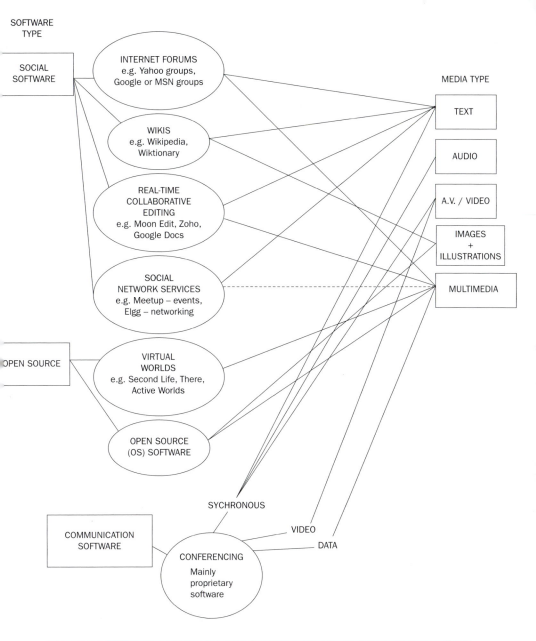

Figure 6.3
Tools for online collaboration for multi-actors

video and/or data communications software. Most tends to be proprietary, although there are a few open source options.

In terms of social software, internet forums, wikis and collaborative real-time text editors offer useful options for iterative discourse and text documentation. An internet forum, such as Yahoo, Google or MSN group, is an easy way of setting up an 'interest' group around a particular design project, while organizing social events can be carried out by notifying these groups, by regular email distribution lists or by using special social events organizing software like Meetup. Elgg is becoming a popular OS social networking software.

Collaboration in virtual worlds, such as Second Life, ActiveWorlds and There, is enabling new possibilities. In these worlds, users create a digital avatar by selecting various personal identity options (gender, clothing, hair style and so on). This avatar can wander around the virtual world landscape to meet and discourse with other avatars. Users create the virtual landscape themselves. Second Life, founded in 2003 by Linden Research,[7] is perhaps the most interesting example because it is providing a vehicle for exchange of ideas and real money making (the currency in Second Life is the Linden dollar, having an exchange value in the order of 260–270 Linden dollars to US$1, at 2007 rates). Today there are more than 15 million registered 'resident' accounts with one avatar per resident, although the appearance of the avatar can change according to the whims of the account holder. Account holders who generate digital content in Second Life retain copyright and there is a permissions and digital rights management service for those who wish to copy content. Commercial companies are experimenting with collaborative design in Second Life, with staff from Philips and Fiat reputedly having engaged in 'crowdsourcing' (see below) and other collaborations to imagine new products and services. This is a form of open innovation tapping into widely distributed knowledge, potentially useful for commercial and educational possibilities. A recent survey revealed that 80 per cent of UK universities have used Second Life for teaching purposes.[8]

Other companies have set up their own platforms for extending collaboration beyond traditional research and development (e.g. IBM set up its Eclipse platform), although the boundary between open innovation, where IP is licensed or shared under agreement, and open source, and the potential to beneficiaries, is the subject of ongoing debate.

Various mass collaboration experiments are occurring through the distributed networks and communities of the internet using social, communications and open source software.[9] Crowdsourcing involves the engagement of large numbers of people in a task traditionally performed within a company or its supply chain.[10] It is invoked and controlled by commercial interests, but nonetheless represents an emergent approach to co-creation and co-design. Organizations can now also use Amazon Mechanical Turk to coordinate crowdsourcing tasks. Successful crowdsourcing initiatives range from internet-based retailing of t-shirts (Threadless) to compilation of data for buildings/builders (Emporis) and even predictive prospecting for a gold mine company (Goldcorp).

Recognizing the power of the crowd, a number of proprietary services have emerged to join together inventors, designers and other partners. These include companies such as CrowdSpirit and Kluster which function as ideas banks within which members can participate in core product development teams and explore the commercial potentiality of ideas. Alternatively, it is possible to take a problem to an open innovation service, like Innocentive, to engage brainpower beyond the normal reach of an R&D department or design agency.[11] Japanese designer Kohei Nishiyama, of Elephant Design, Tokyo, is targeting design agencies to submit their prototypes to his web interface and consumers can get involved in finalizing the design process with what he calls, Design to Order.[12] Once enough 'votes' are received, then a prototype product moves towards being manufactured. Nishiyama is currently testing a trial site for retailer Muji to help develop products for its stores.

Potentially more anarchistic methods of online collaboration involve the act of 'flash mobbing', the coordination of a group of people through internet and mobile telephony systems to quickly assemble in a public place for an event or happening and equally quickly to disperse. Flash mobs are a particular kind of 'smart mob', a term coined by Howard Rheingold in 2002[13] to describe a self-structuring social organization displaying intelligent emergent behaviour that communicates through technology-mediated channels (internet and various wireless devices – laptops, mobile phones, PDAs). The potency of smart mobs is being utilized by everyone from anti-global and anti-capitalist protestors to consumers organizing mass shopping events to level discounts from retailers. Its potential to engage people in designing for positive change remains largely unexplored, although well-known brands such as eBay and Amazon, and phenomena such as internet social tagging, all utilize smart mob thinking in their modus operandi.

Ways of sharing visualizations

Most designers communicate through a wide range of visualization tools using proprietary software to explore concepts, develop scenarios and specify detailed design. In today's networked world, the sharing of multimedia files is a necessity for the modern design agency and involves a considerable skill set. This represents quite a challenge when working with non-designers, the general public and clients. Aside from the proprietary multimedia file formats and software applications there are some straightforward 'entry level' visualization tools, although professional designers may not find them to be very sophisticated. Google introduced SketchUp to make it easier for everyone to create and share 3D models.[14] While this is basic 3D modelling software, it has some potentiality for people to digitally visualize the built environment and has even recently been adopted by an architect, Michelle Kaufmann, promoting eco-housing.[15] There are various open source applications that offer simple 3D visualizations for objects and illustrations (e.g. Wings 3D), very basic sketching (e.g. RateMyDrawings, ImaginationEmbed) and for synchronous whiteboard sessions (e.g. Groupboard). More sophisticated yet easy-to-use visualization tools seem to be needed, so there is a potential gap in the market here.

Certain networks are encouraging the sharing of designers' visualizations. For example, by September 2008 the Open Architecture Network (OAN)[16] had attracted more than 12,500 members in just 18 months and displayed plans, drawings and renderings for 1149 projects ranging from disaster housing to shelter for the poor and marginalized. Subject to certain terms, these designs can be used and adapted for other projects.

Ways of making

The entrepreneurial spirit of the internet is challenging how we make things. This is happening in both mass and niche markets. Various permutations of electronic mass customization are offered by manufacturers. In this context, mass customization means being able to manufacture a product or service to meet a customer's needs with the concurrent efficiencies and gains expected of mass production. Many personal computer manufacturers offer a service that enables customers to tailor the specification of the computer to their personal or business needs – this is what Pine termed 'collaborative customization'[17] as distinct from adaptive customization, when the end-user later alters or changes the product themselves. At the other end of the scale, from a consumer-led perspective, it is now possible for end-users to design their own t-shirts and have a one-off or short print run made.

Designers are also testing emergent ways of designing and making. An outreach programme called FabLabs at the Massachusetts Institute of Technology, led by Neil Gershenfeld at the Center for Bits and Atoms, is investigating the application of 2D and 3D tools in integrated manufacturing centres, to fabricate components using designs delivered digitally to a bank of local machines.[18] The machines include a suite of software applications linked to routers, laser cutters, 3D printers, moulding and casting and circuit-making machines. FabLabs can be adapted to specific prototyping or small batch manufacturing tasks.

The possibilities of distributed manufacturing are being investigated by other designers and engineers. Adrian Bowyer and Vik Oliver of Bath University, UK, have, since the inception of the concept in 2004, successfully developed a rapid prototyping machine that can replicate itself, called RepRap – *Rep*licating *Rap*id-Prototyper (see Figure 4.18, page 104).[19] Material costs for the RepRap are a modest £400 and the open source designs are available under a GNU General Public License. Freedom of Creation in Helsinki, Finland, use a process of laser sintering to create rapid manufactured textiles that can be downloaded to be locally manufactured, preferably at a local CNC router shop. These developments potentially herald a new dawn for distributed manufacturing of certain types of products. Downloading digital designs and making them locally remains a potential revenue stream waiting to be further explored.

In a more prosaic but very effective approach, designers are offering simple cutting plans to enable people to make their own artefacts. In 2003 Tempo, a student-led sustainable design network in Cornwall, UK, led a project called '8 × 4', to create furniture with minimal wastage from standard 8 × 4ft OSB board or ply sheets using only basic tools (Figure 6.4). Cutting patterns for furniture, toys and games are emerging, and no doubt many more will follow as designers (professional and amateur) sell and/or donate designs enabling people to 'make-it-yourself'.[20]

Ambitious open source design-and-make projects, often involving large numbers of designers, include the world's first OS hydrogen car, the c,mm,n,[21] launched at Amsterdam's AutoRAI show in February 2007 (see Figure 4.28, page 111). This joint project between the Netherlands Society for Nature and the Environment, the Technical University of Delft, (TUDelft), University of Eindhoven and University of Enschede, is a zero-emissions vehicle whose technical drawings and blueprints are available online. Other open source car designers include the Society for Sustainable Mobility which is looking to develop a very economical SUV that is designed collaboratively but certain rights are retained to attract potential manufacturing investment.[22]

Open source mapping of cities' green consumer outlets, facilities and spaces has been encouraged by a not-for-profit organization called Green Maps, in New York.[23] Green Maps provides a basic set of universal icons to represent the different 'green' elements within a city, town or location, and a toolbox to help users set up their own map. These can be adopted, modified and new icons added to build up a local and cultural flavour to each map. There are now hundreds of maps in more than 50 countries.

Toolbox for Real World

The main sources of inspiration for collaborative, participatory design come from on-the-ground community-based or community-inspired projects. There is a healthy history of participation through community architecture,[24] action/collaborative planning[25] and more grassroots activities such as the lived experiences of communities creating their own eco-villages[26] and the Slow Food movement.[27] New fields of endeavour are emerging in response to a growing sense of environmental and social crisis. For example, the local activist movements Transition Towns are dealing with a post-peak oil future and 'powering-down' off oil dependence.[28] The community, or at least the idea of a community and it being rooted in a real place, provides a focus. This is more problematic when considering consumer products or services, which tend to be more highly distributed and commercially orientated.

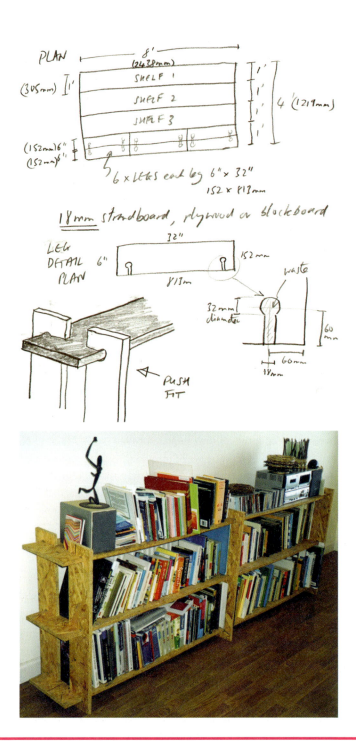

PLAN   8'
(2438mm)

(305mm) 1'   SHELF 1

SHELF 2

SHELF 3

(152mm)6"
(152mm)6"

6 x LEGS each leg 6" x 32"
152 x 813mm

1' 1' 1' 1'   4 (1219mm)

18mm strandboard, plywood or blockboard

LEG
DETAIL   6"
PLAN

32"

813mm

152mm

waste

32mm
diameter

60
mm

60mm
18mm

PUSH
FIT

Figure 6.4
8 × 4 Tempo project

176

Typically, products and services are considered in smaller groups in a more design-led environment. This section examines the range of real-world options for designers wishing to pursue a more co-design or participatory design approach.

Selecting the right kind of co-design event

The right choice of co-design event depends upon the purpose and goal of the design activism, and the intended target audience and beneficiaries. Considerations need to be given to whether the event is designer-led or led by 'non-designers', whether it is public or private, and the size of the event (Figure 6.5, Table 6.1). Community planning and open space events are fine for large numbers of people including a mix of experts, professionals and lay people. These events are well suited to planning or built environment projects. Moderate numbers are suitable for events such as World Café, co-design workshops or design charettes. Small groups or numbers are better for informal/formal 'interest' and 'focus' group work.

Deciding the 'best fit' event for your particular kind of design activism means matching your purpose against the 'designed' purpose of the event. Do you want a formal or informal event? Some events require that the design context is set in some detail prior to the event, others are more open questions intended to help define the design context by means of collective intelligence. A key question is whether an existing design context needs refining or whether there needs to be a full dialogic discourse about the very nature of the design context.

Informal meetings of interest groups do not have a particular format or plan. A successful example of this type of group is Green Drinks, initiated by Edwin Datchefski of Biothinking in 1999.[29] There are more than 350 chapters of Green Drinks worldwide who meet to discuss and network around topical and local environmental issues.

Whatever event is chosen it is likely that its success will depend upon good planning, communication, facilitation, application of appropriate tools and techniques, information capture, dissemination of results, and some form of measurement of action on the ground.

Planning, inspiring, leading and facilitating

Planning is the foundation to all co-design events. Typically, it is important to give consideration to the questions listed in Table 6.2. An appropriate structure for the event including designated people to help control the schedule, flow and communication, will lead to a more successful event. This may include all or one of the following people: a chair, a facilitator(s), an organizing team and a panel of specialists or experts. Small-scale events may only need a facilitator. There is a

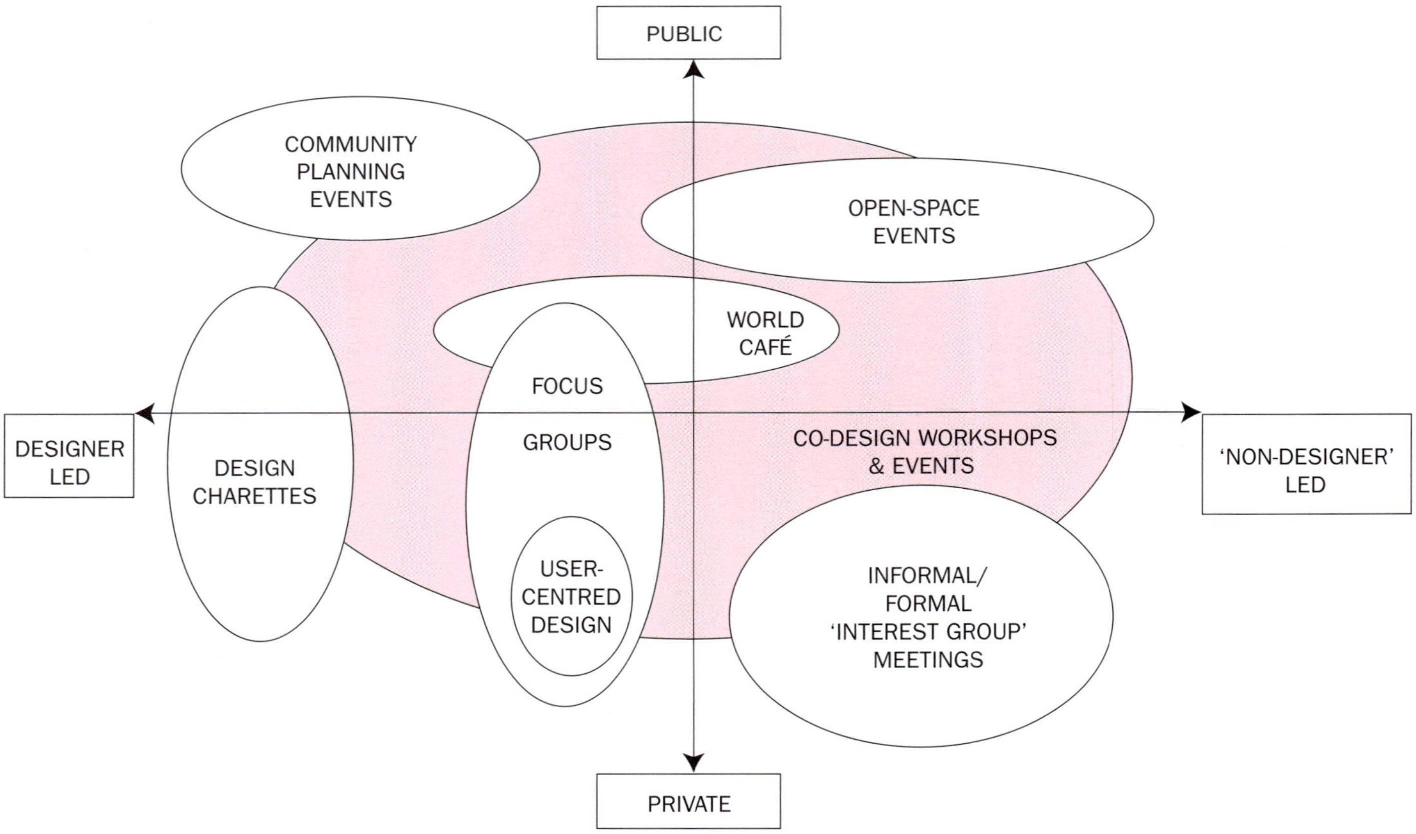
PUBLIC
COMMUNITY PLANNING EVENTS
OPEN-SPACE EVENTS
WORLD CAFÉ
FOCUS
GROUPS
DESIGNER LED
DESIGN CHARETTES
CO-DESIGN WORKSHOPS & EVENTS
'NON-DESIGNER' LED
USER-CENTRED DESIGN
INFORMAL/ FORMAL 'INTEREST GROUP' MEETINGS
PRIVATE

Figure 6.5
Co-design events, designer-led to non-designer-led

Table 6.1
Selecting the right co-design event

Ideal number of people	Type of co-design event	Purpose of event	How is design context typically set?
Large	Community planning events and design charettes	Exploring the views of a wide range of actors and stakeholders by encouraging them to participate in the planning process	Around a proposed development
	Open space events	Engaging large groups in discussions to explore key questions or issues	Around a topical question or issue framed by the title of the event
Moderate	World Café	Exploring specific questions with invited actors and stakeholders	Around a specific topic framed by the organizers of the event
	Co-design workshops or small-group design charettes	Explore the problématique around a particular design context with a view to generating a design brief, process and/or outcomes	Around a specific design context framed by the organizers of the event
Small	Informal/formal 'interest' groups	Exploring particular issues and resolving strategies, actions and ways forward	Around the specific issues defined by the 'interest group'
	Focus groups	Exploring the opinions and views of specific actors and/or stakeholders and/or users invited by the organizers	Around an existing/ proposed development, or prototype product or service

huge array of techniques that can be deployed by these designated people.[30] The work of a facilitator is most important and usually revolves around some basic principles:

- inclusion – getting everyone to voice their opinions
- listening – getting everyone to listen 'deeply', i.e. to the surface and underlying messages
- communicating, capturing and disseminating information during the event
- allowing adequate time for tasks
- applying the most appropriate tools for the tasks and
- summing up and pointing to the next steps.

Table 6.2
Planning for a co-design event

The coordinators
Coordinating individual and/or organization? Any associated individuals or organizations/organizers? e.g. administration, technical, professional or expert inputs? Need for a chair, facilitator and/or panel?
The nature of the event
Reason and purpose of the event? Goal(s) for the event? Which participants? Actors? Stakeholders? Experts? Professionals? Others? Type of event?
The practicalities
Location and venue? Where? Timing? When, why? Lead time for planning? Costs? Prior to, at and after the event? Funding sources?
Other considerations?

The Multi-Stakeholder Processes Resource Portal, the Netherlands, has a diverse range of tools, methodologies and facilitation resources to enable more effective participation for multi-stakeholder situations.[31]

With the appropriate structure in place it is often useful for a keynote speaker, expert, chair or facilitator to frame the context, give some detail and engage the audience in the task ahead, before commencing participatory work. Audiovisual inspiration is critical at this juncture to get the participants involved. Grassroots organizations, such as Transition Towns, give particular advice on running Open Space and World Café type events.[32] Where groups are moderate or smaller it is useful to form the audience in a circle or gather them around tables and for the facilitator to encourage people to briefly introduce themselves in a 'go round'. The more that the event locale and schedule can be configured to maximize an equal input from different voices, the better the outputs will be.

Event techniques (methods, tools, games)

It is important to choose the correct technique for the appropriate part of the cycle of a co-design event. There may be several phases to the event after preliminary introductions and context setting – these can involve exploring, analysing and deciding (Figure 6.6). Exploring is a key part of the early stages of the co-design process and should involve text- and visual-based tools and outputs where possible.

The author finds the application of the 'word circle' technique useful in the early stages of a workshop, but it can be appropriate at any time to help participants

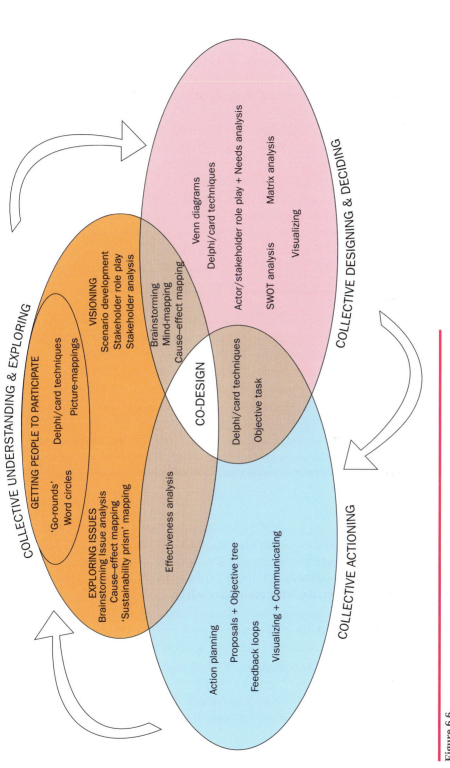

Figure 6.6
Methods and tools to help facilitate a co-design workshop

establish the key concerns or focal points. It is best utilized for smaller groups, between 5 and 15–20 people, but larger groups can be subdivided. Each member of the group is allowed to articulate one word, or phrase of two/three words, about a defined subject area during the workshop (this can be an issue, about understandings or framings of the design context, about a particular development, or artefact, and so on). Each participant's word is captured by the facilitator in a large circle on a flipchart or white/blackboard. Then each participant is asked to join up any two of the circles containing words, using a marker pen/chalk, with a straight line. One participant has one line. When all the participants have marked their line, the facilitator then highlights the words with the most lines, the words that frequently couple and the words that are not as popular. A 'go round' is used for everyone to articulate their thoughts about the word circle (see Figure 5.6 for an example of a word circle from a 'slow design' workshop). Word circles encourage participation, give everyone a 'voice', help delineate synergetic and divergent views and, most importantly, create a sense of collective and individual 'ownership' of the ideas expressed. This tends to elicit better collaboration and co-operation.

Mind-mapping, card techniques (Delphi techniques, metaplanning – use of cards or Post-it notes to group or cluster information, questions and/or issues) and so on, help with the task of gathering and communicating diverse points of view from the participants. Once the key issues have been articulated, summarized and absorbed, then the design context can be given more definition and the participants can move on to further explorations using more visually stimulating tools which help develop stories and scenarios. Typical techniques may involve brainstorming by drawing, using games to stimulate ideas and drawings (e.g. Play ReThink), story-boarding and scenario sketching, the use of proprietary cards that assist with scenario development and understanding actor/user/stakeholder needs (e.g. IDEO cards; Flowmaker cards).

On the ground and active
Towards the end of a co-design event, the chair, facilitator and/or organizers should summarize what happened at the event, what was expressed, what was learnt, what agreements and disagreements exist, and what actions should be taken next (and by whom). This is the most difficult phase of any co-design event as it is easy to gather participants around a topic/issue/design context, feasible to get them to generate ideas and work on concept solutions, but hard to turn words into action. Most of the advice seems to centre around:

- keeping the actions simple, focused on the vision or big idea (and checking that everyone gets the big idea)
- making sure that the relevant people know what is expected of them next
- ensuring adequate communication and networking systems exist to get it all going on the ground and
- setting a follow-on event to track progress and receive feedback to check if it is all heading in the required direction to reach the visionary goal.

At some point, the design activists should try and assess the effectiveness of the strategies, tools and methods applied to reach their goal (refer to Table 4.3). Feedback is essential to readjust the evolving participatory design process or to simply congratulate the participants on having achieved what they (and the design activists) set out to do.

Notes

1 Steffan, A. (ed) (2006) *Worldchanging: A User's Guide for the 21st Century*, Abrams, New York, p536.
2 'Folksonomies' denote ways for collaborative tagging, social classification, social indexing and social tagging in order to mark something as being popular or as having received confirmation of popular validity.
3 'Social software' enables the sharing of data and interactions using a range of software applications.
4 Adbusters, www.adbusters.org/; Architects/Designers/Planners for Social Responsibility, www.adpsr.org/Home.htm; Architects for Peace, www.architectsforpeace.org/index.php; and the O2 network, www.o2nyc.org/, New York, US.
5 Designers Accord, www.designersaccord.org/; and Design Can Change, www.designcanchange.org/#home
6 See more examples of design in the cause of activism, Steffan (2006), op. cit. Note 1; Sinclair, C., Stohr, K. and Architecture for Humanity (2006) *Design Like You Give a Damn: Architectural Responses to Humanitarian Crises*, Thames & Hudson, London.
7 Wikipedia (2008) 'Second Life', http://en.wikipedia.org/wiki/Second_Life
8 Ibid.
9 Tapscott, D. and Williams, A. D. (2007) *Wikinomics: How Mass Collaboration Changes Everything*, Atlantic Books, London; Leadbeater, C. (2008) *We Think: Mass Innovation, Not Mass Production*, Profile Books, London.
10 Wikipedia (2008) 'Crowdsourcing', http://en.wikipedia.org/wiki/Crowdsourcing
11 Innocentive, www.innocentive.com/
12 Sample, I. (2007) 'The future of design? Voters pick the next must-have on the net', *The Guardian*, 24 November 2007, p11.
13 Rheingold, H. (2002) *Smart Mobs: The Next Social Revolution*, Perseus Books, New York.
14 Google SketchUp, http://sketchup.google.com/
15 Michelle Kaufmann Designs, http://sketchup.google.com/green/mkd.html
16 Open Architecture Network, www.openarchitecturenetwork.org/
17 Pine, J. (1999) *Mass Customization: The New Frontier in Business Competition*, Harvard Business School Press, Boston, MA; originally published 1992.
18 MIT FabLabs, http://fab.cba.mit.edu/
19 RepRap, http://reprap.org/bin/view/Main/WebHome
20 See for example, Kith-Kin, www.kith-kin.co.uk/home.asp; Instructables, www.instructables.com/
21 c,mm,n open source car design, www.cmmn.org
22 Leadbeater (2008), op. cit. Note 9, p135.
23 Green Maps, www.greenmap.org/
24 Bell, B. (2004) *Good Deeds, Good Design: Community Service through Architecture*, Princeton Architectural Press, New York.
25 Wates, N. (ed) (2008) *The Community Planning Event Manual*, Earthscan, London.

26 Global Ecovillage Network, http://gen.ecovillage.org/

27 Petrini, C. (2007) *Slow Food Nation: Why Our Food Should Be Good, Clean and Fair*, Rizzoli, New York.

28 Hopkins, R. (2008) *The Transition Handbook: From Oil Dependency to Local Resilience*, Green Books, Totnes; Transition Towns, www.transitiontowns.org

29 Biothinking, www.biothinking.com; Wikipedia (2008) 'Green drinks', http://en.wikipedia. org/wiki/Green_Drinks

30 See for example, Chambers, R. (2002) *Participatory Workshops: A Source Book of 21 Sets of Ideas and Activities*, Earthscan, London.

31 MSP Resource Portal, http://portals.wi.wur.nl/MSP/?page=1180

32 Hopkins (2008), op. cit. Note 28, refer to 'Open Space', pp168–169 and 'World Café', pp184–186.

7

Adaptive Capacity: Design as a Societal Strategy for Designing 'Now' and 'Co-futuring'

'Heads are round so that thoughts can change direction.'　　Francis Picabia

'We are designing nature and we are subject to her laws and powers. This new condition demands that design discourse not be limited to the boardrooms or kept inside tiny disciplines.'

Bruce Mau[1]

During the past two centuries it could be argued that 'design' was self-absorbed in its own culture, besotted in the power bestowed upon it by commercial interests, and assured of its ubiquitous presence in consumers' lives. As has been noted above, design's supreme role has been, and continues to be, about giving form to the concurrent industrial, consumer and information economies, all connected within a greater globalized economy. Design makes the material forms of these economies culturally acceptable. This is not to say that design has been devoid of altruism for broader societal concerns. Nor has design totally ignored the effect of its materialized outcomes on nature. Yet, as we look at man-made artefacts, the built environment, and the manufacturing and public infrastructures, we are gazing on an aesthetic that represents collectively endorsed visions of 'beauty' verified as economically viable. Many other visions of beauty simply do not make it to reality because they do not meet with the current culture of economics. The reality of this 'beauty', from the motor car to the iPod, from the modern housing development to the supermarket, is that it does not reflect 'true cost economics', i.e. it only reflects a market price, economic growth in the form of GDP and the accumulation of economic capital in very powerful transnational companies – all these represent one form or another of financial activity. These economic metrics do not reveal the true ecological and social costs. The supermarket represents the epitome of capitalist success, in its realization of modernity, cleanliness, choice and, of course, its design. The packaging entices the buyer, celebrates the brand and assures the consumer of satisfaction, but is economical with the truth about the story of its birth – the effects of the supply chain; the working conditions of the labourers and factory workers; the destruction of habitat or ecological capacity; the water footprint and energy required to manufacture it; the carbon footprint including 'food miles'; the chemical additives to enhance the longevity and visual seduction of the food; and the potential illnesses that the consumer may be exposed to as the result of the typically high saturated fat, salt and sugar content of many processed foods. Our current notion of beauty in everyday design therefore needs contesting. This beauty will not sustain us in the future.

We need new visions of beauty – we could call this beauty, 'beautiful strangeness', a beauty that is not quite familiar, tinged with newness, ambiguity and intrigue, which appeals to our innate sense of curiosity … beauty that is more than skin deep, beauty that is envisioned by society, because the current version of beauty is largely ordained by big business and governments. We need a beauty that serves all in society, healing society's divides (around wealth, health, education, access to digital and other technologies). We need a beauty that we can adapt as future circumstances change. We need a beauty that does not 'de-future', a phrase coined by Tony Fry,[2] but keeps options open for our grandchildren. We need a beauty that encourages new ideals, values and concept of humankind's 'growth', genuine human flourishing (what the Greeks called 'eudaimonia'), beyond the blinkered thinking of economic growth as 'progress'. To be progressive now and in the future may be to think about 'economic degrowth' as expressed by Herman Daly, as slowing down the economy and putting our energies and efforts into other societal values and measurables.[3] Daly quoted the Victorian author, poet, artist and reformer John Ruskin: 'That which seems to be wealth may in verity be only the gilded index of far-reaching ruin.' Here we return full circle to the dissenters in the first half of the 19th century who witnessed, and dared to critique, the downside of the Industrial Revolution (see Chapter 2, p37), but could not stop the juggernaut of industrial 'progress'. The unsustainability of our present production and consumption patterns, the endemic and growing split between rich and poor, and the real uncertainties of climate change, are our contemporary warning signs. While we are dealing with a very different world to Ruskin, with a global population of more than six times that of the 1850s and with significantly more complexity, there are many more means of democratic participation to help influence the outcome that were available to Ruskin and his followers.

In our search for 'beautiful strangeness' we need to avoid another pitfall that has frequently hijacked design. Design tends to focus on imagining and engineering the future with its emphasis on concepts, prototypes, scenarios and virtual 3D visualizations. These will remain valuable exercises, but sustainability demands that we care for the present much more than the future. The US architect Bruce Goff referred to the 'continuous present' as something we can affect, whereas the past is gone and the future will take care of itself.[4] Stewart Brand says we can affect 'now'[5] and he describes *now* as:

> 'the period in which people feel they live and act and have responsibility. For most of us now is about a week, sometimes a year. For some traditional tribes

in the American northeast and Australia now *is seven generations back and forward (175 years in each direction).'*

We can change now, the present, more easily than the past or future. Recalling Anne-Marie Willis's notions that design is about 'preconfiguration and directionality' (pp36, 87), and noting the urgency of the sustainability debate, suggests we should place more attention on preconfiguring now to give it fresh directionality. To make a choice as to what to preconfigure means bringing design decisions into a wider societal arena, because business and government tend to use design as their strategic futuring tool for *their* directionality and not for society. New products and services about to appear at the retailers, and new buildings about to come onto the market, were conceived and designed months ago by business, and certified as meeting regulatory and legislative requirements by government. The generation of new artefacts and buildings to replace them are currently being designed as you read. In other words, the real decision making has been done by others. Obsolescence of 'old' artefacts and the in-built directionality (and hence 'ecological or sustainability rucksack') of the new artefacts has already been decided. These observations hint at a need to democratize design's role to a wider range of decision makers that better reflect society as a whole. This implies that design needs to take on a more activist role on behalf of society/societies and the environment.

The potential to expand the agenda for design activism therefore seems ripe. If designers wish to contribute to new visions for sustainable development, such as Janis Birkeland's notion of 'positive development' (see p24) or 'economic degrowth' then they have to be prepared to take on the mantle of a design activist. Designers need to rebalance their focus between 'what next' and 'what now'. Aspiring design activists have to be prepared to take on multiple roles as non-aligned social brokers and catalysts, facilitators, authors, co-creators, co-designers and 'happeners' (i.e. making things actually happen). This suggests a much richer and diverse agenda for design than was outlined by Tim Brown, the chief executive officer and president of one of the world's largest design agencies, IDEO, in the *Harvard Business Review* in June 2008.[6] Brown posited design thinking as a means to transform how products, services, processes and strategy are developed, and made special reference to exploring human-centred design as a means to discovering untapped markets. There was no mention of design as a strategic tool for business to address sustainability or its societal responsibilities. Design needs to break out beyond the visions of business. Design research and education are fortunately one step ahead of design practice. At the same time as Brown's article was published, attendees at the conference Changing the Change in Turin set a rather more challenging agenda for the global design community and the results of a European project called DEEDS established a set of 24 core principles for 'designing for sustainability'.[7] Changing the Change set a new agenda:

- Sustainability must be the meta-objective of every possible design research activity.
- Sustainability here is intended as a systemic change to be promoted at the local and global scale. It will be obtained through a wide social learning process, re-orienting the present unsustainable transformations towards a sustainable knowledge society.
- Design research has to feed the social learning process towards sustainability with the needed design knowledge. That is, with visions, proposals, tools and reflections to enable different actors to collaborate and to move concrete steps towards a sustainable knowledge society.

And, on the new 'designer role', Changing the Change noted:

> *'designers as connectors and facilitators, as quality producers, as visualizers and visionaries, as future builders (or co-producers). Designers as promoters of new business models. Designers as catalizers of change.'*

These aspirations, and more, are embraced by the core principles of the DEEDS project under the acronym 'SCALES' representing Special skills, Creating change agents, Awareness, Learning together, Ethical responsibilities and Synergy and co-creating (Appendix 5). The design research and education community is activated and active. The question is what does this agenda mean for the wider design community, especially the practitioners?

There is a strong sense that design activism in a sustainability framework reinvigorates the agenda for design, can genuinely affect 'now' and give fresh directionality towards a more sustainable future (Appendix 6). If this premise is accepted, then where can existing and emergent design activists begin making a contribution?

Design for a Better Future
The happy sustainable planet?

A number of studies by the New Economics Foundation reveal that the wealthiest and most materialistic societies are not necessarily the happiest or most ecologically secure.[8] The Happy Planet Index (HPI) is a new metric measuring 'life satisfaction' multiplied by 'life expectancy' and divided by 'ecological footprint'. An HPI of 100 is best, 0 is worst; a reasonable ideal HPI is 83.5, the highest recorded was Vanuatu at 68.2 and lowest was Zimbabwe at 16.6. This model recognizes human reliance on nature. HPI is a measure of ecological efficiency delivering human well-being. Countries at the top of the list may surprise: first is Vanuatu, the pacific island state, second is Colombia and third is Costa Rica, all blessed with good ecological capacity

Table 7.1

The Happy Planet Index by the New Economics Foundation

Countries	Happy Planet Index
Top three countries	
1 Island state of Vanuatu, Pacific Ocean	68.2
2 Colombia	67.2
3 Costa Rica	66.0
Bottom three countries	
176 Burundi	19.0
177 Swaziland	18.4
178 Zimbabwe	16.6
G8 countries	
66 Italy	48.3
81 Germany	43.8
95 Japan	41.7
108 UK	40.3
111 Canada	39.8
129 France	36.4
150 US	28.8
Other high gross GDP countries	
31 China	56.0
62 India	48.7
63 Brazil	48.6

Source: Marks et al (2006)[9]

and populated with contented, long-lived peoples (Table 7.1). Bottom-ranking countries all come from Africa, a continent where even the top country only has an HPI of 57.9. Despite all their development and wealth, the G8 countries fall in the middle rankings *below* China, India and Brazil, countries with a high gross GDP, although low per capita GDP. Clearly material development and wealth do not necessarily equate with subjective notions of a good or better life. Significantly, the NEF reports also indicate that higher social capital tends to exist where life satisfaction is highest. Building social capital and improving human well-being are therefore two mutual ambitions for design activism. Figure 7.1 gives a schematic of the individual and sustainability dimensions of well-being that need to be balanced, as a means to consider these ambitions. This schematic also aims to reduce the distance between the designer as professional and the designer as citizen and consumer.

Bio-local and bio-regional

Climate change will drive a dramatic re-evaluation of local and regional biotic (living) assets because existing patterns of agriculture, water use, human habitation and biodiversity will change with rising global temperatures (see Figure 3.1).[10] Countries, regions and localities with a high ecological capacity per capita are going

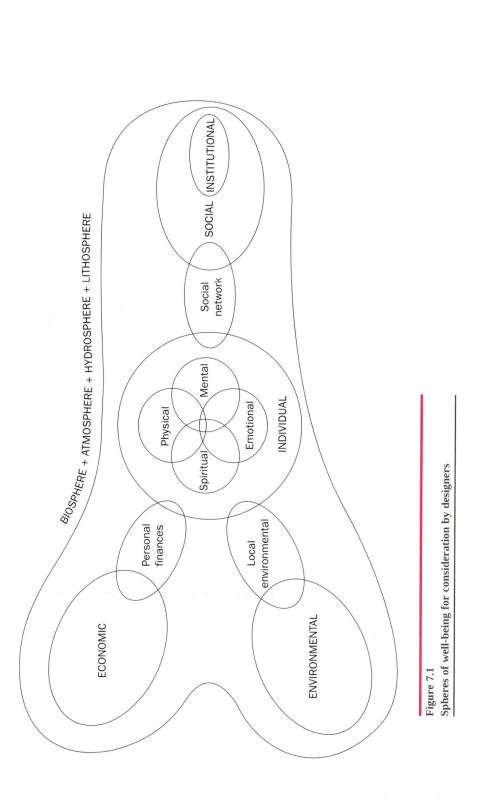

Figure 7.1
Spheres of well-being for consideration by designers

to fare better than those with a low ecological capacity per capita and a reliance on imports. Most countries will have to deeply consider their food, energy and water security in a more uncertain world. Designers like William McDonough are already helping the Chinese address these problems, with ambitious plans for urban rooftop farming.[11] There are also other sources of inspiration. There is a substantive model in Cuba's resilience and transition to a low-input oil economy caused by the 1960 US trade embargo and other embargoes from some members of the international community, deepened further with the demise of the Soviet bloc and communist era starting in the early 1980s. Cuba experienced radical shifts in land ownership, societal organization and application of permaculture design thinking (see p56) to reduce dependence on external synthetic inputs and by regenerating using nature's own ability to maintain levels of fertility. Cuba's approach recognizes a synergistic relationship with its bio-region. Bio-regionalism has also been applied to built environment projects such as Beddington Zero Emissions Development, (BedZED) near Croydon in the UK[12] and is finding new expressions in visions of productive green urban landscapes.[13] Applying co-design to re-examine local resources, ecological and social capacity, can only boost the existing localization movements that are already seeking transition to a more sustainable way of living, producing and consuming.

Emerging enterprise models

The 'credit crunch' emerged in summer 2007 in the US then quickly spread through the global economic systems. Within a year, institutions of the international banking system that have been around for 150 years or more faced severe difficulties, some like Lehman Brothers became bankrupt and ceased trading. Governments across the globe re-nationalized banks and building societies and central banks pumped in vast sums of money to stem the crisis.[14] The game has yet to play out, but this is the most stringent of warnings that the existing models of financial investment and borrowing do not guarantee future economic stability; nor are they promoting sustainability. The capitalized and borrowing structure of most organizations depends on these global financial systems, so there is a profound question mark over the future viability and stability of existing enterprises, both commercial and not-for-profit. Fortunately, there has been a growing interest by some European governments in new enterprise models with an ambition to grow human and social capital rather than just financial capital.[15] These models involve public–private partnerships, social enterprises and community interest companies. How does design work with and offer support to these emerging socially orientated enterprises, with the social entrepreneurs, while making sure that they tread lightly on environmental resources too? The application of co-design approaches offers a means of increasing participation in design processes (see pp147–160), so can potentially improve social networking, cohesion and capacity, in order to build resilience and enable future adaptation.

New ways of making and building

Just 3 per cent of social enterprises in the UK manufacture goods, the remainder provide services to specific target users/groups in the social sector and/or focus on environmental objectives. There is no reason why social enterprises cannot compete with commercial, privately owned enterprises to manufacture goods and deliver product-service systems. These social enterprises are already focused on the institutional, social and economic dimensions of the sustainability prism as part of their *raison d'être*, so are primed to choose some of the emergent markets, for example, the growing markets for better inclusive designs for elderly people in the North; new products, services and housing for the South; more products of sound ethical and environmental standards; and more products and services using local resources and labour.

There are myriad possibilities for distributed local manufacturing by joining up real local centres of production or by using digital networks to deliver replicable files for local rapid prototyping. Another option, again facilitated by the internet, is the retailing of downloadable digital designs to provide cutting patterns and instructions for making, or the sharing of designs with open source and Creative Commons licences. All these possibilities could herald a quiet revolution in production at a local level with new enterprises and/or by individual consumers using locally available materials, saving considerable transportation and other embodied energies associated with the present model of distant factories and extensive distribution chains.

Eco-efficient futures (slowing and powering down)

The design activists focusing on eco-efficiency will need to apply 'best practice' life cycle thinking, light-weighting and use of appropriate emergent technologies in order to deliver the Factor 4 to Factor 10 improvements in efficiency that will ensure sustainable consumption and production for future generations. Closing the loop at the end-of-life of products, by designing for assembly *and* disassembly, and applying the best eco-design strategies, needs to be combined with behavioural change to really deliver efficacy. So, design strategies to slow people down, to create more meaningful, but less energy intense, ways of meeting everyday needs and experiences are of great importance. As the slow movement gathers momentum,[16] design activists at SlowLab[17] are exploring and creating visions and experiences of 'positive slowness'. Perhaps the co-creative power of those who see the benefits of slowing down can encourage step-change solutions.

Regeneration and renewal

The Millennium Assessment Reports by the United Nations painted a pretty grim picture of the state of health of the global ecosystems that support all forms of life, including human.[18] With the global population set to increase by around 30 per cent in the next 40 years (from 6.7 billion at present to 8.9 billion by 2050)[19] the stresses and strains on these ecosystems look set to increase. Restoring the health of these ecosystems, and their capacity to absorb the waste and toxins that human activity generates, is an urgent priority. Cradle-to-cradle thinking, as espoused by William McDonough and Michael Braungart [20] is essential. A simple mantra to follow, established by Edwin Datchefski, is that all design should be 'cyclic, solar and safe'.[21] He later added 'efficient' and 'socially conscious' to this invocation. These are invaluable ways of helping reposition our thinking to help address how we use our ecological capacity per capita more wisely, but the question is how do we *improve* ecological capacity without risking reduced fertility or cataclysmic failure? Again, the lessons are in ecological design, biomimetic design and permaculture design. The design activist must aim for and encourage others to co-design robust ecosystems whatever the location, from urban city centre to suburb or remote rural setting.

Regeneration and renewal is also about restoring our fractured and unequal societies. This requires inclusion of a wider range of actors and stakeholders in the design *and* decision-making processes. Communities are creative if given the right encouragement and resources to prove it. Designers' potential to assist these communities in realizing new visions is considerable, but it needs bringing to life on the ground.

Yet another facet of regeneration and renewal is to care for and retrofit the existing built environment and infrastructure. It is all too easy to be a pioneer with new products, services and buildings but often the reality is that we just need to reconfigure what already exists. We need to re-evaluate what we have already got and add further value by design. Retrofitting buildings to reduce energy and water demand, to improve working and living conditions with restorative plants and mini-ecosystems, or better natural daylighting, are all valid tasks for the design activist in co-operation with the residents, workers, owners, utilities and other stakeholders.

Maverick, solo designer or co-designer?

Designers, like artists, are perceived by the public as possessing 'natural' creativity and the boundary between these two creative agencies is pretty blurred.[22] The public also struggles to really understand who or what designers are, with the exception of architects and graphic/industrial/interior designers.[23] In contrast, designers see themselves as distinct from artists as design is 'purposeful and tied by the boundaries of the client's brief', as well as being a creative activity. The vagueness with which the public perceive designers may be an advantage to the maverick, solo designer who wishes to gain the attention of the public by an act of design activism, since such an activity would be expected of artists. Of course, the maverick designer does not have to consider doing something in the public domain and many of the examples cited in Chapter 4 illustrate work aimed at quietly improving eco-efficiency or creating an artefact with potentiality to encourage positive behavioural change. Each designer may find some projects are more easily pursued solo, whereas others are better suited to more participatory, co-design modes of work. For designers that already hold an 'iconic' status in the profession, and with a wider public, they may bring effective leverage to solo maverick and participatory design projects.

Anticipatory Democracy and the 'MootSpace'

At the root of the concept of design activism is the philosophical and ethical position that design in the service of society has to embrace democracy. This contrasts with design in the service of a client where it has to embrace the client's contract and, but not always, the client's philosophy and ethics. Graphic designer Shawn Wolfe notes that 'whether you are the faithful consumer of cultural products or you're the instrument or mastermind of some faithless cultural production … you are involved and you're accountable for the part you play'.[24] If we are all involved then we should all be part of the decision-making processes, so we can equally share responsibility for the outcomes. Suzi Gablik, in her book *The Re-enchantment of Art*, 'calls for an end to the alienation of artists and aesthetics from social values in a new inter-relational, audience-oriented art'.[25] In the same way, design needs to enjoin with active citizens to co-create and co-design the new 'now', the counter-narrative that points to a new directionality, towards sustaining that which genuinely sustains.

Design activists can contribute to dialogic discourse about new social goals and, in doing so, the creation of new social values. To set out on this road is to quickly realize that design, especially when deploying co-design approaches, becomes a political and democratic act. As Alvin Toffler noted in his polemical book, *Future Shock*, in 1970, we need new forms of anticipatory democracy, 'We need to initiate, in short, a continuing plebiscite on the future'.[26] He called these 'social future assemblies' which would convene in each nation, city and neighbourhood 'charged with defining and assigning priorities to specific social goals'.[27] Today, we may add that the democracy in these assemblies should embrace all people in direct participation, as distinct from traditional representative democracies that tend to dominate models of contemporary politics. 'Participatory democracy' is seen by some as being in the domain of civil society and a community-based activity and is certainly a tenet of green politics.[28] These assemblies would also need to encourage deep democracy which 'suggests that all voices, states of awareness, and frameworks are important', and welcomes both central and marginalized voices.[29] Designers as facilitators and catalysts can use participatory design processes to achieve 'participatory' and 'deep' forms of democracy. These contemporary assemblies would focus on changing 'now', with a view to directing sustainable futures. In doing so they would 'co-future', give new directionality to the future.

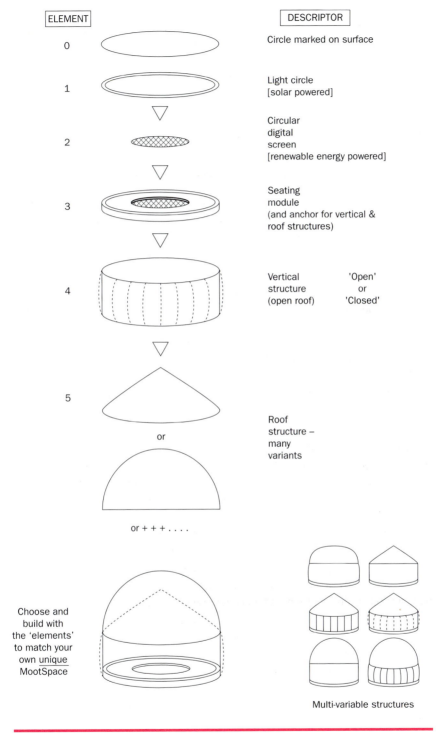

ELEMENT

DESCRIPTOR

0 — Circle marked on surface

1 — Light circle
[solar powered]

2 — Circular
digital
screen
[renewable energy powered]

3 — Seating
module
(and anchor for vertical &
roof structures)

4 — Vertical   'Open'
structure   or
(open roof)   'Closed'

5 — Roof
structure –
many
variants

or

or + + + ...

Choose and
build with
the 'elements'
to match your
own unique
MootSpace

Multi-variable structures

Figure 7.2
MootSpace – a modular build environment for design democracy

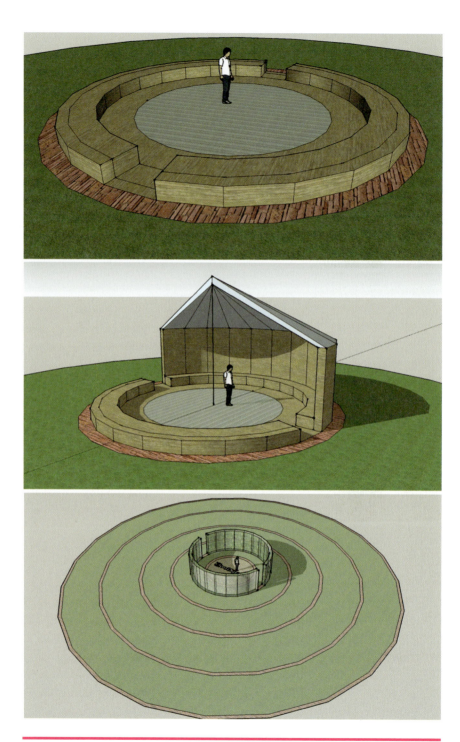

Figure 7.3
MootSpace examples

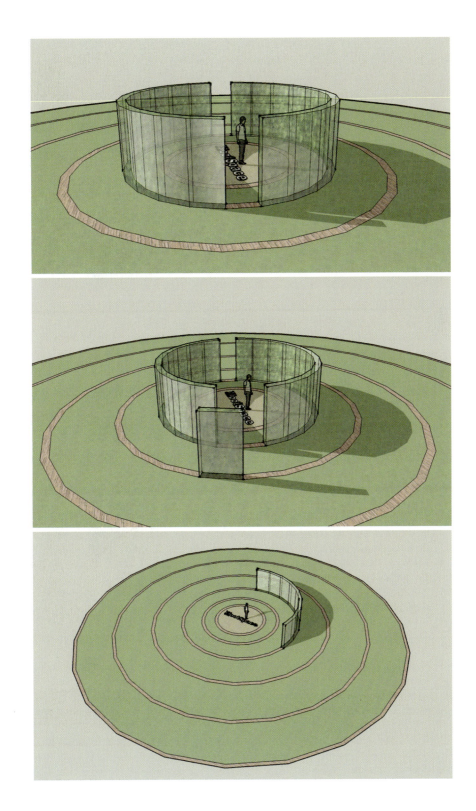

Do these participatory democracy assemblies or something similar already exist? Yes, in the living 'marae' of the Maori in New Zealand, which are also found across Pacific island cultures including the Cook Islands, Tonga, Samoa and Hawaii.[30] There are also historical examples, such as the secular meeting houses and moot halls of Europe, whose origin dates back to the 9th century Anglo-Saxon system of administration called 'hundreds' when meetings would be held outdoors at designated spaces, mounds or hills.[31] Taking these living and past traditions suggests the notion of a new democratic space for design. Let's give it the designation 'MootSpace' where every citizen (and citizen designer) knows their voice will be heard.

Where would these MootSpaces be? Wherever they are needed. They can be ephemeral, temporarily marked or erected – a chalk circle in the city square, a mown circle of grass on the village green, or a mark in the sand on a beach. The MootSpace could occupy an existing building or it can be a new modular structure configurable to suit the needs of the local group, community and environs (Figure 7.2), one that can be assembled locally, perhaps using local materials in combination with rentable modular units. Whatever form the MootSpace takes (Figure 7.3), it should be a space that the group or community 'owns', one where they can comfortably discourse and co-design their 'now' and their future. Perhaps this is one arena where design activism will gather momentum to deliver participatory democracy, human flourishing and ecosystem renewal.

Notes

1 Mau, B. (2003) *Massive Change*, Phaidon, London, p16.
2 Fry, T. (2008) *Design Futuring: Sustainability, Ethics and New Practice*, Berg Publishers, Oxford.
3 See Wikipedia (2008) 'Uneconomic growth', http://en.wikipedia.org/wiki/Uneconomic_growth, and Herman Daly's 1999 lecture on the topic at www.feasta.org/documents/feastareview/daly1.pdf
4 De Long, D. G. (1995) *The Architecture of Bruce Goff, 1904–1982: Design for the Continuous Present*, Prestel Verlag, Munich.
5 Brand, S. (1999) *The Clock of the Long Now: Time and Responsibility*, Phoenix/Orion Books, London, p133.
6 Brown, T. (2008) 'Design thinking', *Harvard Business Review*, June, pp84–92.
7 Changing the Change, 2008, http://emma.polimi.it/emma/showEvent.do?page=645&idEvent=23; the DEEDS project, 2008, www.deedsproject.org
8 Marks, N., Abdallah, S., Simms, A. and Thompson, S. (2006) *The Unhappy Planet Index*, edited by Mary Murphy, New Economics Foundation (NEF), London, available at www.neweconomics.org/gen/uploads/dl44k145g5scuy453044gqbu11072006194758.pdf, accessed September 2008
9 Ibid.
10 IPCC (2007) *Climate Change 2007: Synthesis Report. Contribution of Working Groups I, II and III to the Fourth Assessment*, Report of the Intergovernmental Panel on Climate

Change (edited by Pachauri, R. K and Reisinger, A., Core Writing Team); Lynas, M, (2008) *Six Degrees: Our Future on a Hotter Planet*, Harper Perennial, London.

11 Green Roofs, 2008, www.greenroofs.com/projects/pview.php?id=524; see also William McDonough + Partners, www.mcdonoughpartners.com/

12 Wikipedia (2008) 'BedZED', http://en.wikipedia.org/wiki/BedZED

13 Viljoen, A. (2005) *Continuous Productive Urban Landscapes: Designing Urban Agriculture for Sustainable Cities*, Architectural Press, London.

14 Wikipedia (2008) 'Credit crunch', http://en.wikipedia.org/wiki/Credit_Crunch

15 See for example, the UK government's action plan for social enterprise, www.cabinetoffice.gov.uk/third_sector/social_enterprise/action_plan.aspx

16 The Slow Planet, www.slowplanet.com/

17 SlowLab, www.slowlab.net

18 Millennium Ecosystem Assessments, www.millenniumassessment.org/en/index.aspx

19 UN, 2004, www.un.org/esa/population/publications/sixbillion/sixbilpart1.pdf

20 McDonough, W. and Braungart, M. (2002) *Cradle to Cradle*, North Point Press, New York.

21 Datchefski, E. (2001) *The Total Beauty of Sustainable Products*, RotoVision, Crans-Près-Céligny.

22 Smith, G. and Whitfield, T. W. A. (2005a) 'Profiling the designer: A cognitive perspective', *The Design Journal*, vol 8, no 2, pp3–14.

23 Smith, G. and Whitfield, T. W. A. (2005b) 'The professional status of designers: A national survey of how designers are perceived', *The Design Journal*, vol 8, no 1, pp52–60.

24 Wolfe quoted in Heller, S. (2003) 'Brand name dropper', Steven Heller interviews Shawn Wolfe in Heller, S. and Vienne, V. (eds) *Citizen Designer: Perspectives on Design Responsibility*, Allworth Press, New York, p48.

25 Gablik quoted in McCoy, K. (2003) 'Good citizenship: Design as a social and political force', in Heller, S. and Vienne, V. (eds) *Citizen Designer: Perspectives on Design Responsibility*, Allworth Press, New York, p6.

26 Toffler, A. (1971) *Future Shock*, Pan Books, London, p431.

27 Ibid. p432.

28 Wikipedia (2008) 'Participatory democracy', http://en.wikipedia.org/wiki/Participatory_democracy

29 Wikipedia (2008) 'Deep democracy', http://en.wikipedia.org/wiki/Deep_democracy

30 Wikipedia (2008) 'Marae', http://en.wikipedia.org/wiki/Marae

31 Wikipedia (2008) 'Moot hall', http://en.wikipedia.org/wiki/Moot_hall

Key Design Movements and Groups, 1850–2000: Activist, but Where, and for Whom or What?

British Arts and Crafts (A&C)

Dates: 1850–1914

Motives and intentions: Opposed industrial mass production in favour of the 'useful and beautiful'

Form-giving: Natural ornamentation, clear simple, structured forms, handcrafted with vernacular influences generating simplicity and utility

Target audiences: Art Academies and the Art and Craft Guilds, including the Arts and Crafts Exhibition Society

Beneficiaries: Emergent design culture – Art and Craft Guilds, the emerging Deutscher (German) Werkbund and Art Nouveau movements, bourgeois middle-class socialists?

Sustainability elements:

Economic: Outputs from the A&C movement remained the preserve of the better off, not the masses

Ecological: Anti-industrial pollution

Social: Advocate better working conditions in factory production; artefacts with functionality, usefulness and beauty to improve life and encourage positive social change; believed in the social importance of craft and community

Institutional: Progression of the Art & Craft Guilds but failed in the social experiment to return to handicraft production

Art Nouveau

Dates: 1895–1910

Motives and intentions: Rejected 'historicism' and poor quality industrial production; refined early Arts & Craft thinking for an artistic reformation of life from objects to architecture; heavily influenced by scientific discoveries about natural world

Form-giving: Stylized but organic natural or geometric forms – a style adopted by Belgium, France, Germany (Jugendstil), Austria (Sezesionstil), Italy (Stile Liberty), Spain (Modernista) and so regarded as the first international style

Target audiences: The old Art Academies
Beneficiaries: The rise of individual artists designing everything from glassware to furniture, interiors and complete buildings
Sustainability elements:
Economic: Brought new economic life to ceramics, glassware, furniture and architectur
Institutional: Helped promote individuals as new artists as institutions – the first auteur designers?

Vienna Workshop to Vienna Modern
(Koloman Moser and Josef Hoffman to Adolf Loos)

Dates: 1903–1920s
Motives and intentions: Reduction of décor to rejection of ornamentation and drawn to early geometric abstraction
Form-giving: Increasingly 'modern' pared down, objective designs, with functional styling
Target audiences: Rejection of Jugendstil and, ornamentation, especially by Loos
Beneficiaries: Stimulus for the German Werkbund and Bauhaus movements
Sustainability elements:
Institutional: Helped emerging institutions towards 'modern' industrial design and production

Deutscher Werkbund

Dates: 1907–1935 and 1945–present
Motives and intentions: Seeking a new path towards modern industrial design through the adoption of more formal approaches to function
Form-giving: Early functionalism, standardized furniture and household objects
Target audiences: Reform of industry and its methods of production – blending art, industry and handicrafts – towards mass production
Beneficiaries: Industry, the working class; the emergence of full-blown Functionalism and the Modern Movement
Sustainability elements:
Economic: The creation of inexpensive objects for the working class; utilitarian production methods realized while giving affordable quality by designers such as Richard Riemerschmid, Peter Behrens and Josef Maria Olbrich
Social: Improving people's lives through improved household objects and furniture and living conditions; improved working conditions in factories, e.g. those designed by Walter Gropius and Peter Behrens
Institutional: Internal institutional tussle between the pro-standardization and industrialization advocates and the pro-individualization, craftsmanship advocates

Futurism

Dates: 1909–1917

Motives and intentions: Adulation of technology, speed and abstraction of form, all in the name of progress

Form-giving: Forms suggested the dynamism of the 'machine', separated from nature and glorifying the city; expressive rather than conventional typographic designs

Target audiences: Other artists, designers and architects of the era who affirmed ideas of the Age of the Machine

Beneficiaries: All future design movements allied to the notion of technology for progress

Sustainability elements:

Social: Sought order through extreme radicalism and to upset the existing bourgeois culture

Constructivism

Dates: 1917–1935

Motives and intentions: Rejection of art and design's traditional role of representation; a new culture of materials

Form-giving: Dynamic aesthetic of the Age of the Machine; utopian architecture and planning; anti-emotional, anti-personal; suprematists' motifs – dynamic and modern

Target audiences: In service to a 'new society'; propaganda for Soviet government; mass production; introduction of artistic aesthetic in production

Beneficiaries: Soviet mass-produced goods manufacturers

Sustainability elements:

Social: Aimed at more democratic production and distribution of goods by utilitarian 'production art' and architecture – in reality much of the output of the Constructivists was limited to exhibitions

De Stijl

Dates: 1917–1931

Motives and intentions: Absolute abstraction – form, surface and colour; a new aesthetic purity and philosophy in art and design

Form-giving: Search for a functional aesthetic – simplified geometric form; limited colour palette

Target audiences: Modernization of technical industrial production; radical change to art and design education

Beneficiaries: All future design movements, especially the Bauhaus and early Modern Movement

Bauhaus

Dates: 1919–1933

Motives and intentions: A new educational structure to provide artistic advisory services to industry, trade and craft; to create a foundation for Modernism and Functionalism

Form-giving: Search for a functional aesthetic; unornamented forms of the modern style

Target audiences: Educational establishments of the day in the 'creative arts'; industry – from ceramics, metalwork, furniture, lighting to architecture

Beneficiaries: The students and teachers at the Bauhaus; the lucky few that lived in the new affordable housing created by the Bauhaus; German industry in general; introduction of the concept of the 'white-collar' worker; all subsequent design movements and design education as the Bauhaus remains influential to the Modern Movement today

Sustainability elements:

Social: 1919–1925 'Weimar' Bauhaus (director is Walter Gropius) – 'making' is an important social, symbolic and intellectual endeavour; design in the service of society. 1926–1932 Dessau Bauhaus (directors included Gropius, Hannes Meyer, Mies van der Rohe. Meyer was a Communist and believed in creating practical, affordable products for working class consumers. Inexpensive housing, and 'apartment for minimum living standards' for the masses was a key objective under Ernst May and architect Ferdinand Kramer; under Hannes Meyer. Weissenhof Settlement in Stuttgart 1927 – Gropius, Mies van der Rohe, Jacobus JP Oud and Le Corbusier

Institutional: Challenged the social and political structures of industry and kept 'affordability' at the forefront of the debate – this was perhaps most dramatically hijacked by the emerging fascist regime with the Volksempfänger 'People's Radio' in 1928 and later the Volkswagen car in 1938

International Style

Dates: 1920–1980

Motives and intentions: Creation of an international language of form in architecture and design evolved directly from the Bauhaus and the Modernists such as Le Corbusier, JJP Oud, Walter Gropius and Ludwig Mies van der Rohe

Form-giving: Clarity of design, free of decoration and an emphasis on volume not mass; rationality and a Functionalist aesthetic that gave voice to a universal style able to transcend national (and cultural) boundaries

Target audiences: An emerging design cognoscenti and rich clients, especially the early transnational companies

Beneficiaries: Transnational companies and a few 'iconic' designers that worked in a trans-cultural environment opening the way for manufacturers looking for global solutions

Sustainability elements:

Economic: Transnational companies were able to create a recognizable style, a brand, that had international value

Institutional: Targeting of corporations as a style statement

Art Deco

Dates: 1920–1939

Motives and intentions: Reaction to the Functionalism of the German Werkbund – introduction of luxurious ornamentation and decoration from exotic sources

Form-giving: Luxury crafted artefacts and deliberate stylistic elements of decorative value taken up by industry to 'sell a lifestyle'

Target audiences: The wealthy who could afford Art Deco 'one-offs'; industry who found a new aesthetic to package their wares

Beneficiaries: Corporations who adopted the 'style' as a symbol of luxury and power; raised the aesthetic sensibility of the mass consumer; Hollywood glamour

Sustainability elements:

Economic: Industrial manufacturing of consumer 'style'

Social: Affordable representation of luxury – selling the idea of well-being by consumption;

Institutional: Corporations' realization of the power of design to brand products and the company

Streamlining

Dates: 1930–1950

Motives and intentions: A methodology of aerodynamic design later subverted to styling as 'progress' to facilitate mass consumption

Form-giving: Function and technology discreetly hidden by streamlined, 'teardrop' and biomorphic forms

Target audiences: The mass consumer – buying their way out of the Great Depression in the US

Beneficiaries: The manufacturing industry

Sustainability elements:

Economic: Product obsolescence by restyling and shortening the 'product life cycle' enabled industry to sell new generations of products

Organic Design

Dates: 1930–1960 and 1990–present

Motives and intentions: Contemporary art of 1940s and 1950s expressing ideas of biomorphic, organic forms were introduced into the design world with a holistic approach – to extend the choice for the consumer by reinterpreting spatial and form arrangements

Form-giving: Organic, fluid, anthropomorphic forms where the overall effect is greater than the sum of its parts, capturing the spirit of nature

Target audiences: A growing design cognoscenti willing to acquire designs to differentiate status

Beneficiaries: Organic popular forms of late 1960s designs and 1990s onwards with advent of computer-aided design, CAD; middle- to high-end furniture and lighting manufacturers

Sustainability elements:

Economic: Specialist sectors of the manufacturing industry, especially furniture

Ecological: The context of the surrounding environment was integrated into design considerations

Social: Desire to connect users with the functional, ergonomic, intellectual and emotional dimensions of the artefacts, often through choice of natural materials, to enhance quality of life

Post-War: Utility Design and Good Design

Dates: 1945–1958

Motives and intentions: A phenomenon linked to the establishment of the UK's Council for Industrial Design (later the Design Council) to promote good design values

Form-giving: A combination of Functionalism, Rationalism of production, light-weighting and simplicity – endorsed by the Good Design label, a mark of quality

Target audiences: British industry and the emerging consumers

Beneficiaries: Middle and lower income consumers; some manufacturers; Good Design was similar to and influenced 'Good Form' in Germany

Sustainability elements:

Economic: Specialist sectors of the manufacturing industry, especially furniture

Social: Affordable, durable and reliable design for the masses

Post-War: Good Form and Bel Design

Dates: 1945–1958

Motives and intentions: Introduction of rationalization in the mass production of consumer electronic/electrical goods, furniture and lighting

Form-giving: Combining advances in manufacturing technologies and materials (especially plastics) with new functional aesthetics

Target audiences: German and Italian manufacturing industries; European consumers

Beneficiaries: European manufacturing and consumers

Sustainability elements:

Economic: Growth and differentiation of manufacturing industries in Europe

Social: Increased consumer choice

Pop Design

Dates: 1958–1972

Motives and intentions: Rejection and critique of post-war Functionalism and Modernism by virulent and pluralistic counterculture initiatives; drawing from a palette of 'low art' contemporary life; initially socially conscious later became its own consumerist fiesta of everyday products

Form-giving: Fusion of pop and commercial art, fashion and experimental, exotic forms using a new generation of plastics, often eliciting an ephemeral or gimmicky ethos

Target audiences: New visions of mass consumption via counterculture

Beneficiaries: Mass manufacturers, retailers and consumers; contributed to early ideas of pluralism so vital to the emergence of Postmodernism

Sustainability elements:

Economic: Manufacturing and retailing industries

Social: Initially a flourishing of inexpensive consumer choice replaced by mass production of cheap, poor quality products

Anti-Design

Dates: 1968–1978

Motives and intentions: Italian-led counterculture movement with many Radical design groups (see below) with critical philosophical, political and social consciousness; rejection of 'Bel design' and its use as a status symbol and an attempt to revalidate individual creative expression

Form-giving: Disruption of existing form patterns by exaggeration of size, abstraction of shape, or other means influenced by Surrealism

Target audiences: The design and political 'establishment'; art and design educational institutions

Beneficiaries: Early Postmodernists; specialist manufacturing companies in Italy; individual designers and certain design groups; the root of the 'designer' label cachet

Sustainability elements:

Social: Queried the relationship between artefacts and human existence; anti-consumerist position

Radical Design Groups

Dates: 1968–1978

Motives and intentions: A more theoretical, radicalized and experimental example of Anti-design promoted by groups such as Archizoom, Superstudio, UFO, Gruppo Strum and Global Tools. Focus on utopian projects to reposition the meaning of Modernism – questioned the validity of Rationalism, advanced technology and consumerism

Form-giving: Eclectic, experimental, 'provocative projections', borrowing from everything from Pop design to the classics and Arte Povera

Target audiences: Design and consumer culture

Beneficiaries: The proto-Postmodernists

Sustainability elements:

Social: Examined user interaction and participation through 'happenings' and installations in an attempt to bring some spontaneity back into consumer–product relationships

Institutional: Queried the purpose of design in contemporary culture within design and cultural institutions

Alternative Design

Dates: 1970–1980?

Motives and intentions: Social critique of design by a range of individual designers and groups promoting ideas of appropriate technology, recycling, permaculture design and questioning the implicit rationale of consumerism

Form-giving: Experimental and recycling aesthetic – overt use of materials obviously reused or recycled; practical systems drive aesthetic considerations

Target audiences: Consumer, manufacturing and design culture

Beneficiaries: The designers and design groups themselves; mainstream social and commercial life little affected

Sustainability elements:

Ecological: Recycling, redesign, alternative manufacturing methods

Design for Need

Dates: 1965–1976

Motives and intentions: Social, economic and ecological critique of design; early critique of globalization

Form-giving: Alternative and appropriate technology; light-weighting; efficient resource use; form for 'well-being'; ergonomics that were inclusive and universal access

Target audiences: Design culture and disadvantaged groups

Beneficiaries: Certain disadvantaged sectors of society – people with disabilities; Postmodern ecologists; and much later 'eco-design'

Sustainability elements:

Economic: Suggested new models of manufacturing

Ecological: Localization, use of local materials

Social: Improvements in quality of life for disadvantaged sectors of society; refocusing from 'form' to 'content'

Institutional: Suggested significant institutional change was needed in design education, practice and policy development

Postmodern Ecological Design

Dates: 1969–present
Motives and intentions: Critique of design that does not consider ecological factors or limitations or the strength of local cultural and social knowledge; early critique of globalization
Form-giving: Form strongly influenced by site, locality, local culture
Target audiences: Design culture
Beneficiaries: Other Postmodern ecologists and a raising of the general consciousness of design culture to environmental issues
Sustainability elements:
Ecological: Site and bio-regional considerations balanced with global impacts
Social: Welfare and well-being of users

Postmodernism
(Postmodern Design)

Dates: Started 1960s, emerged mid-1970s and continues to the present day
Motives and intentions: Egoistic, self-interested and elitist control of 'good form' and Functionalism, as represented in late 20th century Modernism, rejected by those who saw a 'classless' society with pluralistic tastes; influenced by the emerging field of semiotics – the study of signs and symbols in cultural communication
Form-giving: Pluralism – any form you want is OK; borrow from any historical, traditional or contemporary source and hybridize new forms to create ambiguity and social friction, e.g. rich ornamentation with minimalist forms; explosion of new electronics and ICT offered new options for form-giving; forms speak to a globalizing world economy
Target audiences: Design and mass consumer culture; the design cognoscenti; design-led manufacturers
Beneficiaries: Design and mass consumer culture; manufacturing industries for consumer markets who exploited the aesthetics of Postmodernism to sell 'status' – especially to the elite who could afford them. Early Postmodernists, e.g. Studio Alchimia, Italy, tried to genuinely forge a new, more meaningful, relationship between people and products thereby humanizing design's impacts; however, their outputs remained the preserve of the elite and intellectual design world
Sustainability elements:
Institutional: Triumph of capitalism over the social ideology of the Modern Movement signalling another surge in mass consumption fuelled by credit borrowing

New Design

Dates: 1980–1990?

Motives and intentions: Celebration of diverse metropolitan life, one-offs to small batch production to remain independent of industry

Form-giving: Eclectic, searching for new subverted forms of Functionalism

Target audiences: Design culture and design cognoscenti and design-led manufacturers

Beneficiaries: Some emerging 'iconic' designers, e.g. Starck, Arad

Sustainability elements:

Ecological: Promotion of the use of recycled, reused and durable materials by some designers

High-Tech Design

Dates: 1972–1985 and 1995–present

Motives and intentions: Celebration of the progress of science and technology

Form-giving: Stylistic convergence to show the technology 'on view' in everything from electronic products to buildings driven by miniaturization, computerization and high-tech materials

Target audiences: Industry and consumer culture

Beneficiaries: Technology-led companies

Sustainability elements:

Economic: Growth of electronic and eco-tech manufacturers

Ecological: Early explorations in renewable power for public and consumer markets

Design for the Environment

Dates: 1986–present

Motives and intentions: Design awakens to its responsibilities and duty of care to the environment

Form-giving: Embeds eco-efficient feature through high-tech solutions and/or light-weighting, use of recycled or recyclable materials

Target audiences: Industry and design culture

Beneficiaries: Helping industry meet increasing regulatory pressures and position 'green marketed' products

Sustainability elements:

Economic: Economic gains through being eco-efficient

Ecological: Reduction of impacts on the environment

Institutional: Encouraging shift to more responsible manufacturing and design practices

Sources

Fiell, C. and Fiell, T. (1999) *Design of the 20th Century*, Taschen, Köln

Hauffe, T. (1998) *Design: A Concise History*, Lawrence King, London

Jencks, C. and Kropf, K. (eds) (1997) *Theories and Manifestoes of Contemporary Architecture*, Wiley-Academy, Chichester

Starke, P. (1987) *Design in Context*, Guild Publishing, London

The Millennium Development Goals, published by the United Nations (2000): Goals, Targets and Indicators

Goal 1: Eradicate extreme poverty and hunger

Indicators

Target 1a: Reduce by half the proportion of people living on less than a dollar a day

1.1 Proportion of population below $1 (PPP) per day

1.2 Poverty gap ratio

1.3 Share of poorest quintile in national consumption

Target 1b: Achieve full and productive employment and decent work for all, including women and young people

1.4 Growth rate of GDP per person employed

1.5 Employment-to-population ratio

1.6 Proportion of employed people living below $1 (PPP) per day

1.7 Proportion of own-account and contributing family workers in total employment

Target 1c: Reduce by half the proportion of people who suffer from hunger

1.8 Prevalence of underweight children under five years of age

1.9 Proportion of population below minimum level of dietary energy consumption

Goal 2: Achieve universal primary education

Indicators

Target 2a: Ensure that all boys and girls complete a full course of primary schooling

2.1 Net enrolment ratio in primary education

2.2 Proportion of pupils starting grade 1 who reach last grade of primary

2.3 Literacy rate of 15–24 year-olds, women and men

Goal 3: Promote gender equality and empower women

Indicators

Target 3a: Eliminate gender disparity in primary and secondary education preferably by 2005, and at all levels by 2015

3.1 Ratios of girls to boys in primary, secondary and tertiary education

3.2 Share of women in wage employment in the non-agricultural sector

3.3 Proportion of seats held by women in national parliament

Goal 4: Reduce child mortality

Indicators

Target 4a: Reduce by two-thirds the mortality rate among children under five

4.1 Under-five mortality rate

4.2 Infant mortality rate

4.3 Proportion of 1 year-old children immunized against measles

Goal 5: Improve maternal health

Indicators

Target 5a: Reduce by three-quarters the maternal mortality ratio

5.1 Maternal mortality ratio

5.2 Proportion of births attended by skilled health personnel

Target 5b: Achieve, by 2015, universal access to reproductive health

5.3 Contraceptive prevalence rate

5.4 Adolescent birth rate

5.5 Antenatal care coverage (at least one visit and at least four visits)

5.6 Unmet need for family planning

Goal 6: Combat HIV/AIDS, malaria and other diseases

Indicators

Target 6a: Halt and begin to reverse the spread of HIV/AIDS

6.1 HIV prevalence among population aged 15–24 years

6.2 Condom use at last high-risk sex

6.3 Proportion of population aged 15–24 years with comprehensive correct knowledge of HIV/AIDS

6.4 Ratio of school attendance of orphans to school attendance of non-orphans aged 10–14 years

Target 6b: Achieve, by 2010, universal access to treatment for HIV/AIDS for all those who need it
6.5 Proportion of population with advanced HIV infection with access to anti-retroviral drugs

Target 6c: Halt and begin to reverse the incidence of malaria and other major diseases
6.6 Incidence and death rates associated with malaria
6.7 Proportion of children under five sleeping under insecticide-treated bednets
6.8 Proportion of children under five with fever who are treated with appropriate anti-malarial drugs
6.9 Incidence, prevalence and death rates associated with tuberculosis
6.10 Proportion of tuberculosis cases detected and cured under directly observed treatment short course

Goal 7: Ensure environmental sustainability

Indicators

Target 7a: Integrate the principles of sustainable development into country policies and programmes; reverse loss of environmental resources

Target 7b: Reduce biodiversity loss, achieving, by 2010, a significant reduction in the rate of loss
7.1 Proportion of land area covered by forest
7.2 CO_2 emissions, total, per capita and per $1 GDP (PPP)
7.3 Consumption of ozone-depleting substances
7.4 Proportion of fish stocks within safe biological limits
7.5 Proportion of total water resources used
7.6 Proportion of terrestrial and marine areas protected
7.7 Proportion of species threatened with extinction

Target 7c: Reduce by half the proportion of people without sustainable access to safe drinking water
7.8 Proportion of population using an improved drinking water source
7.9 Proportion of population using an improved sanitation facility

Target 7d: Achieve significant improvement in lives of at least 100 million slum dwellers, by 2020
7.10 Proportion of urban population living in slums

Goal 8: Develop a global partnership for development

Indicators

Target 8a: Develop further an open, rule-based, predictable, non-discriminatory trading and financial system
Includes a commitment to good governance, development and poverty reduction – both nationally and internationally

Target 8b: Address the special needs of the least developed countries
Includes: tariff and quota free access for the least developed countries' exports; enhanced programme of debt relief for heavily indebted poor countries (HIPC) and cancellation of official bilateral debt; and more generous ODA for countries committed to poverty reduction

Target 8c: Address the special needs of landlocked developing countries and small island developing states (through the Programme of Action for the Sustainable Development of Small Island Developing States and the outcome of the 22nd special session of the General Assembly)

Target 8d: Deal comprehensively with the debt problems of developing countries through national and international measures in order to make debt sustainable in the long term
Some of the indicators listed below are monitored separately for the least developed countries (LDCs), Africa, landlocked developing countries and small island developing states.

Official development assistance (ODA)
8.1 Net ODA, total and to the least developed countries, as percentage of OECD/DAC donors' gross national income
8.2 Proportion of total bilateral, sector-allocable ODA of OECD/DAC donors to basic social services (basic education, primary health care, nutrition, safe water and sanitation)
8.3 Proportion of bilateral official development assistance of OECD/DAC donors that is untied
8.4 ODA received in landlocked developing countries as a proportion of their gross national incomes
8.5 ODA received in small island developing states as a proportion of their gross national incomes

Market access

8.6 Proportion of total developed country imports (by value and excluding arms) from developing countries and least developed countries, admitted free of duty

8.7 Average tariffs imposed by developed countries on agricultural products and textiles and clothing from developing countries

8.8 Agricultural support estimate for OECD countries as a percentage of their gross domestic product

8.9 Proportion of ODA provided to help build trade capacity

Debt sustainability

8.10 Total number of countries that have reached their HIPC decision points and number that have reached their HIPC completion points (cumulative)

8.11 Debt relief committed under HIPC and Multilateral Debt Relief Initiative (MDRI) Initiatives

8.12 Debt service as a percentage of exports of goods and services

Target 8e: In cooperation with pharmaceutical companies, provide access to affordable essential drugs in developing countries

8.13 Proportion of population with access to affordable essential drugs on a sustainable basis

Target 8f: In cooperation with the private sector, make available the benefits of new technologies, especially information and communications

8.14 Telephone lines per 100 population

8.15 Cellular subscribers per 100 population

8.16 Internet users per 100 population

Metadesign Tools Emerging from the Attainable Utopias Project

21 Metadesign Tools

The following tools were chosen from more than 90 that we developed between January 2005 and September 2008 as part of a research project funded by the Arts and Humanities Research Council (AHRC) and based at Goldsmiths, University of London. The tools are intended to operate as an integrated set of methods and techniques that could help society to become more ecological in its ways. This is not a simple task. The discourse of 'sustainability' emerged from an industrial mindset that is mechanistic rather than ecological. This is unfortunate, because it also informs some of the specialist training given to designers. The separation between specialist design practices is convenient for those who market specific goods and services within a consumption-driven economy. Sadly, it renders it virtually impossible for individual designers to change the fundamental tenets of how we live. In our view, rather than improve efficiencies or reduce waste at specific points within the whole system, designers must now find ways to harmonize many apparently incommensurate processes at the same time. In order to do so, they need to upgrade design to work at a higher level, i.e. as 'metadesign'. Here, by 'metadesign' we refer to processes that are still under development. In comparison with traditional specialist design practices – or even with a more 'strategic design' – metadesign is intended to be more flexible, self-reflexive and comprehensive. This is not just a quantitative difference. Where design characteristically prefigures a desired future state, its consensual (therefore non-hierarchical) nature means it must operate as an adaptive 'seeding process' that establishes the conditions for unforeseen opportunities to emerge. Its main task is therefore to orchestrate many levels of synergy, so that human society causes less damage, while proliferating increasing levels of wisdom and fun.

Again, this is not a trivial task. Although many synergies are already recognizable at different scales or orders of existence they may transcend familiar disciplinary boundaries. Where some work at the physical, microscopic level – such as in metallurgy or biochemistry – others may operate at the macroscopic level – say, at the social or cultural level. There are probably countless numbers of other synergies that need to be mapped and understood. However, unless they are joined together appropriately and effectively they may clash or even cancel one another out.

What this means is that the designer's task is far too complex to be undertaken by individual designers. On the other hand it will require new team skills that reconcile intellectual, emotional, intuitive and procedural faculties. This is a key aspect of synergy because it influences many other modes of synergy. All of the following 21 tools are designed to support synergistic, collaborative processes. However, optimizing teamwork is an art, not a science. Our 21 team-tools should not, therefore, be seen as autonomous recipes that guarantee instant success. While they have all been tested with design teams, some may require more special expertise, training, sensitivity and creative insight than others.

1 The Dream Exchange

Our beliefs are always hindered by our assumptions. This tool encourages participants to 'think beyond the possible'.

2 Team Roles and Action Types

Education tends to encourage individual development. This tool helps teams to find and orchestrate their complementary strengths.

3 Casting for Team Members

Team members relate in many ways – skills, emotions, personalities, seniority, etc. This tool helps to balance these factors within the recruitment process.

4 Cultural Props

Designers relate to objects and 'things'. By playing with personally meaningful 'props', colleagues quickly develop good interpersonal relations.

5 The 'I-to-We' Cycle

The balance of self-awareness and selflessness is important to team-play. This tool helps participants to monitor and orchestrate their shifts from one state to the other.

6 Cross-championing

Competitiveness is endemic in many corporate cultures. Asking players to empathize with colleagues can boost confidence and optimize a team's potential.

7 Building Team Identities

New teams sometimes take time to 'bond'. Getting the team to choose values offered by individual members helps it to define itself quickly.

8 The Team Turns Inside-Out

Concentrated teamwork can lead to collective myopia. Asking individual members (one by one) to observe the others 'from the outside' helps the team to remain self-reflexive.

9 Mapping Team Evolution

Teams do not always have a clear model of their own evolution. This eightfold template of suggested values enables the team to monitor its own development.

10 Synergy Mapping

Synergy is not always expected or noticed. This chart of values helps teams to document whether participation is as effective as it could be.

11 Mapping Role and Scale

Agreed values may not always stay within their expected position or scale. This tool enables teams to map the dimensions and relational position of each agent.

12 Mapping Relations in Systems

In a given system we seldom consider all the possible relations between all of the parts. This tool helps team players to notice many otherwise hidden possibilities.

13 Mapping the Equilibrium in Systems

Mapping the salient components and their relations may not be sufficient. This tool helps teams to log the directional effects of dynamic relations between agents.

14 Collective Storytelling

Narrative can be a useful vehicle for enriching the shared understanding within a team. This tool offers guidelines for making this process work effectively.

15 Metaphors Be With You

Teams of designers sometimes become limited by the peculiarities of specific metaphors. This tool helps teams to 'steer' decision-making away from the conventions of a given language.

16 Using Bisociation in Preference to Conflict

In a culture of competition it seems logical to use conflict as a way to find preferred solutions. This tool uses differences of view to locate unexpected opportunities.

17 4-Way Thinking

The human mind is not very good at conceiving highly complex, interdependent situations. This tool offers a simple, multi-purpose topology (the tetrahedron) that can be used to address this problem.

18 4-Way Innovation

Sometimes, we need single artefacts or propositions that satisfy many requirements at once. This template for manifold innovation uses the tetrahedron to offer sufficient complexity.

19 4-Way Ethics

Ethical systems tend to reduce the number of relations that pertain to the designer's task. The tetrahedron is used to offer a simple, shareable format that makes relational ethics easy to apply.

20 Win–Win–Win–Win

The idea of 'environmental sustainability' is usually depicted as a 'lose–win' offer. This tool maps a number of abundances in a way that can be clustered and named as a unified (positive) outcome.

21 Team Diagnosis

It is hard to maintain the positive spirits of a non-hierarchical team, indefinitely. Used with caution and some training, this tool is intended to offer diagnostic methods that can, sometimes, be applied in a more creative way.

Source: Personal communication with John Wood, 30 September 2008.

Acknowledgements: These metadesign tools are an outcome of the 'Benchmarking Synergy-Cultivation within Metadesign' research project at Goldsmiths, University of London, details available at Attainable Utopias, http://attainable-utopias.org/m21. The project was funded by the AHRC between 2005 and the end of 2008. The regular Attainable Utopias team comprised: John Backwell, Jonny Bradley, Hannah Jones, Julia Lockheart, Anette Lundebye and Professor Mathilda Tham, with administration by Ann Schlachter. John Wood was the principal investigator, and there were contributions from scores of consultants in many countries.

Appendix 4

Slow Design Principles, Philosophy, Process and Outcomes

Philosophy and principles

- Design to slow human, economic and resource use metabolisms
- repositioning the focus of design on individual, socio-cultural and environmental well-being
- design to celebrate slowness, diversity and pluralism
- design encouraging a long view
- design dealing with the 'continuous present' (a term coined in the 1950s by Bruce Goff, the US architect who noted that history is past and the future has not arrived but that the 'continuous present' is always with us)
- 'design as a counterbalance to the "fastness" (speed) of the current (industrial and consumer) design paradigm'.

Process

The process of slow design is comprehensive, holistic, inclusive, reflective and considered. It permits evolution and development of the design outcomes. It belongs to the professional and public arenas and emphasizes the importance of democratizing the design process by embracing a wide range of stakeholders.

Outcomes

Slow design is manifest in any object, space or image that encourages a reduction in human, economic, industrial and urban resource flow metabolisms by:

- designing for space to think, react, dream and muse
- designing for people first, commercialization second
- designing for local first, global second
- designing for socio-cultural benefits and well-being
- designing for regenerative environmental benefits and well-being
- democratizing design by encouraging self-initiated design
- catalysing behavioural change and socio-cultural transformation
- creating new economic and business models and opportunities
- outcomes can be represented in eight overlapping themes: ritual, tradition, experiential, evolved, slowness, eco-efficiency, open-source knowledge and (slow) technology.

Source: Alastair Fuad-Luke (2004) 'Slow', www.slowdesign.org, accessed September 2008.

The DEEDS Core Principles

This is a set of interrelated principles to guide designers in their thoughts and actions in 'designing for sustainability'. The principles were developed between November 2006 and July 2007 and underwent several iterations. They were published on the DEEDS website, www.deedsproject.org, in November 2007, and formally at the Changing the Change conference in Turin in July 2008, www.changingthe change.org. An overview of the DEEDS project is to be published in the *International Journal of Innovation and Sustainable Development* in early 2009.

The principles are the most comprehensive manifesto for change published in the past 30 years (see Table A1) based around six themes under the acronym 'SCALES', including two new themes not previously addressed – 'Special skills around communication and leadership' and 'Creating change agents'. The principles are a call to designers to take hold of the sustainability agenda and to inspire, lead and catalyse positive change. SCALES offers a most comprehensive set of criteria that:

- embraces the scope of previous criteria yet adds new ones found to be essential when understanding design for sustainability (DfS) as a broader challenge than design for the environment (DfE)
- can be easily adapted and 'owned' by an individual or a group, initiating a process of learning by doing
- can form a reference point to demonstrate how case studies embed the principles
- allows for each principle to become the basis of a teaching module and/or an example case study
- provide a philosophical and practical foundation for a pluralistic approach to developing DfS teaching and learning (T&L) pedagogy and practical tools serving as a benchmark.

The Core Principles – SCALES

Design for sustainability is a life journey … that expands the context of *your* design life:

Special skills – holistic approach

(S 1) *Develop new skills* for recognizing, framing (looking for systemic connections) and solving problems

(S 2) *Define problems holistically* by systems and life cycle thinking, combined with appropriate technical and social innovation

(S 3) *Analyse problems from multiple perspectives*, including the four sustainability dimensions – economic, social, institutional and environmental – but not forgetting human dimensions too (mental, physical, emotional and spiritual)

Special skills – eco-efficient production and resource usage

(S 4) *Develop LCT, LCA and 'cradle to cradle' skills*, be familiar with technology know-how and appropriate application of light-weighting (materials reduction), renewables/new materials, extended product lives, reusability and recyclability (designing 'quality waste'), waste avoidance, energy issues and dematerialization (moving from products to dematerialized services)

(S 5) *Integrate efficient service provision* in design solutions, by designing product-service systems, products suitable for sharing and pooling, pay per use or per experience

(S 6) *Maximize consumer satisfaction* per service enjoyed by addressing human needs; consider different material and immaterial options to do so and choose the most sustainable one; design fertile products offering users' experience, emotion, relation, pride, self-esteem and awareness

Special skills – communication and leadership

(S 7) *Lead the agenda* – develop leadership skills

(S 8) *Tell engaging stories* – develop presentation, narrative and scenario-setting skills

(S 9) *Forge new visions of enterprise* – understand economic thinking without adopting it (know the language, but do not have the mindset of business)

Creating change agents

(C 1) *Expand your context* – be aware that the sustainability context expands the design context in thinking and practice

(C 2) *Change perceptions* – by making use of the diversity of 'value-added' outcomes of design for sustainability DfS

(C 3) *Set new aspirations* – practice DfS approaches that provide significant, immediate and visible benefits to encourage consumers to aspire to a new, sustainable cultural representation of the 'good life'

Awareness – systemic and context

(A 1) *Be aware of context and connections* (people, planet, prosperity; key drivers and timeframes)

(A 2) *Be aware of positive and negative impacts*, feedback loops and side effects in this context

(A 3) *Be aware of choice and responsibility* under these circumstances

Learning together

(L 1) *Seek to work with other disciplines* – practice inter- and trans-disciplinary thinking and practice

(L 2) *Be a teacher-learner* – practice mutual learning, creativity and team working, understand sharing ideas as a way to stimulate creativity

(L 3) *Participate with your peers* – practice T&L through participation, involving an extended peer community of relevant stakeholders

Ethical responsibilities

(E 1) *Develop design that does no harm* (responsible design, with integrity), but contributes to a sustainable way of a 'good life', long term and globally, also if applied in mass production

(E 2) *Create genuine consumer empowerment* – offer design that enhances personal standing and acceptance, and thus social sustainability and encourages user involvement (consumer empowerment)

(E 3) *Focus on experiences not objects* – develop practical, functional and *fun* design that deepens life experiences and strengthens personal and social cohesion

Synergy and co-creating

(Sy 1) *Activate through participation* – promote the development of teams, communities and networks

(Sy 2) *Engage in synergistic clusters of competence*

(Sy 3) *Practice collaboration, sharing and partnering*, and the involvement of stakeholders in the problem definition and the solution design process

Table A1 Comparison of DEEDS core principles with previously published green design, eco-design, ecological and sustainable design systematiques

Date Author	Special skills Holistic approach			Eco-efficient production and resource usage				Communication and leadership		Creating change agents			Awareness – systemic and context			Learning together			Ethical responsibilities			Synergy and co-creating		
	S1	S2	S3	S4	S5	S6	S7	S8	S9	C1	C2	C3	A1	A2	A3	L1	L2	L3	E1	E2	E3	S1	S2	S3
1968 McHarg	X	X	X							X	X	X		X	X									
1984 Todd & Todd	X	X	X	X	X	X							X	X	X									
1986 John Elkington Associates	X	X	X	X	X	X							X	X						X				
1991 Team Zoo Atelier Zo	X	X	X	X	X	X							X	X	X									
1991 Vale & Vale	X	X	X	X	X	X							X	X	X									
1992 McDonough	X	X	X										X	X	X	X	X	X	X	X	X	X	X	X
1996 Burrall			X	X	X	X								X										

Date Author	Special skills Holistic approach	Eco-efficient production and resource usage	Communication and leadership	Creating change agents	Awareness – systemic and context	Learning together	Ethical responsibilities	Synergy and co-creating
1996 van der Ryn & Cowan	X X X	X X X	X		X X X	X X X	X X	X X
2001 demi	X	X X X	X		X X	X X	X X	X X
2002 Fuad-Luke	X	X X	X	X	X	X X	X X	X X
2004 RIBA	X	X X					X	X
2004 Pre	X X	X X					X	X X
2004 Ryan	X	X X			X			X
2007 Chochinov	X X X	X X			X X	X	X X X	X X

Phrases, or words, that the above sources mention but that are absent from the DEEDS core principles:

Bio-regionality, diversity, symbiosis, fitness/fitting, emotional senses, balance, humanizing designs, respect for place/site, respect for users, humanity and nature co-existence, respect for material and spiritual connections, safe objects, understand limitations of design, humility, responsive to locality (place and people), regenerate do not deplete, make nature visible, involve all stakeholders, design adaptable to future needs, identify and satisfy real needs, ask 'why?' and 'why not?', preserve and restore 'natural capital', move from products to product-services.

Source: Blincoe, K. Fuad-Luke, A., Spangenberg, J. H., Thomson, M., Holmgren, D., Jaschke, K., Ainsworth, T. and Tylka, K. (2009) 'DEEDS: A teaching and learning resource to help mainstream sustainability into everyday design teaching and professional practice', *International Journal of Innovation and Sustainable Development*, vol 4, no 1, pp1–23

Appendix 6

Nodes of Design Activism

A selection of some contemporary nodes of design activism available
via the internet:

Adbusters, www.adbusters.org
Architects for Peace, www.architectsforpeace.org
Architecture 2030, www.architecture2030.org
Architecture for Humanity, www.architectureforhumanity.org
Article 25, www.article-25.org
Attainable Utopias, http://attainable-utopias.org/tiki/tiki-index.php
Design 21: Social Design Network, www.design21sdn.com
Design Activism, blog http://designactivism.net/about-contact
Design Activism festival, www.designactivism.org/2009/Index.htm
Design Can Change, www.designcanchange.org
The Designers Accord www.designersaccord.org
Design Seeds, www.designseeds.org
Design With Intent, http://architectures.danlockton.co.uk
Doors of Perception weblog, www.doorsofperception.com
EcoLabs, http://eco-labs.org/dev
Ecoresonance, www.ecoresonance.org
Experientia blog, www.experientia.com/blog
Futerra, www.futerra.co.uk
Institute Without Boundaries, www.institutewithoutboundaries.com
O2 Global Network, www.o2.org
Open Architecture, Network http://openarchitecturenetwork.org
Platform21, www.platform21.nl
Project H, www.projecthdesign.com
Re-nourish, www.re-nourish.com
Seccoshop, www.seccoshop.com
Slow Cities, www.cittaslow.org.uk
Slow design, www.slowdesign.org
Slow Food, www.slowfood.com
slowLab, www.slowlab.net
SlowPlanet, www.slowplanet.com/blog/home
Social Design Notes, http://backspace.com/notes/about.php
Social Design Site, www.socialdesignsite.com
Society for Sustainable Mobility, www.osgv.org

Sustainable Everyday, www.sustainable-everyday.net
Transition Towns Network, http://transitiontowns.org
Treehugger, www.treehugger.com
Worldchanging, www.worldchanging.com

Illustration credits

The author: p3, Figure 1.1; p4, Figure 1.2; p9, Figure 1.3; pp11–16, Figures 1.4–1.9; p19, Figure 1.10; p25, Figure 1.11; p35, Figure 2.1, adapted from original sources by Will Murray and Charles Jencks; pp44–45, Figure 2.3a; p46 Figure 2.3b; p68–69, Figure 3.6, graphic devised with Earthscan, data extracted from WWF's *Living Planet Report*, 2006; p99, Figure 4.13; p149, Figure 5.3; pp153–154, Figures 5.4 and 5.5 abstracted and drafted by author from Margolin and Margolin (2002) – see Note 13, p160; p158, Figure 5.6, all images, word circle and concepts generated during a workshop facilitated by the author with Rowena Arden, Rod McLaughlin, Steve Bond, Anne Roberts, Nick Swallow, Bunk, Lisa Fuller, Moryl Mamie and Alex Glanville at RANE, University College Falmouth, UK, 29 April 2008; p159, Figure 5.7; p159, Figure 5.8, concept by the author, renders by Ines Sanchez-Calatrava; p168, Figure 6.1; p170, Figure 6.2; p171, Figure 6.3; p176, Figure 6.4; p178, Figure 6.5; p181, Figure 6.6; p192, Figure 7.1; p197, Figure 7.2; p198/199, Figure 7.3.

Other contributors: p40, Figure 2.2, Bauhaus Archiv, Museum of Design, Berlin; p58, Figure 3.1, *Climate Change 2007: Synthesis Report. Contribution of Working Groups I, II and II to the Fourth Assessment Report of the Intergovernmental Panel on Climate Change*, IPCC, Geneva, Switzerland; p62, Figure 3.2, Association for the Study of Peak Oil & Gas; p63, Figure 3.3, Pilot Assessment of Global Ecosystems, World Resources Institute/IFPRI, 2000; p65, Figure 3.4, Jerrad Pierce, 2007, http://pthbb.org/natural/footprint; p66, Figure 3.5, courtesy New Economics Foundation (NEF) from Mary Murphy (ed) (2006) *The UK Interdependence Report*, NEF, 2006; p70, Figure 3.7, courtesy PricewaterhouseCoopers, from James Shaw et al (2000) *Good News: Money Does Grow on Trees*, PWC; pp78–79, Figure 4.1, courtesy François Jégou, Strategic Design Scenarios, Belgium and Ezio Manzini, DIS INDACO Politecnico di Milano, Italy, the Sustainable Everyday Exhibiton, Triennale di Milano, Milan, 2003; p82, Figure 4.2, redrawn after D. Fallman, Note 22, p135; p88, Figure 4.3, the idea, design and development of the Habbit is by Professor David Walker and Rob Holdway, Giraffe Innovations; p89, Figure 4.4, © Copyright 2006 SASI Group (University of Sheffield) and Mark Newman (University of Michigan), see www.worldmapper.org/copyright.html; pp90–91, Figure 4.5, © 2007 Tim Kekeritz, www.traumkrieger.de/virtualwater/; p92, Figure 4.6, Richard Saul Wurman, Nigel Holmes and Radical Media, www.192021.org; p92, Figure 4.7, Mads Hogstroem/FLOWmarket, www.flowmarket.com; p93, Figure 4.8, National Renewable Energy Lab and Futurefarmers team (Amy Franceschini, Jonathan Meuser, Dragisa Krsmanovic, Eric Ratcliffe, Michael Swaine, Noah Murphy-Reinhertz and Stijin Schiffeleers); p94, Figure 4.9, courtesy Thomas Matthews, photo David Spero; pp96–97, Figure 4.10, courtesy Foresight, illustrations Narinder Sagoo/Foster and Partners; p97, Figure 4.11, © Design Council, 2006, www.designcouncil.org.uk; pp98–99, Figure 4.12, © 2007 Cay Green; p100, Figure 4.14, © Martin Ruiz de Azúa; p101, Figure 4.15, courtesy

Natalie Schaap, photo Joost van Blejswijk, 2003; p102, Figure 4.16, courtesy Droog, do Hit chair for Droog by Marijn van der Poll, photo by Robaard/Theuwkens (styling by Marjo Karanenbory, CMK); p105, Figure 4.17, © Stuart Walker, 2006; p104, Figure 4.18, courtesy Adrian Bowyer and Vik Oliver, http://reprap.org; p105, Figure 4.19, © Judith van den Boom, 2007; p105, Figure 4.20, courtesy Droog, Proto Gardening Bench by Jurgen Bey for Droog; p106, Figure 4.21, courtesy Yael Stav, Innivo Design; p107, Figure 4.22, courtesy Richard Liddle, Codha Design Limited; p107, Figure 4.23, courtesy Pli Design and Sprout Design; p108, Figure 4.24, courtesy Trevor Baylis Brands plc; p109, Figure 4.25, © Inga Knölke, Imagekontainer; p110, Figure 4.26, Dr Mitchell Joachim, Lara Greden and Javier Arbona, MIT Team Human Ecology Design, now Terreform 1, www.terreform.org; p111, Figure 4.27, Dr Mitchell Joachim, Terreform 1 and image Franco Vairani, Smart Cities, http://cities.media.mit.edu/; p111, Figure 4.28, c,mm,n open source car project, www.cmmn.org; p112, Figure 4.29, courtesy Force4 Architects, www.force4.dk; p114, Figure 4.30 (top), image by Lucy Jane Batchelor; p114, Figure 4.30 (bottom), image courtesy Kate Fletcher and Becky Earley, photography Tom Gidley; p116, Figure 4.31, courtesy vanhoffontwerpen, www.vanhoffontwerpen.nl; p117, Figure 4.32, courtesy Simon Heijdens, www.simonheijdens.com; p117, Figure 4.33, design and photography Monika Hoinkis, www.livingwiththings.org, www.monikahoinkis.de; p118, Figure 4.34, courtesy FRONT, www.frontdesign.se; p118, Figure 4.35, courtesy Thorunn Arnadottir, www.thorunndesign.com; p119, Figure 4.36, courtesy CuteCircuit; p120, Figure 4.37, courtesy Dunne and Raby, www.dunneandraby.co.uk; p122, Figure 4.38, Dott 07 (Designs of the time) project, © Design Council, www.design council.org.uk; p124, Figure 4.39, courtesy Peter Wouda, The Time Foundation/ eco-cathedral, www.timefoundation.com; p127, Figure 4.40, montage of images, Swee Hong Ng and others from Architecture for Humanity and the Open Architecture Network, www.architectureforhumanity.org and www.openarchitecture network.org; p128, Figure 4.41, Rural Studio, http://cac.auburn.edu/soa/rural-studio/contact.htm; p128, Figure 4.42, courtesy Michael Rakowitz and Lombard-Freid Projects, NY, Michael McGee's ParaSITE shelter, 2000; p129, Figure 4.43, © Smithsonian Institution, Design for the Other 90% exhibition at the Cooper-Hewitt National Design Museum, http://other90.cooperhewitt.org/; p130, Figure 4.44, image Michael Roberts, IDE (International Development Enterprises); p130, Figure 4.45, image P. J. Hendrikse; p131, Figure 4.46, Oxfam's Technical Unit (left) and Carlo Heathcote/Oxfam (right), Pakistan, November 2005, Thuri park IDP camp, Phool Abbasi drinks from an Oxfam bucket; p131, Figure 4.47, courtesy Stephan Augustin, Watercone, the Yemen project, 2004; p132, Figure 4.48, Carla Gomes Monroy of One Laptop per Child (OLPC); p133, Figure 4.49, courtesy Vestergaard Frandsen; p133, Figure 4.50, courtesy Godisa Technologies, Botswana; p142, Figure 5.1, redrawn from J. Wood (2003), see p160, Note 6; p143, Figure 5.2, Liz Sanders and G. K. van Platter conversation, NextD, see p160, Note 12.

Index